Embedded Programming with Modern C++ Cookbook

Practical recipes to help you build robust and secure embedded applications on Linux

Igor Viarheichyk

BIRMINGHAM - MUMBAI

Embedded Programming with Modern C++ Cookbook

Commissioning Editor: Richa Tripathi
Acquisition Editor: Vincy Davis
Content Development Editor: Pathikrit Roy
Senior Editor: Storm Mann
Technical Editor: Pradeep Sahu
Copy Editor: Safis Editing
Project Coordinator: Francy Puthiry
Proofreader: Safis Editing
Indexer: Pratik Shirodkar
Production Designer: Jyoti Chauhan

First published: April 2020

Production reference: 1170420

Published by Packt Publishing Ltd.
Livery Place
35 Livery Street
Birmingham
B3 2PB, UK.

ISBN 978-1-83882-104-3

www.packt.com

To my mother, Tamara, and to the memory of my father, Vyacheslav, for their love and support.

Packt.com

Subscribe to our online digital library for full access to over 7,000 books and videos, as well as industry leading tools to help you plan your personal development and advance your career. For more information, please visit our website.

Why subscribe?

- Spend less time learning and more time coding with practical eBooks and Videos from over 4,000 industry professionals

- Improve your learning with Skill Plans built especially for you

- Get a free eBook or video every month

- Fully searchable for easy access to vital information

- Copy and paste, print, and bookmark content

Did you know that Packt offers eBook versions of every book published, with PDF and ePub files available? You can upgrade to the eBook version at www.packt.com and as a print book customer, you are entitled to a discount on the eBook copy. Get in touch with us at customercare@packtpub.com for more details.

At www.packt.com, you can also read a collection of free technical articles, sign up for a range of free newsletters, and receive exclusive discounts and offers on Packt books and eBooks.

Contributors

About the author

Igor Viarheichyk works as an engineering manager at Samsung, developing a safety-critical middleware platform for advanced driver assistance systems aimed at specialized automotive embedded platforms. Prior to joining Samsung, in the past 20 years of his career, he has played different roles, from software engineer to software architect, to engineering manager in a variety of projects, and he has gained vast experience in the areas of system programming, embedded programming, network protocols, distributed and fault-tolerant systems, and software internationalization. Though he knows and actively uses programming languages such as C, Java, and Python, C++ is his language of choice to implement large-scale, high-performance applications.

I would like to thank Pathikrit Roy, Content Development Editor, and Tanvi Bhatt, Project Manager of this book, for their guidance, attention to detail, and dedication, essential to bring this book to life.

Many thanks go to Antonio Calderone for the technical review of the book and for testing all code samples. Your suggestions were extremely valuable.

Finally, I want to thank my family for their patience and support.

About the reviewer

Antonino Calderone has worked in the computer software industry for over 20 years as a software engineer in various domains, including telecommunications and networks, embedded systems, cybersecurity, machine learning algorithms, and DBMS. He has worked for companies such as Ericsson, Intel, and McAfee. He has also been a security architect, technical writer, and teacher in programming courses in C++ and design patterns. Antonino is an author and maintainer of several open source projects, including mipOS, an RTOS for SoC microcontrollers, and nuBASIC, a language designed for educational purposes. He was also a contributor to the magazine *Computer Programming*, one of the most well-known programming magazines in Italy in the 90s and 2000s.

Packt is searching for authors like you

If you're interested in becoming an author for Packt, please visit `authors.packtpub.com` and apply today. We have worked with thousands of developers and tech professionals, just like you, to help them share their insight with the global tech community. You can make a general application, apply for a specific hot topic that we are recruiting an author for, or submit your own idea.

Table of Contents

Preface

For a long time, development for embedded systems required either plain C or assembly language. There was a host of good reasons for this. The hardware did not have enough resources to run applications written in higher-level programming languages, such as C++, Java, or Python, but more importantly, there was no real need to write software in these languages. Limited hardware resources put a limit on software complexity, the functionality of embedded applications remained relatively simple, and the capabilities of C were sufficient to implement it.

As a result of the progress in hardware development, more and more embedded systems nowadays are powered by inexpensive yet powerful System-on-Chip capable of running a general-purpose multitasking operating system such as Linux.

Growing hardware capabilities demand more complex software, and more and more often C++ becomes the language of choice for new embedded systems. With its *you don't pay for what you don't use* approach it allows developers to create applications that use computational and memory resources, like applications written in C, but gives developers many more tools for dealing with complexity and safer resource management, such as object-oriented programming and the RAII idiom.

Seasoned embedded developers with substantial experience in C often tend to write code in C++ in a similar, habitual way, considering this language just as an object-oriented extension of C, a *C with classes*. Modern C++, however, has its own best practices and concepts that, properly used, help developers avoid common pitfalls and allow them to do a lot in a few lines of code.

On the other side, developers with C++ experience entering the world of embedded systems should be aware of the requirements, limitations, and capabilities of specific hardware platforms and application domains and design their C++ code accordingly.

The goal of this book is to bridge this gap and demonstrate how features and best practices of modern C++ can be applied in the context of embedded systems.

Who this book is for

This book is for developers and electronic hardware, software, and system-on-chip engineers who want to build effective embedded programs in C++.

The world of embedded systems is vast. This book tries to cover one type of them, the SoCs running Linux OS, such as Raspberry Pi or BeagleBoard, briefly touching low-level microcontrollers such as Arduino.

Familiarity with C++ is expected, but no deep knowledge of C++ or experience with embedded systems is required.

What this book covers

Chapter 1, *Fundamentals of Embedded Systems*, defines what embedded systems are, how they are different from other systems, why specific programming techniques are needed, and why C++ is good and in many cases the best choice for embedded development. It outlines the constraints and challenges that embedded developers encounter in their everyday work: limited system resources and CPU performance, dealing with hardware errors, and remote debugging.

Chapter 2, *Setting Up the Environment*, explains the differences in a development environment for embedded systems compared to web or desktop application development and goes through concepts of the build and target system, cross-compilation and cross-toolkits, the serial console, and the remote shell. It provides practical steps for setting up virtualized build and target hosts for the most common desktop configurations running Windows, macOS, or Linux.

Chapter 3, *Working with Different Architectures*, explains how to take into account important differences in CPU architectures and memory configuration of target systems in your C++ code.

Chapter 4, *Handling Interrupts*, covers the low-level concepts of interrupts and interrupt service routines. In modern OSes, even developers or device drivers have to use a higher-level API provided by the OS. That is why we explore the interrupt techniques using the 8051 microcontroller.

Chapter 5, *Debugging, Logging, and Profiling*, covers debugging techniques specific to Linux-based embedded systems, such as running gdb directly on the target board, setting up gdbserver for remote debugging, and the importance of logging for debugging and failure root cause analysis.

Chapter 6, *Memory Management*, provides several recipes and best practices of memory allocation that will be helpful for developers of embedded systems. We discuss why dynamic memory allocation is avoided in embedded applications and what alternatives can be considered for fast, deterministic memory allocation.

Chapter 7, *Multithreading and Synchronization*, explains how to use the functions and classes provided by the standard library of C++ to implement efficient multithreading applications that can utilize all the power of the modern multicore CPUs.

Chapter 8, *Communication and Serialization*, covers the concepts, challenges, and best practices for inter-process and inter-system communications, such as sockets, pipes, shared memory, and memory-efficient serialization using the FlatBuffers library. Decoupling applications into independent components that talk to each other using well-defined asynchronous protocols is a de facto standard way of scaling a software system while keeping it fast and fault-tolerant.

Chapter 9, *Peripherals*, explains how to work with various peripheral devices in C++ programs. Though most device communication APIs do not depend on a particular programming language, we will learn how to use the power of C++ to write wrappers that are convenient for developers and help prevent common resource leaking errors.

Chapter 10, *Reducing Power Consumption*, explores the best practices for writing energy-efficient applications and utilizing the power management functions of the OS. It provides several practical recipes for Linux-based embedded systems, but the same concepts can be expanded to any OS and any platform.

Chapter 11, *Time Points and Intervals*, covers various topics related to time manipulations, from measuring intervals to adding delays. We will learn about the API provided by the standard C++ Chrono library and how it can be used efficiently to build portable embedded applications.

Chapter 12, *Error Handling and Fault Tolerance*, explores possible implementations and best practices of error handling for embedded applications written in C++. It explains how to use C++ exceptions efficiently and compares it to alternatives such as traditional error codes and complex return types. It touches on basic fault-tolerance mechanisms such as watchdog timers and heartbeats.

Chapter 13, *Guidelines for Real-Time Systems*, covers the specifics of real-time systems. It briefly describes how real-time systems are defined and what kinds of real-time systems exist. It contains practical recipes on how to make the behavior of applications more deterministic, a crucial requirement for real-time systems.

Chapter 14, *Guidelines for Safety-Critical Systems*, explains what safety-critical systems are and how they are different from other embedded systems. It covers development methodologies and tools that are required when working on safety-critical systems, from following formalized coding guidelines such as MISRA, AUTOSAR, or JSF to using static code analysis or formal software validation tools.

Chapter 15, *Microcontroller Programming*, outlines basic concepts of writing, compiling, and debugging C++ code for microcontrollers. We will learn how to set up the development environment using the widely used Arduino board as an example.

To get the most out of this book

Development for embedded systems implies that your applications will interact with some sort of specialized hardware—a specific SoC platform, a specific microcontroller, or a specific peripheral device. There is a huge variety of possible hardware configurations, along with specialized OSes or IDEs that are needed to work with those hardware setups.

The goal of this book is to let everyone start learning about programming for embedded systems without investing too much in hardware. That is why most of the recipes are aimed at working in a virtualized Linux environment or an emulator. Some of the recipes, however, may require physical hardware. These recipes were designed to be run on either a Raspberry Pi or an Arduino, the two most widely used and inexpensive platforms that can be obtained relatively easily.

Software/Hardware covered in the book	OS requirements
Docker (https://www.docker.com/products/docker-desktop)	• Microsoft Windows 10 Professional or Enterprise 64-bit • macOS 10.13 or newer • Ubuntu Linux 16.04 or newer • Debian Linux Stretch (9) or Buster (10) • Fedora Linux 30 or newer
QEMU (https://www.qemu.org/download/)	• Windows 8 or newer (32-bit or 64-bit) • macOS 10.7 or newer • Linux (various distributions)
Raspberry Pi 3 Model B+	
Arduino UNO R3 or ELEGOO UNO R3	

If you are using the digital version of this book, we advise you to type the code yourself or access the code via the GitHub repository (link available in the next section). Doing so will help you avoid any potential errors related to the copying and pasting of code.

Download the example code files

You can download the example code files for this book from your account at www.packt.com. If you purchased this book elsewhere, you can visit www.packtpub.com/support and register to have the files emailed directly to you.

You can download the code files by following these steps:

1. Log in or register at `www.packt.com`.
2. Select the **Support** tab.
3. Click on **Code Downloads**.
4. Enter the name of the book in the **Search** box and follow the onscreen instructions.

Once the file is downloaded, please make sure that you unzip or extract the folder using the latest version of:

- WinRAR/7-Zip for Windows
- Zipeg/iZip/UnRarX for Mac
- 7-Zip/PeaZip for Linux

The code bundle for the book is also hosted on GitHub at `https://github.com/ PacktPublishing/Embedded-Programming-with-Modern-CPP-Cookbook`. In case there's an update to the code, it will be updated on the existing GitHub repository.

We also have other code bundles from our rich catalog of books and videos available at `https://github.com/PacktPublishing/`. Check them out!

Download the color images

We also provide a PDF file that has color images of the screenshots/diagrams used in this book. You can download it here: `https://static.packt-cdn.com/downloads/ 9781838821043_ColorImages.pdf`.

Conventions used

There are a number of text conventions used throughout this book.

`CodeInText`: Indicates code words in text, database table names, folder names, filenames, file extensions, pathnames, dummy URLs, user input, and Twitter handles. Here is an example: "Run the `hello` application under `gdbserver`."

A block of code is set as follows:

```cpp
#include <iostream>

int main() {
  std::cout << "Hello, world!" << std::endl;
  return 0;
}
```

When we wish to draw your attention to a particular part of a code block, the relevant lines or items are set in bold:

```cpp
#include <iostream>

int main() {
  std::cout << "Hello, world!" << std::endl;
  return 0;
}
```

Any command-line input or output is written as follows:

```
$ docker run -ti -v $HOME/test:/mnt ubuntu:bionic
```

Bold: Indicates a new term, an important word, or words that you see onscreen. For example, words in menus or dialog boxes appear in the text like this. Here is an example: "The best way to configure cross-compilation for CMake is by using the so-called **toolchain** files"

 Warnings or important notes appear like this.

 Tips and tricks appear like this.

Sections

In this book, you will find several headings that appear frequently (*Getting ready, How to do it..., How it works..., There's more...,* and *See also*).

To give clear instructions on how to complete a recipe, use these sections as follows:

Getting ready

This section tells you what to expect in the recipe and describes how to set up any software or any preliminary settings required for the recipe.

How to do it...

This section contains the steps required to follow the recipe.

How it works...

This section usually consists of a detailed explanation of what happened in the previous section.

There's more...

This section consists of additional information about the recipe in order to make you more knowledgeable about the recipe.

See also

This section provides helpful links to other useful information for the recipe.

Get in touch

Feedback from our readers is always welcome.

General feedback: If you have questions about any aspect of this book, mention the book title in the subject of your message and email us at customercare@packtpub.com.

Errata: Although we have taken every care to ensure the accuracy of our content, mistakes do happen. If you have found a mistake in this book, we would be grateful if you would report this to us. Please visit www.packtpub.com/support/errata, selecting your book, clicking on the Errata Submission Form link, and entering the details.

Piracy: If you come across any illegal copies of our works in any form on the Internet, we would be grateful if you would provide us with the location address or website name. Please contact us at copyright@packt.com with a link to the material.

If you are interested in becoming an author: If there is a topic that you have expertise in and you are interested in either writing or contributing to a book, please visit authors.packtpub.com.

Reviews

Please leave a review. Once you have read and used this book, why not leave a review on the site that you purchased it from? Potential readers can then see and use your unbiased opinion to make purchase decisions, we at Packt can understand what you think about our products, and our authors can see your feedback on their book. Thank you!

For more information about Packt, please visit packt.com.

Fundamentals of Embedded Systems

1

Embedded systems are computer systems that combine hardware and software components to solve a specific task within a larger system or device. Unlike general-purpose computers, they are heavily specialized and optimized to perform only one task but do it really well.

They are everywhere around us, but we rarely notice them. You can find them in virtually every home appliance or gadget, such as a microwave oven, TV set, network-attached storage, or smart thermostat. Your car contains several interconnected embedded systems that handle brakes, fuel injection, and infotainment.

In this chapter, we are going to deal with the following topics on embedded systems:

- Exploring embedded systems
- Working with limited resources
- Looking at performance implications
- Working with different architectures
- Working with hardware errors
- Using C++ for embedded development
- Deploying software remotely
- Running software remotely
- Logging and diagnostics

Exploring embedded systems

Every computer system created to solve a particular problem as part of a larger system or device is an embedded system. Even your general-purpose PC or laptop contains many embedded systems. A keyboard, a hard drive, a network card, or a Wi-Fi module—each of these is an embedded system with a processor, often called a **microcontroller**, and its own software, often called **firmware**.

Let's now dive into the different features of an embedded system.

How are they different from desktop or web applications?

The most distinctive feature of embedded systems compared to desktops or servers is their tight coupling of hardware and software specialized to accomplish a particular task.

Embedded devices work in a wide range of physical and environmental conditions. Most of them are not designed to work only in dedicated conditioned data centers or offices. They have to be functional in uncontrollable environments, often without any supervision and maintenance.

Since they are specialized, hardware requirements are precisely calculated to accomplish the task of being as cost-efficient as possible. As a result, the software aims to utilize 100% of the available resources with minimal or no reserves.

The hardware of embedded systems is much more differentiated compared to regular desktops and servers. The design of each system is individual. They may require very specific CPUs and schematics that connect them to memory and peripheral hardware.

Embedded systems are designed to communicate with peripheral hardware. A major part of an embedded program is checking the status, reading input, sending data, or controlling the external device. It is common for an embedded system to not have a user interface. This makes development, debugging, and diagnostics much more difficult compared to doing the same on traditional desktop or web applications.

Types of embedded systems

Embedded systems span a wide range of use cases and technologies—from powerful systems used for autonomous driving or large-scale storage systems to tiny microcontrollers used to control light bulbs or LED displays.

Based on the level of integration and specialization of hardware, embedded systems can roughly be divided into the following categories:

- **Microcontrollers (MCUs)**
- **A System on Chip (SoC)**
- **Application-Specific Integrated Circuits (ASICs)**
- **Field Programmable Gate Arrays (FPGAs)**

Microcontrollers

MCUs are general-purpose integrated circuits designed for embedded applications. A single MCU chip typically contains one or more CPUs, memory, and programmable input/output peripherals. Their design allows them to interface directly with sensors or actuators without adding any additional components.

MCUs are widely used in automobile engine control systems, medical devices, remote controls, office machines, appliances, power tools, and toys.

Their CPUs vary from simple 8-bit processors to the more complex 32-bit and even 64-bit processors.

Lots of MCUs exist; the most common ones nowadays are the following:

- The Intel MCS-51 or 8051 MCU.
- AVR by Atmel
- The **Programmable Interface Controller** (PIC) from Microchip Technology
- Various ARM-based MCUs

System on Chip

An SoC is an integrated circuit that combines all the electronic circuits and parts needed to solve a particular class of problem on a single chip.

It may contain digital, analog, or mixed-signal functions, depending on the application. The integration of most electronic parts in a single chip gives two major benefits: miniaturization and low power consumption. Compared to a less-integrated hardware design, an SoC requires significantly less power. The optimization of power consumption on the hardware and software levels allows it to create systems that can work for days, months, and even years on a battery without an external power source. Often, it also integrates radio frequency signal processing, which, along with its compact physical size, makes it an ideal solution for mobile applications. Besides that, SoCs are commonly used in the automotive industry, in wearable electronics, and in the **Internet of Things (IoT)**:

Figure 1.1: A Raspberry Pi Model B+

A Raspberry Pi family of single-board computers is an example of a system based on the SoC design. Model B+ is built on top of a Broadcom BCM2837B0 SoC with an integrated quad-core 1.4 Hz ARM-based CPU, 1 GB memory, a network interface controller, and four Ethernet interfaces.

The board has four USB interfaces, a MicroSD card port to boot an operating system and store data, Ethernet and Wi-Fi network interfaces, HDMI video output, and a 40-pin GPIO header to connect custom peripheral hardware.

It is shipped with the Linux operating system and is an excellent choice for educational and **DIY** projects.

Application-specific integrated circuits

Application-specific integrated circuits, or **ASICs**, are integrated circuits customized by their manufactures for a particular use. The customization is an expensive process but allows them to meet the requirements that are often infeasible for solutions based on general-purpose hardware. For example, modern high-efficiency Bitcoin miners are usually built on top of specialized ASIC chips.

To define the functionality of ASICs, hardware designers use one of the hardware description languages, such as Verilog or VHDL.

Field programmable gate arrays

Unlike SoCs, ASICs, and MCUs, **field programmable gate arrays**, or **FPGAs**, are semiconductor devices that can be reprogrammed on a hardware level after manufacturing. They are based around a matrix of **configurable logic blocks** (**CLBs**), which are connected via programmable interconnects. The interconnects can be programmed by developers to perform a specific function according to their requirements. The FPGA is programmed with a **Hardware Definition Language** (**HDL**). It allows the implementation of any combination of digital functions in order to process a massive amount of data very quickly and efficiently.

Working with limited resources

It is a common misconception that embedded systems are based on hardware that is much slower compared to regular desktop or server hardware. Although this is commonly the case, it is not always true.

Some particular applications may require lots of computation power of large amounts of memory. For example, autonomous driving requires both memory and CPU resources to handle the large amount of data that comes from various sensors using AI algorithms in real time. Another example is high-end storage systems that utilize large amounts of memory and resources for data caching, replication, and encryption.

In either case, the embedded system hardware is designed to minimize the cost of the overall system. The results for software engineers working with embedded systems is that resources are scarce. They are expected to utilize all of the available resources and take performance and memory optimizations very seriously.

Looking at performance implications

Most embedded applications are optimized for performance. As discussed earlier, the target CPU is chosen to be cost-efficient and developers extract all the computation power that it is capable of. An additional factor is communication with peripheral hardware. This often requires precise and fast reaction times. As a result, there is only limited room for the scripting, interpretable, bytecode languages such as Python or Java. Most of the embedded programs are written in languages that compile into the native code, primarily C and C++.

To achieve maximum performance, embedded programs utilize all the performance optimization capabilities of compilers. Modern compilers are so good at code optimization that they can outperform code in assembly language written by skilled developers.

However, engineers cannot rely solely on the performance optimizations provided by compilers. To achieve maximum efficiency, they have to take into account the specifics of the target platform. Coding practices that are commonly used for desktop or server applications running on an x86 platform may be inefficient for different architectures such as ARM or MIPS. The utilization of specific features of the target architecture often gives a significant performance boost to the program.

Working with different architectures

Developers of desktop applications usually pay little attention to the hardware architecture. First, they often use high-level programming languages that hide these complexities at the cost of some performance drop. Second, in most cases, their code runs on x86 architecture and they often take its features for granted. For example, they may assume that the size of `int` is 32 bits, which is not true in many cases.

Embedded developers deal with a much wider variety of architectures. Even if they do not write code in assembly language native to the target platform, they should be aware that all C and C++ fundamental types are architecture-dependent; the standard only guarantees that `int` is at least 16 bits. They should also know the traits of particular architectures, such as **endianness** and **alignment**, and take into account that operations with floating point or 64-bit numbers, which are relatively cheap on x86 architecture, may be much more expensive on other architectures.

Endianness

Endianness defines the order in which bytes that represent large numerical values are stored in memory.

There are two types of endianness:

- **Big-endian**: The most significant byte is stored first. The `0x01020304` 32-bit value is stored at the `ptr` address as follows:

Offset in memory	Value
`ptr`	0x01
`ptr + 1`	0x02
`ptr + 2`	0x03
`ptr + 3`	0x04

Examples of big-endian architectures are AVR32 and Motorola 68000.

- **Little-endian**: The least significant byte is stored first. The `0x01020304` 32-bit value is stored at the `ptr` address as follows:

Offset in memory	Value
`ptr`	0x04
`ptr + 1`	0x03
`ptr + 2`	0x02
`ptr + 3`	0x01

The x86 architecture is little-endian.

- **Bi-endian**: Hardware supports switchable endianness. Some examples are PowerPC, ARMv3, and the preceding examples.

Endianness is particularly essential when exchanging data with other systems. If a developer sends the `0x01020304` 32-bit integer as is, it may be read as `0x04030201` if the endianness of the receiver does not match the endianness of the sender. That is why data should be **serialized**.

This C++ snippet can be used to determine the endianness of a system:

```cpp
#include <iostream>
int main() {
  union {
    uint32_t i;
    uint8_t c[4];
  } data;
  data.i = 0x01020304;
  if (data.c[0] == 0x01) {
    std::cout << "Big-endian" << std::endl;
```

```
    } else {
      std::cout << "Little-endian" << std::endl;
    }
  }
```

Alignment

Processors don't read and write data in bytes but in **memory words**—chunks that match their data address size. 32-bit processors work with 32-bit words, 64-bit processors with 64-bit words, and so on.

Reads and writes are most efficient when words are aligned—the data address is a multiple of the word size. For example, for 32-bit architectures, the 0x00000004 address is aligned, while 0x00000005 is unaligned.

Compilers align data automatically to achieve the most efficient data access. When it comes to structures, the result may be surprising for developers who are not aware of alignment:

```
    struct {

        uint8_t c;

        uint32_t i;

    } a = {1, 1};

    std::cout << sizeof(a) << std::endl;
```

What is the output of the preceding code snippet? The size of uint8_t is 1 and the size of uint32_t is 4. A developer may expect that the size of the structure is the sum of the individual sizes. However, the result highly depends on the target architecture.

For x86, the result is 8. Let's add one more uint8_t field before i:

```
    struct {

        uint8_t c;

        uint8_t cc;

        uint32_t i;

    } a = {1, 1};

    std::cout << sizeof(a) << std::endl;
```

The result is still 8! The compiler optimizes the placement of the data fields within a structure according to alignment rules by adding padding bytes. The rules are architecture-dependent and the result may be different for other architectures. As a result, structures cannot be exchanged directly between two different systems without serialization, which will be explained in more depth in `Chapter 8`, *Communication and Serialization*.

Besides the CPU, access data alignment is also crucial for efficient memory mapping through hardware address translation mechanisms. Modern operating systems operate 4 KB memory blocks or pages to map a process virtual address space to physical memory. Aligning data structures on 4 KB boundaries can lead to performance gain.

Fixed-width integer types

C and C++ developers often forget that the size of fundamental data types, such as `char`, `short`, or `int`, is architecture-dependent. To make the code portable, embedded developers often use fixed-size integer types that explicitly specify the size of a data field.

The most commonly used data types are as follows:

Width	Signed	Unsigned
8-bit	int8_t	uint8_t
16-bit	int16_t	uint16_t
32-bit	int32_t	uint32_t

The pointer size also depends on the architecture. Developers often need to address elements of arrays and since arrays are internally represented as pointers, the offset representation depends on the pointer size. `size_t` is a special data type to represent the offset and data sizes in an architecture-independent way.

Working with hardware errors

A significant part of an embedded developer's work is dealing with hardware. Unlike most application developers, embedded developers cannot rely on hardware. Hardware fails for different reasons and embedded developers have to distinguish purely software failures from software failures caused by hardware failures or glitches.

Early versions of hardware

Embedded systems are based on specialized hardware designed and manufactured for a particular use case. This implies that at the time that the software for the embedded system is being developed, its hardware is not yet stable and well tested. When software developers encounter an error in their code behavior, it does not necessarily mean there is a software bug but it might be a result of incorrectly working hardware.

It is hard to triage these kinds of problems. They require knowledge, intuition, and sometimes the use of an oscilloscope to narrow the root cause of an issue down to hardware.

Hardware is unreliable

Hardware is inherently unreliable. Each hardware component has a probability of failure and developers should be aware that hardware can fail at any time. Data stored in memory can be corrupted because of memory failure. Messages being transmitted over a communication channel can be altered because of external noise.

Embedded developers are prepared for these situations. They use checksums or **cyclic redundancy check (CRC)** code to detect and, if possible, correct corrupted data.

The influence of environmental conditions

High temperature, low temperature, high humidity, vibration, dust, and other environmental factors can significantly affect the performance and reliability of hardware. While developers design their software to handle all potential hardware errors, it is common practice to test the system in different environments. Besides that, knowledge of environmental conditions can give an important clue when working on the root-cause analysis of an issue.

Using C++ for embedded development

For many years, the vast majority of an embedded project was developed using the C programming language. This language perfectly fits the needs of embedded software developers. It provides feature-rich and convenient syntax but at the same time, it is relatively low-level and does not hide platform specifics from developers.

Due to its versatility, compactness, and the high performance of the compiled code, it became a de facto standard development language in the embedded world. Compilers for the C language exist for most, if not all, architectures; they are optimized to generate machine code that is more efficient than those that are written manually.

Over time, the complexity of embedded systems increased and developers faced the limitations of C, the most notable being error-prone resource management and a lack of high-level abstractions. The development of complex applications in C requires a lot of effort and time.

At the same time, C++ was evolving, gaining new features and adopting programming techniques that make it the best choice for developers of modern embedded systems. These new features and techniques are as follows:

- You don't pay for what you don't use.
- Object-oriented programming to time the code complexity.
- **Resource acquisition is initialization** (**RAII**).
- Exceptions.
- A powerful standard library.
- Threads and memory model as part of the language specification.

You don't pay for what you don't use

One of the mottos of C++ is *You don't pay for what you don't use*. This language is packed with many more features than C, yet it promises zero overhead for those that are not used.

Take, for example, virtual functions:

```
#include <iostream>

class A {

public:

  void print() {

    std::cout << "A" << std::endl;

  }

};

class B: public A {
```

```
public:

  void print() {

    std::cout << "B" << std::endl;

  }

};

int main() {

  A* obj = new B;

  obj->print();

}
```

The preceding code will output A, despite obj pointing to the object of the B class. To make it work as expected, the developer adds a keyword—virtual:

```
#include <iostream>

class A {

public:

  virtual void print() {

    std::cout << "A" << std::endl;

  }

};

class B: public A {

public:

  void print() {

    std::cout << "B" << std::endl;

  }

};

int main() {
```

```
    A* obj = new B;

    obj->print();

}
```

After this change, the code outputs B, which is what most developers expect to get as a result. You may ask why C++ does not enforce every method to be virtual by default. This approach is adopted by Java and doesn't seem to have any downsides.

The reason is that virtual functions are not free. Function resolution is performed at runtime via the virtual table—an array of function pointers. It adds a slight overhead to the function invocation time. If you do not need dynamic polymorphism, you do not pay for it. That is why C++ developers add the virtual keyboard, to explicitly agree with functionality that adds performance overhead.

Object-oriented programming to time the code complexity

As the complexity of embedded programs grows over time, it becomes more and more difficult to manage them using the traditional procedural approach provided by the C language. If you take a look at a large C project, such as the Linux kernel, you will see that it adopts many aspects of object-oriented programming.

The Linux kernel extensively uses encapsulation, hiding implementation details and providing object interfaces using C structures.

Though it is possible to write object-oriented code in C, it is much easier and convenient to do it in C++, where a compiler does all the heavy lifting for the developers.

Resource acquisition is initialization

Embedded developers work a lot with the resources provided by the operating system: memory, files, and network sockets. C developers use pairs of API functions to acquire and free resources; for example, `malloc` to claim a block of memory and `free` to return it to the system. If for some reason the developer forgets to invoke `free`, this block of memory leaks. Memory leaking, or resource leaking, is generally a common problem in applications written in C:

```c
#include <stdio.h>

#include <unistd.h>

#include <fcntl.h>

#include <string.h>

int AppendString(const char* str) {

  int fd = open("test.txt", O_CREAT|O_RDWR|O_APPEND);

 if (fd < 0) {

    printf("Can't open file\n");

    return -1;

  }

  size_t len = strlen(str);

  if (write(fd, str, len) < len) {

    printf("Can't append a string to a file\n");

    return -1;

  }

  close(fd);

  return 0;

}
```

This preceding code looks correct, but it contains several serious issues. If the `write` function returns an error or writes less data than requested (and this is correct behavior), the `AppendString` function logs an error and returns. However, if it forgets to close the file descriptor, it leaks. Over time, more and more file descriptors leak and at some point, the program reaches the limit of open file descriptors, making *all* calls to the `open` function fail.

C++ provides a powerful programming idiom that prevents resource leakage: **RAII**. A resource is allocated in an object constructor and deallocated in the object destructor. This means that the resource is only held while the object is alive. It is automatically freed when the object is destroyed:

```cpp
#include <fstream>

void AppendString(const std::string& str) {

  std::ofstream output("test.txt", std::ofstream::app);

  if (!output.is_open()){

    throw std::runtime_error("Can't open file");

  }

  output << str;

}
```

Note that this function does not call `close` explicitly. The file is closed in the destructor of the output object, which is automatically invoked when the `AppendString` function returns.

Exceptions

Traditionally, C developers handled errors using error codes. This approach requires lots of attention from the coders and is a constant source of hard-to-find bugs in C programs. It is too easy to omit or overlook missing check-for-a-return code, masking the error:

```cpp
#include <stdio.h>

#include <unistd.h>

#include <fcntl.h>

#include <iostream>
```

```
#include <fstream>

char read_last_byte(const char* filename) {

        char result = 0;

        int fd = open(filename, O_RDONLY);

        if (fd < 0) {

                printf("Can't open file\n");

                return -1;

        }

        lseek(fd, -1, SEEK_END);

        size_t s = read(fd, &result, sizeof(result));

        if (s != sizeof(result)) {

                printf("Can't read from file: %lu\n", s);

                close(fd);

                return -1;

        }

        close(fd);

        return result;

}
```

The preceding code has at least two issues related to error handling. First, the result of the lseek function call is not checked. If lseek returns an error, the function will work incorrectly. The second issue is more subtle, yet more important and harder to fix. The read_last_byte function returns −1 to indicate an error, but it is also a valid value of a byte. It is not possible to distinguish whether the last byte of a file is 0xFF or whether the function encountered an error. To correctly handle this case, the function interface should be redefined as follows:

```
int read_last_byte(const char* filename, char* result);
```

The function returns -1 in the case of an error and 0 otherwise. The result is stored in a `char` variable passed by reference. Although this interface is correct, it is not as convenient for developers as the original one.

A program that eventually crashes randomly may be considered the best outcome for these kinds of errors. It would be worse if it keeps working, silently corrupting data or generating incorrect results.

Besides that, the code that implements the logic and the code responsible for error checks are intertwined. The code becomes hard to read and hard to understand and, as a result, even more error-prone.

Although developers can still keep using return codes, the recommended way of error handling in modern C++ is exceptions. Correctly designed and correctly used exceptions significantly reduce the complexity of error handling, making code readable and robust.

The same function written in C++ using exceptions looks much cleaner:

```cpp
char read_last_byte2(const char* filename) {

    char result = 0;

    std::fstream file;

    file.exceptions (

        std::ifstream::failbit | std::ifstream::badbit );

    file.open(filename);

    file.seekg(-1, file.end);

    file.read(&result, sizeof(result));

    return result;

}
```

The powerful standard library

C++ comes with a feature-rich and powerful standard library. Many functions that required C developers to use third-party libraries are now part of the standard C++ library. This means less external dependencies, more stable and predictable behavior, and improved portability between hardware architectures.

The C++ standard library comes with containers built on top of the most commonly used data structures, such as arrays, binary trees, and hash tables. These containers are generic and efficiently cover most of the developer's everyday needs. Developers do not need to spend time and effort creating their own, often error-prone, implementations of the essential data structures.

The containers are carefully designed in a way that minimizes the need for explicit resources, allocation, or deallocation, leading to significantly lower chances of memory or other system resources leaking.

The standard library also provides many standard algorithms, such as `find`, `sort`, `replace`, binary search, operations with sets, and permutations. The algorithms can be applied to any containers that expose integrator interfaces. Combined with standard containers, they help developers focus on high-level abstractions and build them on top of well-tested functionality with a minimal amount of additional code.

Threads and a memory model as part of the language specification

The C++11 standard introduced a memory model that clearly defines the behavior of a C++ program in a multithreaded environment.

For the C language specifications, the memory model was out of scope. The language itself was not aware of threads or parallel execution semantics. It was up to the third-party libraries, such as pthreads, to provide all the necessary support for multithread applications.

Earlier versions of C++ followed the same principle. Multithreading was out of the scope of the language specification. However, modern CPUs with multiple pipelines supporting instruction reordering demanded more deterministic behavior of compilers.

As a result, modern specifications of C++ explicitly define classes for threads, various types of locks and mutexes, condition variables, and atomic variables. This gives embedded developers a powerful tool kit to design and implement applications capable of utilizing all the power of modern multicore CPUs. Since the tool kit is part of the language specification, these applications have deterministic behavior and are portable to all supported architectures.

Deploying software remotely

The deployment of software for embedded systems is often a complex procedure that should be carefully designed, implemented, and tested. There are two major challenges:

- Embedded systems are often deployed in places that are difficult or impractical for a human operator to access.
- If software deployment fails, the system can become inoperable. It will require the intervention of a skilled technician and additional tools for recovery. This is expensive and often impossible.

A solution for the first challenge of embedded systems that are connected to the internet was found in the form of **Over-the-Air** (**OTA**) updates. A system periodically connects to the dedicated server and checks for available updates. If the updated version of the software is found, it is downloaded to the device and installed to the persistent memory.

This approach is widely adopted by manufacturers of smartphones, **Set-Top-Box** (**STB**) appliances, smart TVs, and game consoles connected to the internet.

When designing OTA updates, system architects should take into account many factors that affect the scalability and reliability of the overall solution. For example, if all devices check for updates at approximately the same time, it creates high peak loads in the update servers, while leaving them idle all other time. Randomizing the check time keeps the load distributed evenly. The target system should be designed to reserve enough persistent memory to download the complete update image before applying it. The code implementing the updated software image download should handle network connection drops and resume download once the connection is recovered, rather than start over. Another important factor of OTA update is security. The updated process should only accept genuine update images. Updates are cryptographically signed by the manufacturer and an image is not accepted by the installer running on the device unless the signature matches.

Developers of embedded systems are aware that the update may fail for different reasons; for example, a power outage during the update. Even if the update completes successfully, the new version of the software may be unstable and crash on startup. It is expected that even in such situations the system will be able to recover.

This is achieved by separating the main software components and the bootloader. The bootloader validates the consistency of the main components, such as the operating system kernel and root filesystem that contains all the executables, data, and scripts. Then, it tries to run the operating system. In the case of failure, it switches to the previous version, which should be kept in the persistent memory along with the new one. Hardware watchdog timers are used to detect and prevent situations where a software update causes the system to hang.

It is impractical to use OTA or complete image re-flashing during software development and testing. It significantly slows down the development process. Engineers use other ways to deploy their software builds to the development systems, such as a remote shell or network filesystems that allow file sharing between developers' workstations and target boards.

Running software remotely

Embedded systems are designed to solve a particular problem using a specific combination of hardware and software components. That is why all software components in a system are tailored to fulfill this goal. Everything non-essential is disabled and all custom software is integrated into the boot sequence.

Users do not launch embedded programs; they start on system boot. However, during the development process, engineers need to run their applications without rebooting the system.

This is done differently depending on the type of the target platform. For powerful-enough systems based on SoC and running a preemptive multitasking operating system such as Linux, it can be done using a remote shell.

Modern systems usually use a **secure shell** (**SSH**) as a remote shell. The target system runs an SSH daemon waiting for incoming connections. Developers connect using a client SSH program, such as SSH in Linux or PuTTY in Windows, to get access to the target system. Once connected, they can work with the Linux shell on the embedded board in the same way as on a local computer.

The common workflow for running the program remotely is as follows:

1. Build a program executable in your local system using a cross-compilation toolkit.
2. Copy it to the remote system using the `scp` tool.

3. Connect to the remote system using SSH and run the executable from the command line.
4. Using the same SSH connection, analyze the program output.
5. When the program terminates or gets interrupted by the developer, fetch its logs back to the developer's workstation for in-depth analysis.

MCUs do not have enough resources for a remote shell. Developers usually upload the compiled code directly into the platform memory and initiate the code execution from the particular memory address.

Logging and diagnostics

Logging and diagnostics are an important aspect of any embedded project.

In many cases, using an interactive debugger is not possible or practical. Hardware state can change in a few milliseconds. After a program stops on a breakpoint, a developer does not have enough time to analyze it. Collecting detailed log data and using tools for their analysis and visualization is a better approach for high-performance, multithreaded, time-sensitive embedded systems.

Since in most cases resources are limited, developers often have to make tradeoffs. On the one hand, they need to collect as much data as possible to identify the root cause of failure—whether it is the software or hardware, the status of the hardware components at the time of the failure, and the accurate timing of the hardware and software events handled by the system. On the other hand, the space available for the log is limited, and each time writing the log affects the overall performance.

The solution is buffering log data locally on a device and sending it to a remote system for detailed analysis.

This approach works fine for the development of embedded software. However, the diagnostics of the deployed systems require more sophisticated techniques.

Many embedded systems work offline and do not provide convenient access to internal logs. Developers need to design and implement other ways of diagnostics and reporting carefully. If a system does not have a display, LED indicators or beeps are often used to encode various error conditions. They are sufficient for giving information about the failure category but in most cases cannot provide the necessary details to nail it down to the root cause.

Embedded devices have dedicated diagnostics modes that are used to test the hardware components. After powering up, virtually any device or appliance performs a **Power-On Self-Test** (**POST**), which runs quick tests of the hardware. These tests are supposed to be fast and do not cover all testing scenarios. That is why many devices have hidden **service modes** that can be activated by developers or field engineers to perform more thorough tests.

Summary

In this chapter, we discussed a high-level overview of embedded software, what makes it different, and also learned why and how C++ can be used efficiently in this area.

Setting Up the Environment

2

To start working with an embedded system, we need to set up an environment. Unlike the environment we use for desktop development, the environment for embedded programming requires two systems:

- **A build system**: The system you use to write the code
- **A target system**: The system your code is going to be run on

In this chapter, we will learn how to set up these two systems and connect them together. Configurations of build systems may vary significantly— there may be different operating systems, compilers, and IDEs. The variance in target system configurations is even greater since each embedded system is unique. Moreover, while you can use your laptop or desktop as a build system, you do need some sort of embedded board as a target system.

It would be impossible to cover all the possible combinations of build and target systems. Instead, we will just learn how to use one popular configuration:

- Ubuntu 18.04 as the build system
- Raspberry Pi as the target system

We will use Docker to run Ubuntu in a virtual environment on your laptop or desktop. Docker supports Windows, macOS, and Linux, but, if you already use Linux, you can use it directly without running a container on top of it.

We will use **Quick EMUlator** (**QEMU**) to emulate the Raspberry Pi board. This will teach us how to build applications for embedded boards even without access to the real hardware. Carrying out the initial phases of development in an emulated environment is common and, in many cases, the only possible practical solution, given that the target hardware may not be available when the software development starts.

This chapter will cover the following topics:

- Setting up the build system in a Docker container
- Working with emulators
- Cross-compilation
- Connecting to an embedded system
- Debugging embedded applications
- Using gdbserver for remote debugging
- Using CMake as a build system

Setting up the build system in a Docker container

In this recipe, we will set up a Docker container to run Ubuntu 18.04 on your desktop or laptop. It does not matter what operating system runs on your machine, as Docker supports Windows, macOS, and Linux. As a result of this recipe, you will have a unified, virtualized Ubuntu Linux build system running within your host operating system.

If your operating system already runs Ubuntu Linux, feel free to skip to the next recipe.

How to do it...

We are going to install the Docker application on our laptop or desktop and then use a ready-made image of Ubuntu to run this operating system in a virtual environment:

1. In your web browser, open the following link and follow the instructions to set up Docker for your operating system:
2. For Windows: `https://docs.docker.com/docker-for-windows/install/`
3. For macOS: `https://docs.docker.com/docker-for-mac/install/`
4. Open a terminal window (Command Prompt in Windows, the Terminal app in macOS) and run the following command to check that it has been installed correctly:

```
$ docker --version
```

5. Run this command to use an Ubuntu image:

   ```
   $ docker pull ubuntu:bionic
   ```

6. Create a working directory. In either macOS, Linux shell, or Windows PowerShell, run the following command:

   ```
   $ mkdir ~/test
   ```

7. Now, run the downloaded image in the container:

   ```
   $ docker run -ti -v $HOME/test:/mnt ubuntu:bionic
   ```

8. Next, run the uname -a command to get information about the system:

   ```
   # uname -a
   ```

   You are now in a virtual Linux environment, which we will use for the subsequent recipes in this book.

How it works...

In the first step, we install Docker—a virtualization environment that allows an isolated Linux operating system to run on Windows, macOS, or Linux. This is a convenient way of distributing and deploying containers that uniformly encapsulate all of the libraries and programs required for any operating system you use.

After installing Docker, run a quick command to check whether it has been installed correctly:

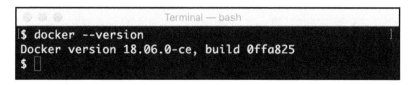

After checking the installation, we need to fetch the ready-made Ubuntu image from the Docker repository. Docker images have tags; we can use the `bionic` tag to find Ubuntu version 18.04:

```
●  ●  ●                        Terminal — bash
$
$ docker pull ubuntu:bionic
bionic: Pulling from library/ubuntu
35c102085707: Pull complete
251f5509d51d: Pull complete
8e829fe70a46: Pull complete
6001e1789921: Pull complete
Digest: sha256:d1d454df0f579c6be4d8161d227462d69e163a8ff9d20a847533989cf0c94d90
Status: Downloaded newer image for ubuntu:bionic
$ 
```

It takes time for the image to download. Once the image is fetched, we can create a directory, which we will use for development. The directory content will be shared between your operating system and Linux, running in Docker. This way, you can use your favorite text editor to work on code but still use the Linux build tools to compile the code into the binary executable files.

Then, we can start a Docker container using the Ubuntu image fetched in step 4. The `option -v $HOME/test:/mnt` command line makes the folder created in step 5 visible to Ubuntu as the `/mnt` directory. This means that all of the files you create in the `~/test` directory automatically appear in `/mnt`. The `-ti` option makes the container interactive, giving you access to the Linux shell environment (bash):

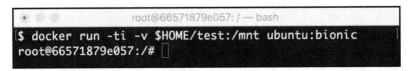

Finally, we run a quick sanity check of the . `uname` container, which displays information about the Linux kernel, as shown here:

```
● ● ●                    root@66571879e057: / — bash
$ docker run -ti -v $HOME/test:/mnt ubuntu:bionic
root@66571879e057:/# uname -a
Linux 66571879e057 4.9.93-linuxkit-aufs #1 SMP Wed Jun 6 16:55:56 UTC 2018 x86_6
4 x86_64 x86_64 GNU/Linux
root@66571879e057:/# 
```

Although the exact version of your kernel may differ, we can see that we are running Linux and our architecture is `x86`. This means we have set up our build environment, where we will be able to compile our code in a unified way, whatever operating system is running on our computer. However, we are still not able to run the compiled code because our target architecture is **Acorn RISC Machines** (**ARM**), not `x86`. We will learn how to set up an emulated ARM environment in the next recipe.

There's more...

Docker is a powerful and flexible system. Moreover, its repository contains lots of ready-made images that contain tools that are useful to most developers.

Go to `https://hub.docker.com/search?q=type=image` and browse through the most popular images. You can also search for images using keywords, such as *embedded*.

Working with emulators

Using a real embedded board is not always possible or practical—hardware is not yet ready, or the number of boards is limited. Emulators help developers use an environment that's as close to the target system as possible, yet do not depend on hardware availability. It is also the best way to start learning embedded development.

In this recipe, we will learn how to set up QEMU (a hardware emulator) and configure it to emulate an ARM-based embedded system running Debian Linux.

How to do it...

We need a virtual environment that, unlike Docker, can emulate processors with architectures that differ from the architecture of our computer:

1. Navigate to `https://www.qemu.org/download/` and click on the tab that matches your operating system—**Linux**, **macOS**, or **Windows**—and follow the installation instructions.

2. Create a test directory, unless one already exists:

   ```
   $ mkdir -p $HOME/raspberry
   ```

3. Download the following files and copy them over to the `~/raspberry` directory you created in the previous step:
   - **Raspbian Lite zip-archive**: `http://downloads.raspberrypi.org/raspbian_lite/images/raspbian_lite-2019-07-12/2019-07-10-raspbian-buster-lite.zip`
   - **Kernel image**: `https://github.com/dhruvvyas90/qemu-rpi-kernel/raw/master/kernel-qemu-4.14.79-stretch`
   - **Device tree blob**: `https://github.com/dhruvvyas90/qemu-rpi-kernel/raw/master/versatile-pb.dtb`

4. Change the directory to `~/raspberry` and extract the Raspbian Lite zip archive downloaded in the previous step. It contains a single file named `2019-07-10-raspbian-buster-lite.img`.

5. Open a terminal window and run QEMU. For Windows and Linux, the command line is as follows:

   ```
   $ qemu-system-arm -M versatilepb -dtb versatile-pb.dtb -cpu arm1176
   -kernel kernel-qemu-4.14.79-stretch -m 256 -drive file=2019-07-10-
   raspbian-buster-lite.img,format=raw -append "rw console=ttyAMA0
   rootfstype=ext4 root=/dev/sda2 loglevel=8" -net
   user,hostfwd=tcp::22023-:22,hostfwd=tcp::9090-:9090 -net nic -
   serial stdio
   ```

6. A new window should show up, displaying the Linux boot process. In a few seconds, a login prompt will be displayed.

7. Log in using `pi` as the username and `raspberry` as the password. Then, type the following command:

   ```
   # uname -a
   ```

8. Check the output of the command. It indicates that our system architecture is ARM, not x86. Now we can use this environment to test applications built for the ARM platform.

How it works...

In the first step, we install the QEMU emulator. Without the loadable code images, this virtual machine doesn't have much use. Then, we can fetch the three images required to run a Linux operating system:

- **The Linux root filesystem**: Contains a snapshot of Raspbian Linux, used on Raspberry Pi devices
- **The Linux kernel**
- **The Device tree blob**: Contains a description of the hardware components of a system

Once all the images are fetched and put into the `~/raspberry` directory, we run QEMU, providing paths to the images as command-line parameters. Additionally, we configure the virtual network, which allows us to connect to the Linux system running in the virtual environment from our native environment.

After QEMU starts, we can see a window with a Linux login prompt:

After logging into the system, we can run a quick sanity check by running the `uname` command:

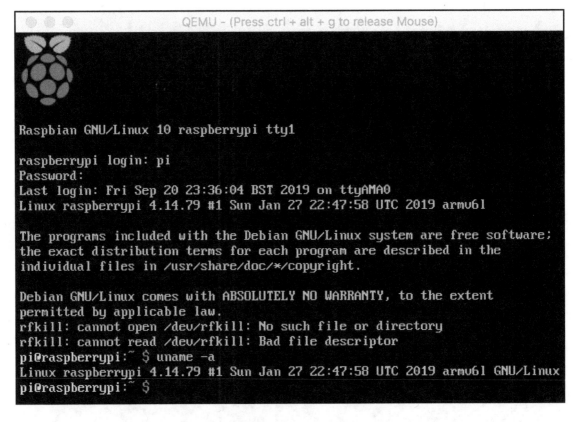

Similar to the sanity check we ran in the previous recipe, *Setting up the build system in a Docker container*, this shows that we are running a Linux operating system, but, in this case, we can see that the target architecture is ARM.

There's more...

QEMU is a powerful processor emulator that supports other multiple architectures aside from x86 and ARM, such as PowerPC, SPARC64, SPARC32, and **Microprocessor without Interlocked Pipelined Stages** (**MIPS**). One aspect that makes it so powerful is its flexibility, due to its many configuration options. Go to `https://qemu.weilnetz.de/doc/qemu-doc.html` to configure QEMU to your needs.

Microcontroller vendors also often provide emulators and simulators. When starting development for particular hardware, check for the available emulation options, as it might significantly affect the development time and effort.

Cross-compilation

We have already learned that the environment for embedded development consists of two systems: the build system, where you write and build code, and the host system, which runs the code.

We now have two virtualized environments set up:

- Ubuntu Linux in a Docker container, which will be our build system
- QEMU running Raspbian Linux, which will be our host system

In this recipe, we will set up the cross-compilation tools required to build Linux applications for the ARM platform and build a simple *Hello, world!* application to test the setup.

Getting ready

To set up the cross-compilation toolkit, we will need to use Ubuntu Linux, which we set up in the *Setting up the build system in a Docker container* recipe.

We also need the ~/test directory to exchange our source code between our operating system and the Ubuntu container.

How to do it...

Let's start by creating a simple C++ program, which we want to compile for our target platform:

1. Create a file named hello.cpp in the ~/test directory.
2. Use your favorite text editor to add the following code snippet to it:

```
#include <iostream>

int main() {
  std::cout << "Hello, world!" << std::endl;
```

```
    return 0;
}
```

3. Now that we have the code for the `Hello, world!` program, we need to compile it.

4. Switch to the Ubuntu (our build system) console.

5. Get the up-to-date list of packages available for the installation by running the following command:

   # apt update -y

6. It will take some time to fetch the package descriptions from the Ubuntu servers. Run the following command to install the cross-compilation tools:

   # apt install -y crossbuild-essential-armel

7. You will see a long list of packages to install. Press *Y* to confirm the installation.As a sanity check, run a cross-compiler with no parameters:

   # arm-linux-gnueabi-g++

8. Change the directory to /mnt

   # cd /mnt

9. The `hello.cpp` file that we created in step 1 is located here. Let's now build it:

   # arm-linux-gnueabi-g++ hello.cpp -o hello

10. This command generates an executable file named `hello`. You may be wondering why it doesn't have any extensions. In Unix systems, extensions are completely optional and binary executable files usually do not have any extensions. Try to run the file. It should fail with an error.

11. Let's generate the details about the executable binary using the `file` tool.

How it works...

In the first step, we created a simple *Hello, World!* C++ program. We put this into the ~/test directory, which makes it accessible from the Docker container running Linux.

To build the source code, we switched to the Ubuntu shell.

If we try to run a standard Linux g++ compiler to build it, we will get an executable for the build platform, which is x86. However, we need an executable for the ARM platform. To build it, we need a version of the compiler that can run on x86, building the ARM code.

As a preliminary step, we need to update the information about the packages available in the Ubuntu packages distributive:

```
root@66571879e057: / — bash
root@66571879e057:/# apt-get update
Get:1 http://security.ubuntu.com/ubuntu bionic-security InRelease [88.7 kB]
Get:2 http://archive.ubuntu.com/ubuntu bionic InRelease [242 kB]
Get:3 http://security.ubuntu.com/ubuntu bionic-security/restricted amd64 Package
s [6222 B]
Get:4 http://security.ubuntu.com/ubuntu bionic-security/universe amd64 Packages
[760 kB]
Get:5 http://archive.ubuntu.com/ubuntu bionic-updates InRelease [88.7 kB]
Get:6 http://archive.ubuntu.com/ubuntu bionic-backports InRelease [74.6 kB]
Get:7 http://archive.ubuntu.com/ubuntu bionic/universe amd64 Packages [11.3 MB]
Get:8 http://security.ubuntu.com/ubuntu bionic-security/main amd64 Packages [628
 kB]
Get:9 http://security.ubuntu.com/ubuntu bionic-security/multiverse amd64 Package
s [4173 B]
Get:10 http://archive.ubuntu.com/ubuntu bionic/main amd64 Packages [1344 kB]
Get:11 http://archive.ubuntu.com/ubuntu bionic/multiverse amd64 Packages [186 kB
]
Get:12 http://archive.ubuntu.com/ubuntu bionic/restricted amd64 Packages [13.5 k
B]
Get:13 http://archive.ubuntu.com/ubuntu bionic-updates/universe amd64 Packages [
1279 kB]
Get:14 http://archive.ubuntu.com/ubuntu bionic-updates/main amd64 Packages [926
kB]
Get:15 http://archive.ubuntu.com/ubuntu bionic-updates/multiverse amd64 Packages
 [7216 B]
```

We can install this compiler, along with a set of related tools, by running `apt-get install crossbuild-essential-armel`:

```
root@66571879e057: / — bash
libgdbm-compat4 libgdbm5 libgomp1 libgomp1-armel-cross libgssapi3-heimdal
libhcrypto4-heimdal libheimbase1-heimdal libheimntlm0-heimdal
libhtml-form-perl libhtml-format-perl libhtml-parser-perl
libhtml-tagset-perl libhtml-tree-perl libhttp-cookies-perl
libhttp-daemon-perl libhttp-date-perl libhttp-message-perl
libhttp-negotiate-perl libhx509-5-heimdal libicu60 libio-html-perl
libio-socket-ssl-perl libio-string-perl libisl19 libitm1 libkrb5-26-heimdal
libksba8 libldap-2.4-2 libldap-common liblocale-gettext-perl liblsan0
liblwp-mediatypes-perl liblwp-protocol-https-perl libmagic-mgc libmagic1
libmailtools-perl libmpc3 libmpfr6 libmpx2 libnet-http-perl
libnet-smtp-ssl-perl libnet-ssleay-perl libnpth0 libperl5.26 libquadmath0
libreadline7 libroken18-heimdal libsasl2-2 libsasl2-modules
libsasl2-modules-db libsqlite3-0 libssl1.1 libstdc++-7-dev
libstdc++-7-dev-armel-cross libstdc++6-armel-cross libtimedate-perl
libtry-tiny-perl libtsan0 libubsan0 libubsan0-armel-cross liburi-perl
libwind0-heimdal libwww-perl libwww-robotrules-perl libxml-libxml-perl
libxml-namespacesupport-perl libxml-parser-perl libxml-sax-base-perl
libxml-sax-expat-perl libxml-sax-perl libxml-simple-perl libxml2 libyaml-0-2
libyaml-libyaml-perl libyaml-perl linux-libc-dev linux-libc-dev-armel-cross
make manpages manpages-dev netbase openssl patch perl perl-modules-5.26
perl-openssl-defaults pinentry-curses readline-common ucf xz-utils
0 upgraded, 161 newly installed, 0 to remove and 4 not upgraded.
Need to get 92.8 MB of archives.
After this operation, 377 MB of additional disk space will be used.
Do you want to continue? [Y/n]
```

The quick sanity check carried out in step 9 shows that it was properly installed:

```
root@66571879e057: / — bash
[root@66571879e057:/# arm-linux-gnueabi-g++                               ]
arm-linux-gnueabi-g++: fatal error: no input files
compilation terminated.
root@66571879e057:/#
```

Now, we need to build `hello.cpp` using the cross-compiler. It generates the executable for the ARM platform, which is why our attempt to run it in the build system in step 12 fails.

To make sure it is really an ARM executable, we need to run the `file` command. Its output is as follows:

```
root@66571879e057: /mnt — bash
[root@66571879e057:/mnt# arm-linux-gnueabi-g++ hello.cpp -o hello
[root@66571879e057:/mnt# ./hello
/lib/ld-linux.so.3: No such file or directory
[root@66571879e057:/mnt# file hello
hello: ELF 32-bit LSB executable, ARM, EABI5 version 1 (SYSV), dynamically linke
d, interpreter /lib/ld-, for GNU/Linux 3.2.0, BuildID[sha1]=5cb7eaf6f52c7d6188ce
9095008b50b39d9a6f1e, not stripped
root@66571879e057:/mnt#
```

As you can see, the binary is built for the ARM platform, which is why it fails to run on a build system.

There's more...

Many cross-compilation toolkits exist for various architectures. Some of them are readily available in the Ubuntu repository; some may require manual installation.

Connecting to the embedded system

After an embedded application is built on a build system using a cross-compiler, it should be transferred to the target system. The best way to do this on Linux-based embedded systems is by using networking connectivity and a remote shell. **Secure Shell** (**SSH**) is widely used due to its security and versatility. It allows you to not only run shell commands on a remote host but also copy files from one machine to another using cryptographic encryption and key-based authentication.

In this recipe, we will learn how to copy the application binary to the emulated ARM system using secure copy, connect to it using SSH, and run the executable in SSH.

Getting ready

We will use the Raspberry Pi emulator we set up in the *Working with emulators* recipe as our target system. Also, we need our Ubuntu build system and the executable `hello` file we built in the *Cross-compilation* recipe.

How to do it...

We are going to access our target system via the network. QEMU provides a virtual network interface for the emulated machine, and we can use it without connecting to a real network. In order to do so, we need to figure out an IP address to use and make sure that the SSH server is running in our virtual environment:

In your native operating system environment, work out the IP address of your machine. Open a Terminal window or PowerShell. Run `ifconfig` on macOS, or Linux, or `ipconfig` for Windows, and check its output.

In the next steps, we will use `192.168.1.5` as a template IP address; you will need to replace it with your actual IP address.

1. Switch to the Raspberry Pi emulator and enable SSH services by running the following command:

   ```
   $ sudo systemctl start ssh
   ```

2. Switch to the Ubuntu window and install the SSH client:

   ```
   # apt install -y ssh
   ```

3. Now, we can copy the `hello` executable to the target system:

   ```
   # scp -P22023 /mnt/hello pi@192.168.1.5:~
   ```

4. When asked for a password, type `raspberry`. Switch back to the Raspberry Pi emulator window. Check that the executable we just copied is there:

   ```
   $ ls hello
   hello
   ```

5. Now, run the program:

   ```
   $ ./hello
   ```

   As we can see, the program is now running as expected.

How it works...

In this recipe, we set up a data exchange between two virtual environments—Docker and QEMU—using SSH. To do this, we need an SSH server to be running and accepting connections on the target system (QEMU), and an SSH client initiating connections on the build system.

In step 2, we set up the SSH client on our build system. Our target system, running in QEMU, already had an SSH server up and running. During the *Working with emulators* recipe, we configured QEMU to forward connections from our host port, 22023, to our virtual machine port, 22, which is SSH.

Now, we can use scp to copy a file from the build system to the target system using a secure network connection. We can specify our system IP address (discovered in step 1) and port 22023, configured for QEMU forwarding, as parameters for scp to connect to:

```
root@3324138cc2c7: / — bash
[root@3324138cc2c7:/# scp -P22023 /mnt/hello/hello pi@192.168.1.5:~/hello2
[pi@192.168.1.5's password:
hello                                   100% 8920    798.0KB/s    00:00
root@3324138cc2c7:/# 
```

After we have copied the file, we can log in to the target system with SSH using the same IP address, port, and username as we used for scp. It opens a login prompt similar to the local console and, after authorization, we get the same command shell as the local terminal.

The hello application we copied in the previous step should be available in the home directory. We checked this in step 5 by running the ls command.

Finally, we can run the application:

When we tried to run it on our build system, we received an error. Now, the output is `Hello, world!`. This is what we would expect, since our application is built for the ARM platform and being run on the ARM platform.

There's more...

Although we ran the recipe to connect to the emulated system, the same steps are applicable for real embedded systems. Even if a target system does not have a display, you can set up SSH using the serial console connection.

In this recipe, we only copied files to our target system. Besides copying, it is a common practice to open an interactive SSH session to the embedded system. Usually, it is more efficient and convenient to use than a serial console. It is established in a similar way to `scp`:

```
# ssh pi@192.168.1.5 -p22023
```

SSH provides various authentication mechanisms. Once you enable and set up public key authentication, there is no need to type in your password for every copy or login. This makes the development process faster and more convenient for developers.

To learn more about ss keys, go to `https://www.ssh.com/ssh/key/`.

Debugging embedded applications

Debugging embedded applications depends significantly on the type of the target embedded systems. Microcontroller manufacturers often provide specialized debuggers for their **microcontroller units** (**MCUs**) as well as hardware support for remote debugging using a **Joint Test Action Group** (**JTAG**) protocol. It allows developers to debug the microcontroller code immediately after the MCU starts executing instructions.

If the target board runs Linux, the most practical method of debugging is to use an extensive debug output and to use GDB as an interactive debugger.

In this recipe, we will learn how to run our application in a command-line debugger: GDB.

Getting ready

We have already learned how to transfer executable files to the target system. We will use the *Connecting to the embedded system* recipe as a starting point to learn how to use a debugger on the target system.

How to do it...

We have learned how to copy an application to the target system and run it there. Now, let's learn how to start debugging an application on a target system using GDB. In this recipe, we will only learn how to invoke the debugger and run applications in the debugger environment. It will be used as a foundation for more advanced and practical debugging techniques later:

1. Switch to the QEMU window.
2. If you have not done so already, log in using pi as the username and raspberry as the password.
3. Run the following command:

   ```
   $ gdb ./hello
   ```

4. This will open the gdb command line.
5. Type run to run the application:

   ```
   (gdb) run
   ```

5. You should see Hello, world in the output.
6. Now, run the quit command, or just q:

   ```
   (gdb) q
   ```

   This terminates the debugging session and returns us back to the Linux shell.

How it works...

The Raspberry Pi image we use for emulation comes with a pre-installed GNU debugger, so we can use it right away.

In the home user directory, we should find the hello executable file, which we copied from our build system as part of the *Connecting to the embedded system* recipe.

We run gdb, passing the path to the hello executable as a parameter. This command opens the gdb shell but does not run the application itself. To run it, we type in the run command:

```
QEMU - (Press ctrl + alt + g to release Mouse)
pi@raspberrypi:~ $ gdb ./hello
GNU gdb (Raspbian 8.2.1-2) 8.2.1
Copyright (C) 2018 Free Software Foundation, Inc.
License GPLv3+: GNU GPL version 3 or later <http://gnu.org/licenses/gpl.html>
This is free software: you are free to change and redistribute it.
There is NO WARRANTY, to the extent permitted by law.
Type "show copying" and "show warranty" for details.
This GDB was configured as "arm-linux-gnueabihf".
Type "show configuration" for configuration details.
For bug reporting instructions, please see:
<http://www.gnu.org/software/gdb/bugs/>.
Find the GDB manual and other documentation resources online at:
    <http://www.gnu.org/software/gdb/documentation/>.

For help, type "help".
Type "apropos word" to search for commands related to "word"...
Reading symbols from ./hello...(no debugging symbols found)...done.
(gdb) run
Starting program: /home/pi/hello
Hello, world!
[Inferior 1 (process 676) exited normally]
(gdb) _
```

The application runs, printing the `Hello world!` message on the screen, and then terminates. However, we are still in the debugger. To exit the debugger, we type the `quit` command:

```
QEMU - (Press ctrl + alt + g to release Mouse)
pi@raspberrypi:~ $ gdb ./hello
GNU gdb (Raspbian 8.2.1-2) 8.2.1
Copyright (C) 2018 Free Software Foundation, Inc.
License GPLv3+: GNU GPL version 3 or later <http://gnu.org/licenses/gpl.html>
This is free software: you are free to change and redistribute it.
There is NO WARRANTY, to the extent permitted by law.
Type "show copying" and "show warranty" for details.
This GDB was configured as "arm-linux-gnueabihf".
Type "show configuration" for configuration details.
For bug reporting instructions, please see:
<http://www.gnu.org/software/gdb/bugs/>.
Find the GDB manual and other documentation resources online at:
    <http://www.gnu.org/software/gdb/documentation/>.

For help, type "help".
Type "apropos word" to search for commands related to "word"...
Reading symbols from ./hello...(no debugging symbols found)...done.
(gdb) run
Starting program: /home/pi/hello
Hello, world!
[Inferior 1 (process 676) exited normally]
(gdb) q
pi@raspberrypi:~ $
```

You can see that the command-line prompt has changed. It is an indication that we are not in the gdb environment anymore. We have returned to the default shell environment of Raspberry Pi Linux, which we were using before running GDB.

There's more...

A GNU debugger is pre-installed in this case, but it may not be in your real target system. If it is Debian-based, you can install it by running the following command:

```
# apt install gdb gdb-multiarch
```

In other Linux-based systems, different commands to install GDB are required. In many cases, you will need to build it from source code and install it manually, similarly to the hello application we have built and tested as part of the recipes in this chapter.

In this recipe, we only learned how to run an application using GDB, which is a complex tool with lots of commands, techniques, and best practices. We will discuss some of them in the Chapter 5, *Debugging, Logging, and Profiling*.

Using gdbserver for remote debugging

As we have discussed, the environment for embedded development usually involves two systems—a build system and a target system (or emulator). Sometimes, interactive debugging on the target system is impractical because of the high latency of remote communication.

In such situations, developers can use remote debugging support provided by GDB. In this setup, an embedded application is launched on the target system using **gdbserver**. Developers run GDB on a build system and connect to gdbserver over the network.

In this recipe, we will learn how to start debugging an application using GDB and gdbserver.

Getting ready

In the *Connecting to the embedded system* recipe, we learned how to make our application available on the target system. We will use that recipe as a starting point to learn a remote debugging technique.

How to do it...

We are going to install and run the gdbserver application, which will allow us to run GDB on our build system and forward all commands to the target system. Switch to the Raspberry Pi emulator window.

1. Log in as `pi` using the `raspberry` password, unless you're already logged in.
2. To install gdbserver, run the following command:

   ```
   # sudo apt-get install gdbserver
   ```

3. Run the `hello` application under `gdbserver`:

   ```
   $ gdbserver 0.0.0.0:9090 ./hello
   ```

4. Switch to the build system terminal and change the directory to `/mnt/hello`:

   ```
   # cd /mnt/hello
   ```

5. Install the `gdb-multiarch` package, which provides the necessary support for the ARM platform:

   ```
   # apt install -y gdb-multiarch
   ```

6. Next, run `gdb`:

   ```
   # gdb-multiarch -q ./hello
   ```

7. Configure the remote connection by typing the following command in the `gdb` command line (make sure you replace `192.168.1.5` with your actual IP address):

   ```
   target remote 192.168.1.5:9090
   ```

8. Type the following command:

   ```
   continue
   ```

   The program will now run.

How it works...

In the Raspberry Pi image we used, `gdbserver` is not installed by default. So, as a first step, we install `gdbserver`:

```
                              QEMU
pi@raspberrypi:~ $ sudo apt-get install gdbserver
Reading package lists... Done
Building dependency tree
Reading state information... Done
The following NEW packages will be installed:
  gdbserver
0 upgraded, 1 newly installed, 0 to remove and 0 not upgraded.
Need to get 362 kB of archives.
After this operation, 703 kB of additional disk space will be used.
Get:1 http://mirrors.ocf.berkeley.edu/raspbian/raspbian buster/main armhf gdbser
ver armhf 8.2.1-2 [362 kB]
Fetched 362 kB in 21s (16.9 kB/s)
Selecting previously unselected package gdbserver.
(Reading database ... 37620 files and directories currently installed.)
Preparing to unpack .../gdbserver_8.2.1-2_armhf.deb ...
Unpacking gdbserver (8.2.1-2) ...
Setting up gdbserver (8.2.1-2) ...
pi@raspberrypi:~ $ _
```

After the installation is complete, we run `gdbserver`, passing the name of the application that needs to be debugged, the IP address, and the port to listen out for incoming connections as its parameters. We use `0.0.0.0` as the IP address to indicate that we want to accept connections on any IP address:

```
              QEMU - (Press ctrl + alt + g to release Mouse)
pi@raspberrypi:~ $ gdbserver 0.0.0.0:9090 ./hello
Process ./hello created; pid = 766
Listening on port 9090
_
```

Then, we switch to our build system and run `gdb` there. But, instead of running the application in GDB directly, we instruct `gdb` to initiate a connection to a remote host using the IP address and port provided:

```
user@3324138cc2c7: /mnt/hello — bash
user@3324138cc2c7:/mnt/hello$ gdb -q hello
Reading symbols from hello...(no debugging symbols found)...done.
(gdb) target remote 192.168.1.5:9090
Remote debugging using 192.168.1.5:9090
warning: while parsing target description (at line 10): Target description speci
fied unknown architecture "arm"
warning: Could not load XML target description; ignoring
Reply contains invalid hex digit 59
(gdb)
```

After that, all the commands you type at the gdb prompt will be transferred to gdbserver and executed there. When we run the application, we will see the resulting output in the gdb console of the build system, even if we run the ARM executable:

```
user@3324138cc2c7: /mnt/hello — bash
user@3324138cc2c7:/mnt/hello$ gdb -q hello
Reading symbols from hello...(no debugging symbols found)...done.
(gdb) target remote 192.168.1.5:9090
Remote debugging using 192.168.1.5:9090
warning: while parsing target description (at line 10): Target description speci
fied unknown architecture "arm"
warning: Could not load XML target description; ignoring
Reply contains invalid hex digit 59
(gdb) run
Starting program: /mnt/hello/hello
Hello, world!
[Inferior 1 (process 2781) exited normally]
(gdb)
```

An explanation is simple—the binary runs on a remote ARM system: our Raspberry Pi emulator. This is a convenient way of debugging applications on a target platform, allowing you to remain in the more comfortable environment of your build system.

There's more...

Make sure that the versions of GDB and gdbserver that you are using match, otherwise there can be issues with communication between them.

Using CMake as a build system

In the previous recipes, we learned how to compile a program that consists of one C++ file. Real applications, however, usually have a more complex structure. They can contain multiple source files, depend on other libraries, and be split into independent projects.

We need a way to conveniently define build rules for any type of application. CMake is one of the most well-known and widely used tools that allow developers to define high-level rules and translate them into a lower-level build system, such as a Unix make.

In this recipe, we will learn how to set up CMake and create a simple project definition for our *Hello, world!* application.

Getting ready

As discussed earlier, a common embedded development workflow includes two environments: a build system and a target system. CMake is part of the build system. We are going to use the Ubuntu build system, created as a result of the *Setting up the build system in a Docker container* recipe, as a starting point.

How to do it...

1. Our build system does not have CMake installed yet. To install it, run the following command:

   ```
   # apt install -y cmake
   ```

2. Switch back to your native operating system environment.
3. In the ~/test directory, create a subdirectory, hello. Use your favorite text editor to create a file, called CMakeLists.txt, in the hello subdirectory.
4. Enter the following lines:

   ```
   cmake_minimum_required(VERSION 3.5.1)
   project(hello)
   add_executable(hello hello.cpp)
   ```

5. Save the file and switch to the Ubuntu console.
6. Switch to the hello directory:

   ```
   # cd /mnt/hello
   ```

7. Run CMake:

```
# mkdir build && cd build && cmake ..
```

8. Now, build the application by running the following:

```
# make
```

9. Get information about the resulting executable binary using the `file` command:

```
# file hello
```

9. As you can see, the build is native to the x86 platform. We need to add cross-compilation support. Switch back to the text editor, open `CMakeLists.txt`, and add the following lines:

```
set(CMAKE_C_COMPILER /usr/bin/arm-linux-gnueabi-gcc)
set(CMAKE_CXX_COMPILER /usr/bin/arm-linux-gnueabi-g++)
set(CMAKE_FIND_ROOT_PATH_MODE_PROGRAM NEVER)
set(CMAKE_FIND_ROOT_PATH_MODE_LIBRARY ONLY)
set(CMAKE_FIND_ROOT_PATH_MODE_INCLUDE ONLY)
set(CMAKE_FIND_ROOT_PATH_MODE_PACKAGE ONLY)
```

10. Save it and switch to the Ubuntu terminal.
11. Run the `cmake` command again to re-generate the build files:

```
# cmake ..
```

12. Build the code by running `make`:

```
# make
```

13. Check the type of the resulting output file again:

```
# file hello
```

Now, we have an executable file built for our target system using CMake.

How it works...

First, we install CMake to our build system. Once the installation is complete, we switch to the native environment to create `CMakeLists.txt`. This file contains high-level build instructions about the project's composition and properties.

We name our project *hello*, which creates an executable, called `hello`, from a source file named `hello.cpp`. Additionally, we specify the minimal version of CMake required to build our application.

After we have created the project definition, we can switch back to the build system shell and generate low-level build instructions by running `make`.

It is common practice to create a dedicated build directory to keep all our build artifacts. By doing this, the object files generated by a compiler or files generated by CMake do not pollute the source code directories.

In a single command line, we create a `build` directory, change to the newly-created directory, and run CMake.

We pass the parent directory as a parameter to let CMake know where to look for `CMakeListst.txt`:

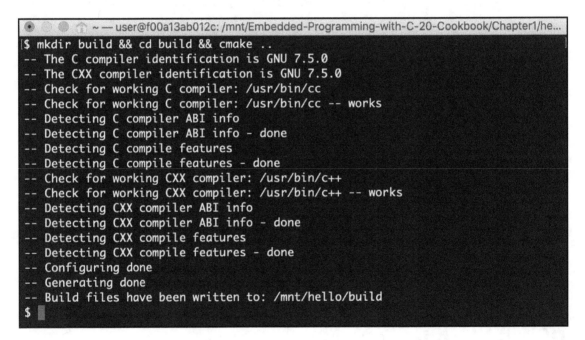

```
$ mkdir build && cd build && cmake ..
-- The C compiler identification is GNU 7.5.0
-- The CXX compiler identification is GNU 7.5.0
-- Check for working C compiler: /usr/bin/cc
-- Check for working C compiler: /usr/bin/cc -- works
-- Detecting C compiler ABI info
-- Detecting C compiler ABI info - done
-- Detecting C compile features
-- Detecting C compile features - done
-- Check for working CXX compiler: /usr/bin/c++
-- Check for working CXX compiler: /usr/bin/c++ -- works
-- Detecting CXX compiler ABI info
-- Detecting CXX compiler ABI info - done
-- Detecting CXX compile features
-- Detecting CXX compile features - done
-- Configuring done
-- Generating done
-- Build files have been written to: /mnt/hello/build
$
```

By default, CMake generates the `Makefile` files for the traditional Unix `make` utility. We run `make` to actually build the application:

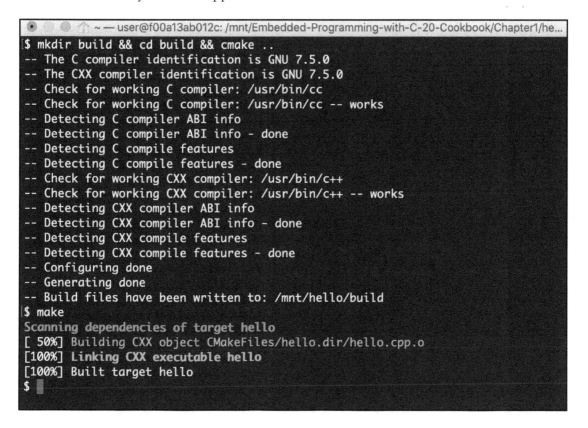

It works, but results in an executable binary built for the x86 platform, while our target system is ARM:

```
-- Check for working C compiler: /usr/bin/cc
-- Check for working C compiler: /usr/bin/cc -- works
-- Detecting C compiler ABI info
-- Detecting C compiler ABI info - done
-- Detecting C compile features
-- Detecting C compile features - done
-- Check for working CXX compiler: /usr/bin/c++
-- Check for working CXX compiler: /usr/bin/c++ -- works
-- Detecting CXX compiler ABI info
-- Detecting CXX compiler ABI info - done
-- Detecting CXX compile features
-- Detecting CXX compile features - done
-- Configuring done
-- Generating done
-- Build files have been written to: /mnt/hello/build
$ make
Scanning dependencies of target hello
[ 50%] Building CXX object CMakeFiles/hello.dir/hello.cpp.o
[100%] Linking CXX executable hello
[100%] Built target hello
$ file hello
hello: ELF 64-bit LSB shared object, x86-64, version 1 (SYSV), dynamically linke
d, interpreter /lib64/l, for GNU/Linux 3.2.0, BuildID[sha1]=170ef6e9b2fd8a9a15b2
6f85b40d0b8e7047a3f5, not stripped
$ 
```

To solve this, we add several options to our `CMakeLists.txt` file to configure cross-compilation. Repeating the build steps again, we get a new `hello` binary, now for the ARM platform:

```
●  ●  ●  🏠 ~ — user@f00a13ab012c: /mnt/Embedded-Programming-with-C-20-Cookbook/Chapter1/he...
-- Configuring done
-- Generating done
-- Build files have been written to: /mnt/hello/build
$ make
Scanning dependencies of target hello
[ 50%] Building CXX object CMakeFiles/hello.dir/hello.cpp.o
[100%] Linking CXX executable hello
[100%] Built target hello
$ file hello
hello: ELF 64-bit LSB shared object, x86-64, version 1 (SYSV), dynamically linke
d, interpreter /lib64/l, for GNU/Linux 3.2.0, BuildID[sha1]=170ef6e9b2fd8a9a15b2
6f85b40d0b8e7047a3f5, not stripped
$ cmake ..
-- Configuring done
-- Generating done
-- Build files have been written to: /mnt/hello/build
$ make
[ 50%] Building CXX object CMakeFiles/hello.dir/hello.cpp.o
[100%] Linking CXX executable hello
[100%] Built target hello
$ file hello
hello: ELF 32-bit LSB executable, ARM, EABI5 version 1 (SYSV), dynamically linke
d, interpreter /lib/ld-, for GNU/Linux 3.2.0, BuildID[sha1]=d12c5182fd3ec0dd07f8
106f4787850cbcc113d7, not stripped
$ ▏
```

As we can see in the output of the `file` command, we have built the executable file for the ARM platform, not x86, which we used as a build platform. This means that this program will not run on the build machine, but can be successfully copied to our target platform and run there.

There's more...

The best way to configure cross-compilation for CMake is by using the so-called **toolchain** files. Toolchain files define all the settings and parameters of the build rules specific to the particular target platform, such as a compiler prefix, compilation flags, and the location of the libraries pre-built on the target platform. An application can be rebuilt for different target platforms by using different toolchain files. See the CMake toolchains documentation at `https://cmake.org/cmake/help/v3.6/manual/cmake-toolchains.7.html` for more details.

3
Working with Different Architectures

The developers of desktop applications usually pay little attention to the hardware architecture. First, they often use high-level programming languages that hide these complexities at the cost of performance. Second, in most cases, their code runs on the x86 architecture, and they often take its features for granted. For example, they may assume that the size of int is 32 bits, but that is not true in many cases.

Embedded developers deal with a much wider variety of architectures. Even if they do not write code in an assembly language that's native to the target platform, they should be aware that all C and C++ fundamental types are architecture-dependent; the standard only guarantees that int is at least 16-bit. They should also know the traits of particular architectures, such as endianness and alignment, and take into account that operations that are performed with the floating-point or 64-bit numbers, which are relatively cheap on the x86 architecture, can be much more expensive on other architectures.

Since they aim to achieve maximal possible performance from embedded hardware, they should understand how to organize data in memory to get the most efficient use out of the CPU cache and operating system paging mechanisms.

In this chapter, we will cover the following topics:

- Exploring fixed-width integer types
- Working with the size_t type
- Detecting the endianness of the platform
- Converting the endianness
- Working with data alignment
- Working with packed structures
- Aligning data with cache lines

By looking at these topics, we will learn how to tailor our code to target platforms to achieve maximum performance and portability.

Exploring fixed-width integer types

C and C++ developers often forget that the size of fundamental data types such as char, short, and int are architecture-dependent. At the same time, most of the hardware peripherals define specific requirements regarding the size of the fields that are used for data exchanges. To make the code working with the external hardware or communication protocols portable, embedded developers use fixed-size integer types, which explicitly specify the size of a data field.

Some of the most commonly used data types are as follows:

Width	Signed	Unsigned
8-bit	int8_t	uint8_t
16-bit	int16_t	uint16_t
32-bit	int32_t	uint32_t

The pointer size also depends on the architecture. Developers often need to address the elements of arrays, and since arrays are internally represented as pointers, the offset representation depends on the pointer's size. size_t is a special data type as it represents the offset and data sizes in an architecture-independent way.

In this recipe, we will learn how to use fixed-size data types in our code to make it portable across architectures. This way, we can make our application work with other target platforms faster and with fewer code modifications.

How to do it...

We are going to create an application that emulates data exchange with a peripheral device. Follow these steps to do so:

1. In your working directory, that is, ~/test, create a subdirectory called fixed_types.

2. Use your favorite text editor to create a file called `fixed_types.cpp` in the `fixed_types` subdirectory. Copy the following code snippet into the `fixed_types.cpp` file:

```
#include <iostream>
void SendDataToDevice(void* buffer, uint32_t size) {
  // This is a stub function to send data pointer by
  // buffer.
  std::cout << "Sending data chunk of size " << size << std::endl;
}

int main() {
  char buffer[] = "Hello, world!";
  uint32_t size = sizeof(buffer);
  SendDataToDevice(&size, sizeof(size));
  SendDataToDevice(buffer, size);
  return 0;
}
```

3. Create a file called `CMakeLists.txt` in the loop subdirectory with the following content:

```
cmake_minimum_required(VERSION 3.5.1)
project(fixed_types)
add_executable(fixed_types fixed_types.cpp)

set(CMAKE_SYSTEM_NAME Linux)
set(CMAKE_SYSTEM_PROCESSOR arm)

SET(CMAKE_CXX_FLAGS "--std=c++11")
set(CMAKE_CXX_COMPILER /usr/bin/arm-linux-gnueabi-g++)
```

4. Build the application and copy the resulting executable binary to the target system. Use the recipes from `Chapter 2`, *Setting Up the Environment*, to do so.

5. Switch to the target system's Terminal. Log in using your user credentials, if needed.

6. Run the binary to see how it works.

How it works...

When you run the binary, you will see the following output:

```
● ● ●              user@feb23236b84c: /mnt/test/fixed_types — bash
user@feb23236b84c:/mnt/test/fixed_types$ ./fixed_types
Sending data chunk of size 4
Sending data chunk of size 14
user@feb23236b84c:/mnt/test/fixed_types$ 
```

In this simple program, we're simulating communication with an external device. Since we don't have a real device, the SendDataToDevice function just prints the size of the data it is supposed to send to the target device.

Suppose the device can operate on chunks of data of a variable size. Each chunk of data is prepended by its size and encoded as a 32-bit unsigned integer. This can be described as follows:

Size	Payload
0-4 bytes	5 - N bytes, where N is Size

In our code, we declare size as uint32_t:

```
uint32_t size = sizeof(buffer);
```

This means that it will take 32 bits exactly on every platform – 16-, 32-, or 64-bit.

Now, we will send the size to the device:

```
SendDataToDevice(&size, sizeof(size));
```

SendDataToDevice doesn't send the actual data; instead, it reports the size of the data to be sent. As we can see, the size is 4 bytes, as expected:

```
Sending data chunk of size 4
```

Suppose that we declare the int data type, as follows:

```
int size = sizeof(buffer);
```

In this case, this code can only work on 32- and 64-bit systems, and silently produce incorrect results on 16-bit systems, since sizeof(int) is 16 here.

There's more...

The code we implemented in this recipe is not fully portable since it doesn't take the order of bytes in a 32-bit word into account. This order is called **endianness**, and its implications will be discussed later in this chapter.

Working with the size_t type

The pointer size also depends on the architecture. Developers often need to address the elements of arrays, and, since arrays are internally represented as pointers, the offset representation depends on the pointer's size.

For example, in a 32-bit system, pointers are 32-bit, the same as `int`. However, in a 64-bit system, the size of `int` is still 32-bit, while pointers are 64-bit.

`size_t` is a special data type since it represents offset and data sizes in an architecture-independent way.

In this recipe, we will learn how to use `size_t` when working with arrays.

How to do it...

We will create an application that handles a data buffer of a variable size. We need an ability to access any address of memory provided by a target platform if needed. Follow these steps to do so:

1. In your working directory, that is, `~/test`, create a subdirectory called `sizet`.
2. Use your favorite text editor to create a file called `sizet.cpp` in the `sizet` subdirectory. Copy the following code snippet into the `sizet.cpp` file:

```
#include <iostream>
void StoreData(const char* buffer, size_t size) {
  std::cout << "Store " << size << " bytes of data" << std::endl;
}

int main() {
  char data[] = "Hello,\x1b\a\x03world!";
  const char *buffer = data;
  std::cout << "Size of buffer pointer is " << sizeof(buffer) <<
std::endl;
```

```
std::cout << "Size of int is " << sizeof(int) << std::endl;
std::cout << "Size of size_t is " << sizeof(size_t) << std::endl;
StoreData(data, sizeof(data));
return 0;
}
```

3. Create a file called `CMakeLists.txt` in the loop subdirectory with the following content:

```
cmake_minimum_required(VERSION 3.5.1)
project(sizet)
add_executable(sizet sizet.cpp)

set(CMAKE_SYSTEM_NAME Linux)
set(CMAKE_SYSTEM_PROCESSOR arm)

SET(CMAKE_CXX_FLAGS "--std=c++11")
set(CMAKE_CXX_COMPILER /usr/bin/arm-linux-gnueabi-g++)
```

4. Build the application and copy the resulting executable binary to the target system. Use the recipes from `Chapter 2`, *Setting Up the Environment*, to do so.
5. Switch to the target system's Terminal. Log in using your user credentials if needed.
6. Run the `sizet` application executable file.

How it works...

In this example, we're emulating a function that stores arbitrary data in a file or a database. The function accepts a pointer to the data and data size. But what type should we use to represent the size? If we use an unsigned int in a 64-bit system, we're artificially limiting the capability of our function to handle only up to 4 GB of data.

To avoid such limitations, we use `size_t` as a data type for `size`:

```
void StoreData(const char* buffer, size_t size) {
```

Most standard library APIs that accept indices and sizes also deal with `size_t` parameters. For example, the `memcpy` C function, which copies a chunk of data from the source buffer to the destination buffer, is declared as follows:

```
void *memset(void *b, int c, size_t len);
```

Running the preceding code produces the following output:

```
user@feb23236b84c: /mnt/test/sizet — bash
user@feb23236b84c:/mnt/test/sizet$ ./sizet
Size of buffer pointer is 8
Size of int is 4
Size of size_t is 8
Store 16 bytes of data
user@feb23236b84c:/mnt/test/sizet$
```

As we can see, the size of the pointer on the target system is 64-bit, despite the size of `int` being 32-bit. Using `size_t` in our program allows it to use all the memory of the embedded board.

There's more...

The C++ standard defines an `std::size_t` type. It is identical to the plain C `size_t`, except it is defined in the `std` namespace. Usage of `std::size_t` is preferable in your C++ code since it is part of the standard, but both `std::size_t` and `size_t` are interchangeable.

Detecting the endianness of the platform

Endianness defines the order in which bytes that represent large numerical values are stored in memory.

There are two types of endianness:

- **Big-endian**: The most significant byte is stored first. A 32-bit value, *0x01020304*, is stored at the `ptr` address, as follows:

Offset in memory (byte)	Value
ptr	0x01
ptr + 1	0x02
ptr + 2	0x03
ptr + 3	0x04

Examples of big-endian architectures include AVR32 and Motorola 68000.

- **Little-endian**: The least significant byte is stored first. A 32-bit value, *0x01020304*, is stored at the `ptr` address, as follows:

Offset in memory (byte)	Value
ptr	0x04
ptr + 1	0x03
ptr + 2	0x02
ptr + 3	0x01

The x86 architecture is little-endian.

Taking care of endianness is especially essential when exchanging data with other systems. If a developer sends a 32-bit integer, say, 0x01020304, as it is, it may be read as 0x04030201 if the endianness of the receiver does not match the endianness of the sender. That is why data should be serialized.

In this recipe, we will learn how to determine the endianness of our target system.

How to do it...

We will create a simple program that can detect the endianness of the target platform. Follow these steps to do so:

1. In your working directory, that is, `~/test`, create a subdirectory called `endianness`.

2. Use your favorite text editor to create a file called `loop.cpp` in the loop subdirectory. Copy the following code snippet into the `endianness.cpp` file:

```cpp
#include <iostream>

int main() {
  union {
    uint32_t i;
    uint8_t  c[4];
  } data;
  data.i = 0x01020304;
  if (data.c[0] == 0x01) {
    std::cout << "Big-endian" << std::endl;
  } else {
    std::cout << "Little-endian" << std::endl;
  }
}
```

3. Create a file called `CMakeLists.txt` in the loop subdirectory with the following content:

```
cmake_minimum_required(VERSION 3.5.1)
project(endianness)
add_executable(endianness endianness.cpp)

set(CMAKE_SYSTEM_NAME Linux)
set(CMAKE_SYSTEM_PROCESSOR arm)

SET(CMAKE_CXX_FLAGS "--std=c++11")
set(CMAKE_CXX_COMPILER /usr/bin/arm-linux-gnueabi-g++)
```

4. Build the application and copy the resulting executable binary to the target system. Use the recipes from `Chapter 2`, *Setting Up the Environment*, to do so.
5. Switch to the target system's Terminal. Log in using your user credentials, if needed.
6. Run the binary.

How it works...

In this recipe, we utilized the capability of C's `union` function to map the representation of different data types to the same memory space.

We define a union with two data fields – an array of 8-bit integers and a single 32-bit integer. These data fields share the same memory, so changes that are made in one field are automatically reflected in another field:

```
union {
  uint32_t i;
  uint8_t c[4];
} data
```

Next, we assign the 32-bit integer field a specially crafted value, where each byte is known in advance and different from any of the others. We used bytes with values of one, two, three, and four to compose the target value.

When the value is assigned to the 32-bit field, `i`, it automatically rewrites all the fields into the `c` byte array field. Now, we can read the first element of the array, and, depending on what we read, we can infer the endianness of the hardware platform.

If the value is one, this means that the first byte contains the most significant byte, and hence the architecture is big-endian. Otherwise, it is little-endian. When we run the binary, it produces the following output:

As we can see, the program detected our system as little-endian. This technique can be used to detect the endianness in our runtime and adjust the application logic accordingly.

There's more...

Nowadays, most widespread platforms, such as x86 and **Acorn RISC Machine** (**ARM**), are little-endian. However, your code should never assume the endianness of the system implicitly.

If you need to exchange data between applications running on the same system, it is safe to stick with the target platform's endianness. However, if your application needs to exchange data with other systems, either via network protocols or common data storage, consider converting your binary data into the common endianness.

Text-based data formats do not have issues with endianness. Use JSON format for platform-independent and human-readable representations of your data.

 Note: Converting from a binary representation and back can be costly for your target embedded platform.

Converting the endianness

While serialization libraries deal with the endianness under the hood, there are situations where developers might want to implement a lightweight communication protocol themselves.

While the C++ Standard Library does not provide functions for serialization, developers may utilize the fact that, in binary network protocols, byte order is defined and is always big-endian.

The Standard Library provides a set of functions that can be used for conversion between the current platform (hardware) and big-endian (network) byte orders:

- uint32_t htonl (uint32_t value): Converts uint32_t from hardware to network order
- uint32_t ntohl (uint32_t value): Converts uint32_t from network to hardware order
- uint16_t htons (uint16_t value): Converts uint16_t from hardware to network order
- uint16_t ntohl (uint16_t value): Converts uint16_t from network to hardware order

Developers can use these functions to exchange binary data between applications running on different platforms.

In this recipe, we will learn how to encode strings so that they can be exchanged between two systems that may have the same or different endianness.

How to do it...

In this recipe, we are going to create two applications: a sender and a receiver. The sender will write data for the receiver, thus encoding them in a platform-independent way. Follow these steps to do so:

1. In your working directory, that is, ~/test, create a subdirectory called enconv.
2. Use your favorite text editor to create and edit a file called sender.cpp in the enconv subdirectory. Include the required header files, as follows:

```
#include <stdexcept>
#include <arpa/inet.h>
#include <fcntl.h>
#include <stdint.h>
#include <string.h>
#include <unistd.h>
```

3. Then, define a function that writes data to the file descriptor:

```
void WriteData(int fd, const void* ptr, size_t size) {
  size_t offset =0;
  while (size) {
    const char *buffer = (const char*)ptr + offset;
    int written = write(fd, buffer, size);
    if (written < 0) {
```

```
                throw std::runtime_error("Can not write to file");
            }
            offset += written;
            size -= written;
        }
    }
```

4. Now, we need to define a function that formats and writes messages, along with the main function that invokes it:

```
void WriteMessage(int fd, const char* str) {
    uint32_t size = strlen(str);
    uint32_t encoded_size = htonl(size);
    WriteData(fd, &encoded_size, sizeof(encoded_size));
    WriteData(fd, str, size);
}

int main(int argc, char** argv) {
    int fd = open("envconv.data",
                  O_WRONLY|O_APPEND|O_CREAT, 0666);
    for (int i = 1; i < argc; i++) {
        WriteMessage(fd, argv[i]);
    }
}
```

5. Similarly, create a file called `receiver.cpp` with the same set of includes:

```
#include <stdexcept>
#include <arpa/inet.h>
#include <fcntl.h>
#include <stdint.h>
#include <string.h>
#include <unistd.h>
```

6. Add the following code, which reads data from a file descriptor:

```
void ReadData(int fd, void* ptr, size_t size) {
    size_t offset =0;
    while (size) {
        char *buffer = (char*)ptr + offset;
        int received = read(fd, buffer, size);
        if (received < 0) {
            throw std::runtime_error("Can not read from file");
        } else if (received == 0) {
            throw std::runtime_error("No more data");
        }
        offset += received;
        size -= received;
```

```
        }
    }
```

7. Now, define a function that will read messages, along with the main function that invokes it:

```cpp
std::string ReadMessage(int fd) {
    uint32_t encoded_size = 0;
    ReadData(fd, &encoded_size, sizeof(encoded_size));
    uint32_t size = ntohl(encoded_size);
    auto data = std::make_unique<char[]>(size);
    ReadData(fd, data.get(), size);
    return std::string(data.get(), size);
}

int main(void) {
    int fd = open("envconv.data", O_RDONLY, 0666);
    while(true) {
        try {
            auto s = ReadMessage(fd);
            std::cout << "Read: " << s << std::endl;
        } catch(const std::runtime_error& e) {
            std::cout << e.what() << std::endl;
            break;
        }
    }
}
```

8. Create a file called CMakeLists.txt in the loop subdirectory with the following content:

```cmake
cmake_minimum_required(VERSION 3.5.1)
project(conv)
add_executable(sender sender.cpp)
add_executable(receiver receiver.cpp)

set(CMAKE_SYSTEM_NAME Linux)
set(CMAKE_SYSTEM_PROCESSOR arm)

SET(CMAKE_CXX_FLAGS "--std=c++14")
set(CMAKE_CXX_COMPILER /usr/bin/arm-linux-gnueabi-g++)
```

9. Build the application and copy the two resulting executable binaries, sender and receiver, to the target system. Use the recipes from Chapter 2, *Setting Up the Environment*, to do so.

10. Switch to the target system's Terminal. Log in using your user credentials, if needed.

11. Run the `sender` binary and pass two command-line arguments: `Hello` and `Worlds`. This won't generate any output.

12. Then, run the receiver.

13. Now, check the content of the file for both the `sender` and `receiver` that were used for data exchange. It will be in binary format, so we need to use the `xxd` tool to convert it into hexadecimal format:

```
$ xxd envconv.data
0000000: 0000 0005 4865 6c6c 6f00 0000 0557 6f72  ....Hello....Wor
0000010: 6c64 1d
```

14. The file contains two strings, `hello` and `world`, prepended by their sizes. The `size` fields are always stored in big-endian byte order, independent of the architecture. This allows the sender and the receiver to be run on two different machines with different endianness.

How it works...

In this recipe, we created two binaries, sender and receiver, that emulate data exchange between two hosts. We can't make any assumptions regarding their endianness, which is why the data exchange format has to be unambiguous.

The sender and receiver exchange data blocks of variable size. We encoded each block as a 4-byte integer in order to define the upcoming block size, followed by the block content.

While the sender does not generate any output on the screen, it saves an encoded block of data in a file. When we run the receiver, it is able to read, decode, and display any information that was saved by the sender, as shown in the following screenshot:

```
user@84627761cf77: /mnt/enconv — bash
user@84627761cf77:/mnt/enconv$ ./sender Hello World
user@84627761cf77:/mnt/enconv$ ./receiver
Read: Hello
Read: World
No more data
user@84627761cf77:/mnt/enconv$ 
```

While we keep the block size in the platform format locally, we need to convert it into a unified representation when sending it out. We use the `htonl` function to do so:

```
uint32_t encoded_size = htonl(size);
```

At this point, we can write the encoded size to the output stream:

```
WriteData(fd, &encoded_size, sizeof(encoded_size));
```

The block's content is as follows:

```
WriteData(fd, str, size);
```

The receiver, in turn, reads the size from the input stream:

```
uint32_t encoded_size = 0;
ReadData(fd, &encoded_size, sizeof(encoded_size));
```

The size is encoded and cannot be used directly until the receiver converts it into a platform representation using the ntohl function:

```
uint32_t size = ntohl(encoded_size);
```

Only after doing this, will it know the size of the block that follows and can allocate and read it:

```
auto data = std::make_unique<char[]>(size);
ReadData(fd, data.get(), size);
```

Since the serialized data size is always represented as big-endian, the read function doesn't need to make assumptions about the endianness of the platform where the data was written. It can deal with data coming from any processor architecture.

Working with data alignment

Processors read and write data not in bytes, but in memory words – chunks that match their data address size. 32-bit processors work with 32-bit words, 64-bit processors with 64-bit words, and so on.

Reads and writes are most efficient when words are aligned – the data address is a multiple of the word size. For example, for 32-bit architectures, the address 0x00000004 is aligned, while 0x00000005 is unaligned. On x86 platform, access to unaligned data is slower that to aligned. On ARM, however, access to unaligned data generates a hardware exception and lead to program termination:

```
Compilers align data automatically. When it comes to structures, the result
may be surprising for developers who are not aware of alignment.
struct {
    uint8_t c;
    uint32_t i;
```

```
} a = {1, 1};

std::cout << sizeof(a) << std::endl;
```

What is the output of the preceding code snippet? `sizeof(uint8_t)` is 1, while `sizeof(uint32_t)` is 4. A developer may expect the size of the structure to be the sum of the individual sizes; however, the result highly depends on the target architecture.

For x86, the result is 8. Let's add one more `uint8_t` field before `i`:

```
struct {
    uint8_t c;
    uint8_t cc;
    uint32_t i;
} a = {1, 1};

std::cout << sizeof(a) << std::endl;
```

The result is still 8! The compiler optimizes the placement of the data fields within a structure according to the alignment rules by adding padding bytes. The rules are architecture-dependent, and the result may be different for other architectures. As a result, structures cannot be exchanged directly between two different systems without *serialization*, which will be explained in depth in `Chapter 8`, *Communication and Serialization*.

In this recipe, we will learn how to use the rules that compilers implicitly apply to align data to write more memory-efficient code.

How to do it...

We will create a program that allocates an array of structures and check how the order of the fields affects memory consumption. Follow these steps to do so:

1. In your working directory, that is, `~/test`, create a subdirectory called `alignment`.

2. Use your favorite text editor to create a file called `alignment.cpp` in the loop subdirectory. Add the required header and define two data types, that is, `Category` and `ObjectMetadata1`:

    ```
    #include <iostream>
    enum class Category: uint8_t {
      file, directory, socket
    };
    struct ObjectMetadata1 {
    ```

```
    uint8_t access_flags;
    uint32_t size;
    uint32_t owner_id;
    Category category;
};
```

3. Now, let's define another data type, called `ObjectMetadata2`, along with the code that uses all of them:

```
struct ObjectMetadata2 {
    uint32_t size;
    uint32_t owner_id;
    uint8_t access_flags;
    Category category;
};

int main() {
    ObjectMetadata1 object_pool1[1000];
    ObjectMetadata2 object_pool2[1000];
    std::cout << "Poorly aligned:" << sizeof(object_pool1) <<
std::endl;
    std::cout << "Well aligned:" << sizeof(object_pool2) <<
std::endl;
    return 0;
}
```

4. Create a file called `CMakeLists.txt` in the loop subdirectory with the following content:

```
cmake_minimum_required(VERSION 3.5.1)
project(alignment)
add_executable(alignment alignment.cpp)

set(CMAKE_SYSTEM_NAME Linux)
set(CMAKE_SYSTEM_PROCESSOR arm)

SET(CMAKE_CXX_FLAGS "--std=c++11")
set(CMAKE_CXX_COMPILER /usr/bin/arm-linux-gnueabi-g++)
```

5. Build the application and copy the resulting executable binary to the target system. Use the recipes from Chapter 2, *Setting Up the Environment*, to do so.

6. Switch to the target system's Terminal. Log in using your user credentials if needed.

7. Run the binary.

How it works...

In our sample application, we defined two data structures, ObjectMetadata1 and ObjectMetadata2, that will hold some metadata about file objects. We defined four fields that represent an object:

- **Access flags**: A combination of bits representing a type of file access, such as read, write, or execute. All bit fields are packed into a single uint8_t field.
- **Size**: Object size as a 32-bit unsigned integer. It limits the supported object size to 4 GB, but it is sufficient for our goal to demonstrate the importance of proper data alignment.
- **Owner ID**: A 32-bit integer that identifies a user in our system.
- **Category**: The category of the object. This can be a file, a directory, or a socket. Since we've only defined three categories, the uint8_t data type is sufficient to represent all of them. This is why we declare them using the enum class:

```
enum class Category: uint8_t {
```

Both ObjectMetadata1 and ObjectMetadata2 contain exactly the same fields; the only difference is how they are ordered within their structures.

Now, we declare two pools of objects. Both pools contain 1,000 objects; object_pool1 holds metadata in ObjectMetadata1 structures, while object_pool2 uses ObjectMetadata2 structures. Now, let's check the output of the application:

```
user@feb23236b84c: /mnt/test/alignment — bash
user@feb23236b84c:/mnt/test/alignment$ ./alignment
Poorly aligned:16000
Well aligned:12000
user@feb23236b84c:/mnt/test/alignment
```

Both object pools are identical in terms of functionality and performance. However, if we check how much memory they occupy, we can see a significant difference: object_pool1 is 4 KB larger than object_pool2. Given the size of object_pool2 is 12 KB, we wasted 33% of memory by not paying attention to data alignment. Be aware of alignment and padding when working on your data structures, as improper field ordering may lead to inefficient memory usage, as in the case of object_pool2. Use these simple rules to organize your data fields in order to keep them properly aligned:

- Group them by their size.
- Order the groups from largest to smallest data types.

Well-aligned data structures are fast, memory-efficient, and do not require any additional code to be implemented.

There's more...

Each hardware platform has its own alignment requirements, and some of them are tricky. You might need to consult the target platform compiler documentation and best practices to get the most out of the hardware. If your target platform is ARM, consider reading the ARM technical article at `http://infocenter.arm.com/help/index.jsp?topic=/com.arm.doc.faqs/ka15414.html` on alignment expectations.

While the proper alignment of data fields within a structure can result in a more compact data representation, be aware of performance implications. Keeping data that's used together in the same memory region is called **data locality** and may significantly improve data access performance. Data elements that fit into the same cache line can be read or written much faster than elements that span the cache line boundaries. In many cases, it is preferable to get a performance gain at the cost of additional memory use. We will review this technique in more detail in the *Aligning data with cache lines* recipe.

Working with packed structures

In this recipe, we will learn how to define structures that do not have any padding bytes between their data members. This may significantly reduce the amount of memory that's used by your application if it works with a large number of objects.

Note, though, that this has a cost. Unaligned memory access is slower, which results in sub-optimal performance. For some architectures, unaligned access is forbidden, thus requiring the C++ compiler to generate much more code to access the data fields than for aligned access.

Although packing your structs may result in more efficient memory usage, avoid using this technique unless it's really necessary. It has too many implied limitations that may lead to obscure, hard-to-find issues in your application later.

Consider packed structures as transport encoding and only use them to store, load, or exchange data outside of your application. But, even in these cases, using a proper data serialize is a better solution.

How to do it...

In this simple application, we will define an array of packed structures and see how this affects the amount of memory it requires. Follow these steps to do so:

1. In your working directory, that is, ~/test, create a copy of the alignment subdirectory. Name it packed_alignment.

2. Modify the alignment.cpp file by adding __attribute__((packed)) to the definition of each structure:

```
struct ObjectMetadata1 {
    uint8_t access_flags;
    uint32_t size;
    uint32_t owner_id;
    Category category;
} __attribute__((packed));

struct ObjectMetadata2 {
    uint32_t size;
    uint32_t owner_id;
    uint8_t access_flags;
    Category category;
} __attribute__((packed));
```

3. Build the application and copy the resulting executable binary to the target system. Use the recipes from Chapter 2, *Setting Up the Environment*, to do so.

4. Switch to the target system's Terminal. Log in using your user credentials, if needed.

5. Run the binary.

How it works...

In this recipe, we modified the code from the *Working with data alignment* recipe by adding a packed attribute to each struct:

```
} __attribute__((packed));
```

This attribute instructs the compiler to not add padding bytes to the structs in order to conform to the alignment requirements of the target platform.

Running the preceding code gives us the following output:

If the compiler does not add padding bytes, the order of the data fields becomes insignificant. Given that the `ObjectMetadata1` and `ObjectMetadata2` structs have exactly the same data fields, their size in packed form becomes identical.

There's more...

The `GNU Compiler Collection` (**GCC**) gives developers lots of control over data layout using its attributes. You can find out about all of the supported attributes and their meaning by going to the `GCC Type Attributes` page.

Other compilers provide similar functionality, but their APIs might differ. For example, Microsoft compilers define the `#pragma pack` compiler directive to declare packed structures. More details can be found on the `Pragma Pack Reference` page.

Aligning data with cache lines

In this recipe, we will learn how to align data structures with cache lines. Data alignment can significantly affect the performance of your system, especially in the case of a multithreaded application that works in a multicore system.

Firstly, frequently accessing data that's used together is much faster if they live in the same cache line. If you program accesses variable A and then variable B consistently, a processor has to invalidate and reload its cache every time, if they are not in the same line.

Secondly, you don't want to keep data that's used independently by different threads in the same cache line. If the same cache line is modified by different CPU cores, this requires cache synchronization, which affects the overall performance of a multithreaded application that uses shared data, since in this scenario memory access time significantly increases.

How to do it...

We are going to create an application that allocates four buffers using four different methods to learn how to align statically and dynamically allocated memory. Follow these steps to do so:

1. In your working directory, that is, ~/test, create a subdirectory called cache_align.

2. Use your favorite text editor to create a file called cache_align.cpp in the cache_align subdirectory. Copy the following code snippet into the cache_align.cpp file to define the necessary constants and a function that detects the alignment:

```
#include <stdlib.h>
#include <stdio.h>

constexpr int kAlignSize = 128;
constexpr int kAllocBytes = 128;

constexpr int overlap(void* ptr) {
  size_t addr = (size_t)ptr;
  return addr & (kAlignSize - 1);
}
```

3. Now, define several buffers that are allocated in different ways:

```
int main() {
  char static_buffer[kAllocBytes];
  char* dynamic_buffer = new char[kAllocBytes];


  alignas(kAlignSize) char aligned_static_buffer[kAllocBytes];
  char* aligned_dynamic_buffer = nullptr;
  if (posix_memalign((void**)&aligned_dynamic_buffer,
      kAlignSize, kAllocBytes)) {
    printf("Failed to allocate aligned memory buffer\n");
  }
```

4. Add the following code, which uses them:

```
printf("Static buffer address: %p (%d)\n", static_buffer,
      overlap(static_buffer));
printf("Dynamic buffer address: %p (%d)\n", dynamic_buffer,
      overlap(dynamic_buffer));
printf("Aligned static buffer address: %p (%d)\n",
aligned_static_buffer,
```

```
              overlap(aligned_static_buffer));
    printf("Aligned dynamic buffer address: %p (%d)\n",
aligned_dynamic_buffer,
              overlap(aligned_dynamic_buffer));
    delete[] dynamic_buffer;
    free(aligned_dynamic_buffer);
    return 0;
    }
```

5. Create a file called CMakeLists.txt in the loop subdirectory with the following content:

```
cmake_minimum_required(VERSION 3.5.1)
project(cache_align)
add_executable(cache_align cache_align.cpp)

set(CMAKE_SYSTEM_NAME Linux)
set(CMAKE_SYSTEM_PROCESSOR arm)

SET(CMAKE_CXX_FLAGS "-std=c++11")
set(CMAKE_CXX_COMPILER /usr/bin/arm-linux-gnueabi-g++)
```

6. Build the application and copy the resulting executable binary to the target system. Use the recipes from Chapter 2, *Setting Up the Environment,* to do so.
7. Switch to the target system's Terminal. Log in using your user credentials, if needed.
8. Run the binary.

How it works...

In the first code snippet, we created two pairs of memory buffers. In each pair, the first buffer is allocated to the stack, while the second one is allocated to the heap.

The first pair is created using the standard C++ technique. The static buffer on the stack is declared as an array:

```
char static_buffer[kAllocBytes];
```

To create a dynamic buffer, we use the new C++ keyword:

```
char* dynamic_buffer = new char[kAllocBytes];
```

In the second pair, we create memory-aligned buffers. Declaring the static buffer on the stack is similar to the regular static buffer. We use an additional attribute, `alignas`, which was introduced in C++11 as a standardized and platform-independent way to align data in memory:

```
alignas(kAlignSize) char aligned_static_buffer[kAllocBytes];
```

This attribute requires an alignment size as a parameter. We want to have data aligned by the cache line boundaries. Depending on the platform, the cache line size may differ. The most common sizes are 32, 64, and 128 bytes. Using 128 bytes makes our buffer aligned for any of them.

There is no standard way to do the same for a dynamic buffer. To allocate memory on the heap, we use a C function called `posix_memalign`. This is available only in **Portable Operating System Interface** (**POSIX**) systems (mostly Unix-like), but this doesn't require the support of the C++11 standard:

```
if (posix_memalign((void**)&aligned_dynamic_buffer,
    kAlignSize, kAllocBytes)) {
```

`posix_memalign` is similar to `malloc`, but has three parameters instead of one. The second parameter is an alignment size, the same as it is for the align attribute. The third is the size of the memory to allocate. The first parameter is used to return a pointer to the allocated memory. Unlike `malloc`, `posix_memalign` may fail not only if it can't allocate memory, but also if the alignment size passed to the function is not a power of two. `posix_memalign` returns an error code as its result value to help developers differentiate between these two cases.

We define function overlap to calculate an unaligned part of a pointer by masking out all the aligned bits:

```
size_t addr = (size_t)ptr;
return addr & (kAlignSize - 1);
```

When we run the application, we can see the difference:

```
user@feb23236b84c: /mnt/test/cache_align — bash
user@feb23236b84c:/mnt/test/cache_align$ ./cache_align
Static buffer address: 0x7fff64310f70 (112)
Dynamic buffer address: 0x56464583fe70 (112)
Aligned static buffer address: 0x7fff64310e00 (0)
Aligned dynamic buffer address: 0x564645840400 (0)
user@feb23236b84c:/mnt/test/cache_align$
```

The addresses of both buffers in the first pair have unaligned parts, while the addresses of the second pair are aligned – the unaligned part is zero. As a result, random access to the elements of the second pair of buffers is faster, because all of them are available in the cache at the same time.

There's more...

CPU access data alignment is also crucial for efficiently mapping memory through a hardware address translation mechanism. Modern operating systems operate 4 KB memory blocks or pages to map a process' virtual address space to physical memory. Aligning data structures on 4 KB boundaries can lead to performance gains.

The same technique we described in this recipe can be applied to align data to the memory page boundaries. Note, however, that posix_memalign may require twice as much memory than what was requested to fulfill this request. This memory overhead growth may be significant for larger alignment blocks.

4
Handling Interrupts

One of the primary tasks of embedded applications is communicating with external hardware peripherals. Sending data to peripherals using the output port is easy to understand. When it comes to reading, though, things become more complicated.

Embedded developers have to know when data is available to be read. Since the peripheral is external to the processor, this can happen at any moment in time.

In this chapter, we will learn about what interrupts are and how to work with them. While using an 8-bit microcontroller, 8051, as a target platform, we will learn about the following topics:

- How to implement a basic interrupt handling
- How to generate a signal on the output pin of the **Microcontroller Unit** (MCU) using interrupts from the timer
- How to use interrupts to count events on the external pins of the MCU
- How to use interrupts to communicate over the serial channel

We will learn about these topics by completing the following recipes:

- Implementing an interrupt service routine
- Generating a 5 kHz square signal using 8-bit auto-reload mode
- Using Timer 1 as an event counter to count a 1 Hz pulse
- Receiving and transmitting data serially

Understanding the core concepts of how to handle interrupts will help you implement responsive and power-efficient embedded applications.

Before we do this, however, we'll acquire some background knowledge of a few concepts.

Data polling

The first approach to waiting for data from an external source is called **polling**. An application periodically queries the input port of an external device to check if it has new data. It is easy to implement but has significant downsides.

First, it wastes processor resources. Most poll calls report that data is not available yet and we need keep waiting. Since these calls do not lead to some data processing, it is waste of computing resources. Moreover, the polling interval should be short enough that it responds to an external event quickly. Developers should look for a compromise between the efficient utilization of processor power and reaction time.

Secondly, it makes the logic of the program convoluted. If the program should poll for events, for example, every 5 milliseconds, none of its subroutines should take longer than 5 milliseconds. As a result, developers artificially split the code into smaller chunks and organize complex switching between them to allow polling.

Interrupt service routines

Interrupts are an alternative to polling. Once an external device has new data, it triggers an event in a processor called an **interrupt**. As its name suggests, it interrupts the normal workflow of executing instructions. The processor saves its current state and starts executing instructions from a different address until it encounters the return from an interrupt instruction. Then, it reads the saved state to continue executing the instruction stream from the moment it was interrupted. This alternative sequence of instructions is called an **Interrupt Service Routine (ISR)**.

Each processor defines its own set of instructions and conventions to work with interrupts; however, all of them use the same general approach while dealing with interrupts:

- Interrupts are identified by numbers, starting with 0. The numbers are mapped to the hardware **interrupt request lines (IRQ)** that physically correspond to specific processor pins.
- When an IRQ line is activated, the processor uses its number as an offset in the interrupt vector array to locate the address of the interrupt service routine. The interrupt vector array is stored in memory on a fixed address.
- Developers can define or redefine ISRs by updating the entries in the interrupt vector arrays.

- A processor can be programmed to enable or disable interrupts, either for specific IRQ lines or all interrupts at once. When interrupts are disabled, the processor does not invoke the corresponding ISRs, although the status of the IRQ lines can be read.
- IRQ lines can be programmed to trigger interrupts, depending on the signal on the physical pin. This can be at the low level of the signal, the high level of the signal, or the edge (which is a transition from low to high or high to low).

General considerations for ISRs

This approach does not waste processor resources for polling and provides a very short reaction time since interrupt processing is performed at the hardware level. However, developers should be aware of its specifics to avoid critical or hard-to-detect issues in the future.

First of all, dealing with multiple interrupts at the same time, or responding to the same interrupt while still handling the previous interrupt, is hard to implement. That is why ISRs are executed with interrupts disabled. This prevents the ISR from being interrupted with another interrupt, but it also means that the reaction time for the pending interrupt can be longer. Worse, this can lead to data or events being lost if interrupts are not re-enabled quickly.

To avoid such situations, all ISRs are written to be short. They only do a minimal amount of work to read or acknowledge data from a device. Complex data analysis and processing are performed outside of the ISR.

8051 microcontroller interrupts

The 8051 microcontroller supports six interrupt sources – reset, two hardware interrupts, two timer interrupts, and a serial communication interrupt:

Interrupt number	Description	Offset in bytes
	Reset	0
0	External interrupt INT0	3
1	Timer 0 (TF0)	11
2	External interrupt INT1	19
3	Timer 1 (TF1)	27
4	Serial	36

The interrupt vector array is located at address 0; each entry except reset is 8 bytes in size. Though a minimal ISR can fit into 8 bytes, normally, the entries contain code that redirects execution to the actual ISR located elsewhere.

The reset entry is special. It is activated by the reset signal and immediately jumps to the address where the main program is located.

8051 defines a special register called **Interrupt Enable** (**EA**), which is used to enable and disable interrupts. Its 8-bits are allocated in the following way:

Bit	Name	Meaning
0	EX0	External Interrupt 0
1	ET0	Timer 0 Interrupt
2	EX1	External Interrupt 1
3	ET1	Timer 1 Interrupt
4	ES	Serial Port Interrupt
5	-	Not used
6	-	Not used
7	EA	Global Interrupt Control

Setting these bits to 1 enables corresponding interrupts, to 0 disables them. The EA bit enables or disables all interrupts.

Implementing an interrupt service routine

In this recipe, we will learn how to define an interrupt service routine for the 8051 microcontroller.

How to do it...

Follow these steps to complete this recipe:

1. Switch to the build system we set up in Chapter 2, *Setting Up the Environment*.
2. Make sure that the 8051 emulator is installed:

   ```
   # apt install -y mcu8051ide
   ```

3. Launch mcu8051ide and create a new project called Test.

4. Create a new file called `test.c` and put the following code snippet into it. This increments an internal `counter` for each timer interrupt:

```c
#include<mcs51reg.h>

volatile int Counter = 0;
void timer0_ISR (void) __interrupt(1) /*interrupt no. 1 for Timer0
*/
{

  Counter++;
}

void main(void)
{
  TMOD = 0x03;
  TH0 = 0x0;
  TL0 = 0x0;
  ET0 = 1;
  TR0 = 1;
  EA = 1;
  while (1); /* do nothing */
}
```

5. Select **Tools** | **Compile** to build the code. The messages window will display the following output:

```
Starting compiler ...

cd "/home/dev"
sdcc -mmcs51 --iram-size 128 --xram-size 0 --code-size 4096 --
nooverlay --noinduction --verbose --debug -V --std-sdcc89 --model-
small "test.c"
sdcc: Calling preprocessor...
+ /usr/bin/sdcpp -nostdinc -Wall -obj-ext=.rel -D__SDCC_NOOVERLAY -
DSDCC_NOOVERLAY -D__SDCC_MODEL_SMALL -DSDCC_MODEL_SMALL -
D__SDCC_FLOAT_REENT -DSDCC_FLOAT_REENT -D__SDCC=3_4_0 -DSDCC=340 -
D__SDCC_REVISION=8981 -DSDCC_REVISION=8981 -D__SDCC_mcs51 -
DSDCC_mcs51 -D__mcs51 -D__STDC_NO_COMPLEX__ -D__STDC_NO_THREADS__ -
D__STDC_NO_ATOMICS__ -D__STDC_NO_VLA__ -isystem
/usr/bin/../share/sdcc/include/mcs51 -isystem
/usr/share/sdcc/include/mcs51 -isystem
/usr/bin/../share/sdcc/include -isystem /usr/share/sdcc/include
test.c
sdcc: Generating code...
sdcc: Calling assembler...
+ /usr/bin/sdas8051 -plosgffwy test.rel test.asm
sdcc: Calling linker...
```

```
sdcc: Calling linker...
+ /usr/bin/sdld -nf test.lk

Compilation successful
```

6. Select the **Simulator | Start/Shutdown** menu entry to activate a simulator.
7. Select **Simulator | Animate** to run the program in slow mode.
8. Switch to the **C variables** panel and scroll down until it shows **Counter variable**.
9. Observe how it increases over time:

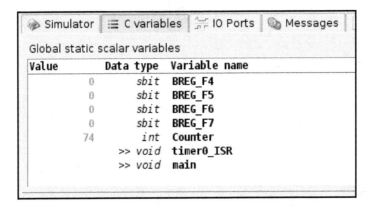

As you can see, the **Value** field for the `Counter` variable is now **74**.

How it works...

For our sample applications, we are going to use an emulator for the 8051 microcontroller. Several of them are available; however, we will be using MCU8051IDE since it's readily available in the Ubuntu repository.

We install it as a regular Ubuntu package, as follows:

```
# apt install -y mcu8051ide
```

This is a GUI IDE and requires an X Window system to run. If you use Linux or Windows as your working environment, consider installing and running it directly from `https://sourceforge.net/projects/mcu8051ide/files/`.

The simple program we created defines a global variable called `Counter`, as shown here:

```
volatile int Counter = 0;
```

This is defined as `volatile`, indicating that it can be changed externally and that a compiler shouldn't try to optimize the code to eliminate it.

Next, we define a simple function called `timer0_ISR`:

```
void timer0_ISR (void) __interrupt(1)
```

It doesn't accept any parameters and doesn't return any values. The only thing it does is increment the `Counter` variable. It is declared with an important attribute called `__interrupt(1)` to let the compiler know that it is an interrupt handler and that it serves the interrupt number 1. The compiler generates code that updates the corresponding entry of the interrupt vector array automatically.

After defining the ISR itself, we configure the parameters of the timer:

```
TMOD = 0x03;
TH0  = 0x0;
TL0  = 0x0;
```

Then, we turn on Timer 0, as shown here:

```
TR0 = 1;
```

The following command enables interrupts from Timer 0:

```
ET0 = 1;
```

The following code enables all interrupts:

```
EA = 1;
```

At this point, our ISR is being periodically activated by the timer's interrupt. We run an endless loop that does nothing since all the work is done within ISR:

```
while (1); // do nothing
```

When we run the preceding code in the simulator, we will see that the actual value of the `counter` variable changes over time, indicating that our ISR is being activated by the timer.

Generating a 5 kHz square signal using 8-bit auto-reload mode

In the preceding recipe, we learned how to create a simple ISR that only does a counter increment. Let's make the interrupt routine do something more useful. In this recipe, we will learn how to program the 8051 microcontroller so that it generates a signal with a given frequency.

The 8051 microcontroller has two timers – Timer 0 and Timer 1 – both of which are configured using two special function registers: **Timer Mode (TMOD)** and **Timer Control (TCON)**. The timer's values are stored in the TH0 and TL0 timer registers for Timer 0 and the TH1 and TL1 timer registers for Timer 1.

The TMOD and TCON bits have special meanings. The bits of the TMOD registers are defined as follows:

Bit	Timer	Name	Purpose
0	0	M0	Timer mode selector – lower bit.
1	0	M1	Timer mode selector – upper bit.
2	0	CT	Counter (1) or Timer (0) mode.
3	0	GATE	Enable Timer 1, but only if the external interrupt of INT0 is high.
4	1	M0	Timer mode selector – lower bit.
5	1	M1	Timer mode selector – upper bit.
6	1	CT	Counter (1) or Timer (0) mode.
7	1	GATE	Enable Timer 1, but only if the external interrupt of INT1 is high.

The lower 4 bits are assigned to Timer 0, while the upper 4 bits are assigned to Timer 1.

The M0 and M1 bits allow us to configure the timers in one of four modes:

Mode	M0	M1	Description
0	0	0	13-bit mode. TL0 or TL1 registers contain lower 5 bits, TH0 or TH1 registers contain upper 8 bits of the corresponding timer value.
1	0	1	16-bit mode. TL0 or TL1 registers contain lower 8-bits, TH0 or TH1 registers contain upper 8 bits of the corresponding timer value.
2	1	0	8 bits mode with auto-reload. TL0 or TL1 contains the corresponding timer value, while TH0 or TL1 contains the reload value.
3	1	1	Special 8 bits mode for Timer 0

The **Timer Control** (**TCON**) registers the control's timer interrupts. Its bits are defined as follows:

Bit	Name	Purpose
0	IT0	External interrupt 0 control bit.
1	IE0	External interrupt 0 edge flag. Set to 1 when high-to-low edge signal received at INT0.
2	IT1	External interrupt 1 control bit.
3	IE1	External interrupt 1 edge flag. Set to 1 when high-to-low edge signal received at INT1.
4	TR0	Run Control for Timer 0. Set to 1 to start, 0 to halt the timer.
5	TF0	Timer 0 overflow. Set to 1 when the timer reaches its maximal value.
6	TR1	Run Control for Timer 1. Set to 1 to start, 0 to halt the timer.
7	TF1	Timer 1 overflow. Set to 1 when the timer reaches its maximal value.

We are going to use the specific mode of 8051 timers called auto-reload. In this mode, the TL0 (TL1 for Timer 1) register contains the timer value, while TH0 (TH1 for Timer 1) contains a reload value. Once TL0 reaches the maximum value of 255, it generates the overflow interrupt and is automatically reset to the reload value.

How to do it...

Follow these steps to complete this recipe:

1. Launch *mce8051ide* and create a new project called `Test`.
2. Create a new file called `generator.c` and put the following code snippet into it. This will generate a 5 kHz signal on the `P0_0` pin of the MCU:

```
#include<8051.h>

void timer0_ISR (void) __interrupt(1)
```

```
    {
      P0_0 = !P0_0;
    }

    void main(void)
    {
      TMOD = 0x02;
      TH0 = 0xa3;
      TL0 = 0x0;
      TR0 = 1;
      EA = 1;
      while (1); // do nothing
    }
```

3. Select **Tools** | **Compile** to build the code.
4. Select the **Simulator** | **Start/Shutdown** menu entry to activate a simulator.
5. Select **Simulator** | **Animate** to run the program in slow mode.

How it works...

The following code defines an ISR for Timer 0:

```
    void timer0_ISR (void) __interrupt(1)
```

On every timer interrupt, we flip the 0 bit of P0's input-output register. This will efficiently generate the square wave signal on a P0 output pin.

Now, we need to figure out how to program the timer to generate interrupts with the given frequency. To generate the 5 kHz signal, we need to flip the bit with the 10 kHz frequency since each wave consists of one high and one low phase.

The 8051 MCU uses an external oscillator as a clock source. The timer unit divides the external frequency by 12. For the 11.0592 MHz oscillator, which is commonly used as a time source for 8051, the timer is activated every 1/11059200*12 = 1.085 milliseconds.

Our timer ISR should be activated with 10 kHz frequency, or every 100 milliseconds, or after every 100/1.085 = 92 timer ticks.

We programmed Timer 0 to run in mode two, as follows:

```
    TMOD = 0x02;
```

In this mode, we store the reset value of the timer in the TH0 register. The ISR is activated by the timer overflow, which happens after the timer counter reaches the maximum value. Mode two is an 8-bit mode, meaning the maximum value is 255. To activate the ISR every 92 ticks, the auto-reload value should be 255-92 = 163, or `0xa3` in hexadecimal representation.

We store the auto-reload value along with the initial timer value in the timer registers:

```
TH0 = 0xa3;
TL0 = 0x0;
```

Timer 0 is activated, as shown here:

```
TR0 = 1;
```

Then, we enable timer interrupts:

```
TR0 = 1;
```

Finally, all the interrupts are activated:

```
EA = 1;
```

From now on, our ISR is invoked every 100 microseconds, as shown in the following code:

```
P0_0 = !P0_0;
```

This flips the `0` bit of the `P0` register, resulting in the 5 kHz square signal being produced on the corresponding output pin.

Using Timer 1 as an event counter to count a 1 Hz pulse

8051 timers have dual functionality. When they are activated by the clock oscillator, they act as timers. However, they can also be activated by the signal pulse on the external pins, that is, P3.4 (Timer 0) and P3.5 (Timer 1), acting as counters.

In this recipe, we will learn how to program Timer 1 so that it counts the activations of the P3.5 pin of the 8051 processor.

How to do it...

Follow these steps to complete this recipe:

1. Open mcu8051ide.
2. Create a new project called `Counters`.
3. Create a new file called `generator.c` and put the following code snippet into it. This increments a counter variable each time a timer interrupt is triggered:

```
#include<8051.h>

volatile int counter = 0;
void timer1_ISR (void) __interrupt(3)
{
   counter++;
}

void main(void)
{
   TMOD = 0x60;
   TH1 = 254;
   TL1 = 254;
   TR1 = 1;
   ET1 = 1;
   EA = 1;
   while (1); // do nothing
}
```

4. Select **Tools | Compile** to build the code.
5. Open the **Virtual HW** menu and select the **Simple Key...** entry. A new window will open.
6. In the **Simple Keypad** window, assign **PORT 3** and **BIT 5** to the first key. Then, click the **ON or OFF** button to activate it:

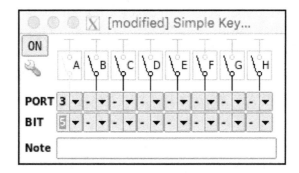

7. Select the **Simulator** | **Start/Shutdown** menu entry to activate the simulator.
8. Select **Simulator** | **Animate** to run the program in the animation mode that displays all changes to the special registers in the debugger window.
9. Switch to the **Simple Keypad** window and click the first key.

How it works...

In this recipe, we utilize the capability of 8051 timers so that they act as counters. We define an interrupt service routine in exactly the same way as we do for ordinary timers. Since we use Timer 1 as a counter, we use interrupt line number 3, as follows:

```
void timer1_ISR (void) __interrupt(3)
```

The body of the interrupt routine is simple. We only increment the counter variable.

Now, let's ensure the ISR is activated by the external source rather than the clock oscillator. To do so, we configure Timer 1 by setting the C/T bit of the TMOD special function register to one:

```
TMOD = 0x60;
```

The same line configures Timer 1 to run in Mode 2 – 8-bit mode with auto-reload. Since our goal is to make the interrupt routine invoked on every external pin activation, we set the auto-reload and initial values to the maximum value of 254:

```
TH1 = 254;
TL1 = 254;
```

Next, we enable Timer 1:

```
TR1 = 1;
```

Then, all the interrupts from Timer 1 are activated, as shown here:

```
ET1 = 1;
EA = 1;
```

After that, we can enter the endless loop that does nothing since all the work is done in the Interrupt Service Routine:

```
while (1); // do nothing
```

At this point, we can run the code in the emulator. However, we need to configure the external source of events. For this purpose, we utilize one of the virtual external hardware components supported by MCU8051IDE – the virtual keypad.

We configure one of its keys to activate pin P3.5 of 8051. This pin is used as a source for Timer 1 when it is used in counting mode.

Now, we run the code. Pressing the virtual key activates the counter. Once the timer value overflows, our ISR is triggered, incrementing the `counter` variable.

There's more...

In this recipe, we used Timer 1 as a counter. The same can be applied to Counter 0. In this case, pin P3.4 should be used as an external source.

Receiving and transmitting data serially

8051 microcontrollers come with a built-in **Universal Asynchronous Receiver Transmitter (UART)** port for serial data exchange.

The serial port is controlled by a **Special Function Register (SFR)** called **Serial Control (SCON)**. Its bits are defined as follows:

Bit	Name	Purpose
0	**RI** (short for **Receive Interrupt**)	Set by UART when a byte is received completely
1	**TI** (short for **Transmit Interrupt**)	Set by UART when a byte is transmitted completely
2	**RB8** (short for **Receive Bit 8**)	Stores the ninth bit of the received data in 9-bit mode.
3	**TB8** (short for **Transmit Bit 8**)	Stores the ninth bit of data to be transmitted in 9-bit mode (see below)
4	**REN** (short for **Receiver Enabled**)	Enables (1) or disables (0) the receive operation
5	**SM2** (Enable Multiprocessor)	Enables (1) or disables (0) multiprocessor communication for 9-bit mode
6	**SM1** (Serial Mode, high bit)	Defines the serial communication mode
7	**SM0** (Serial Mode, low bit)	Defines the serial communication mode

8051 UART supports four m of serial communication modes, all of which are defined by the SM1 and SM0 bits:

Mode	SM0	SM1	Description
0	0	0	Shift-register, fixed baud rate
1	0	1	8-bit UART, baud rate set with Timer 1
2	1	0	9-bit UART, fixed baud rate
3	1	1	9-bit UART, baud rate set with Timer 1

In this recipe, we will learn how to use interrupts to implement a simple data exchange over a serial port using the 8-bit UART mode with a programmable baud rate (mode 1).

How to do it...

Follow these steps to complete this recipe:

1. Open mcu8051ide and create a new project.
2. Create a new file called `serial.c` and copy the following code snippet into it. This code copies the bytes that were received over the serial link to the `P0` output register. This is associated with the general-purpose input/output pins on the MCU:

```c
#include<8051.h>

void serial_isr() __interrupt(4) {
    if(RI == 1) {
        P0 = SBUF;
        RI = 0;
    }
}

void main() {
    SCON = 0x50;
    TMOD = 0x20;
    TH1 = 0xFD;
    TR1 = 1;
    ES = 1;
    EA = 1;

    while(1);
}
```

3. Select **Tools** | **Compile** to build the code.

4. Select the **Simulator** | **Start/Shutdown** menu entry to activate the simulator.

How it works...

We define an ISR for interrupt line 4, which is triggered for serial port events:

```
void serial_isr() __interrupt(4)
```

The interrupt routine is invoked as soon as a full byte is received and stored in the **Serial buffer register (SBUF)**. Our implementation of ISR just copies the received byte to the input/output port, that is, P0 :

```
P0 = SBUF;
```

Then, it resets the RI flag to enable the interrupt for the upcoming byte.

To make the interrupts work as expected, we configure both the serial port and the timer. First, the serial port is configured, as follows:

```
SCON = 0x50;
```

According to the preceding table, this means only the SM1 and REN bits of the **Serial Control Register (SCON)** are set to 1, resulting in the selection of communication mode 1. This is an 8-bit UARS with a baud rate defined via Timer 1. Then, it enables the receiver.

Since the baud rate is defined by Timer 1, the next step is to configure the timer, as follows:

```
TMOD = 0x20;
```

The preceding code configures Timer 1 to use mode 2, which is the 8-bit auto-reload mode.

Loading 0xFD into the TH1 register sets the baud rate to 9600 bps. Then, we enable Timer 1, serial interrupts, and all interrupts.

There's more...

Data transmission can be implemented in a similar way. If you write data to the SBUF special register, the 8051 UART will start transmission. Once completed, a serial interrupt will be invoked and the TI flag will be set to 1.

5
Debugging, Logging, and Profiling

Debugging and profiling is an important part of the development workflow for any type of application. In the case of an embedded environment, these tasks require special attention from developers. Embedded applications run on a system that might be very different from a developer's workstation, and that often has limited resources and user interface capabilities.

Developers should plan in advance how they are going to debug their application during the development phase, and how they are going to determine the root causes of, as well as fix, the issues in the production environment.

Often, the solution is to use an emulator for a target device along with an interactive debugger that is provided by the embedded system vendor. For more complex systems, however, complete and accurate emulation is hardly feasible, and remote debugging is the most viable solution.

In many cases, using an interactive debugger is not possible or not practical at all. Hardware states can change in a few milliseconds after a program stops on a breakpoint, and a developer has insufficient time to analyze it. In such cases, developers have to use extensive logging for root cause analysis.

In this chapter, we will focus on debugging approaches for the more powerful systems based on **SoC** (short for **System On a Chip**) and running Linux OS. We will cover the following topics:

- Running your applications in the **GDB** (short for **GNU Project Debugger)**
- Working with breakpoints
- Working with core dumps

- Using gdbserver for debugging
- Adding debug logging
- Working with debug and release builds

These basic debugging techniques will help significantly while working with the recipes in this book as well as in your work on embedded applications of any kind.

Technical requirements

In this chapter, we will learn how to debug embedded applications in the **ARM** (short for **Acorn RISC Machines**) platform emulator. At this point, you should already have two systems configured in a virtualized Linux environment running on your laptop or desktop:

- Ubuntu Linux in a Docker container as a build system
- Debian Linux in a **QEMU** (short for **Quick EMUlato**) ARM emulator as a target system

To learn the theory of cross-compilation and set up the development environment, please refer to the recipes in `Chapter 2`, *Setting Up the Environment*.

Running your applications in the GDB

In this recipe, we will learn how to run a sample application in a debugger on a target system, as well as try out some basic debugging techniques.

GDB is an open source and widely used interactive debugger. Unlike most of the debuggers that come as part of **Integrated Development Environment (IDE)** products, the GDB is a standalone, command-line debugger. This means that it does not depend on any particular IDE. As you can see in the example, you can use a plain text editor to work on the code of your application, while still being able to debug it interactively, use breakpoints, view the content of variables and stack traces, and much more.

The user interface of the GDB is minimalist. You run with it in the same way as you work with a Linux console— by typing in commands and analyzing their output. This simplicity makes it extremely suitable for embedded projects. It can run on a system that does not have a graphical subsystem. It is especially handy if the target system can only be accessed over a serial connection or ssh shell. Since it does not have a fancy user interface, it can work on systems with limited resources.

In this recipe, we will use an artificial sample application that crashes with an exception. It does not log any useful information and the exception message is too vague to determine the root cause of the crash. We will use the GDB to determine the root cause of the issue.

How to do it...

We are now going to create a simple application that crashes under specific conditions:

1. In your working directory, ~/test, create a subdirectory called loop.

2. Use your favorite text editor to create a loop.cpp file in the loop subdirectory.

3. Let's put some code into the loop.cpp file. We start with includes:

```
#include <iostream>
#include <chrono>
#include <thread>
#include <functional>
```

4. Now, we define three functions that our program will consist of. The first one is runner:

```
void runner(std::chrono::milliseconds limit,
            std::function<void(int)> fn,
            int value) {
  auto start = std::chrono::system_clock::now();
  fn(value);
  auto end = std::chrono::system_clock::now();
  std::chrono::milliseconds delta =
      std::chrono::duration_cast<std::chrono::milliseconds>(end -
start);
  if (delta > limit) {
    throw std::runtime_error("Time limit exceeded");
  }
}
```

5. The second function is delay_ms:

```
void delay_ms(int count) {
  for (int i = 0; i < count; i++) {
    std::this_thread::sleep_for(std::chrono::microseconds(1050));
  }
}
```

6. And finally, we add the entry-point function, `main`:

```
int main() {
  int max_delay = 10;
  for (int i = 0; i < max_delay; i++) {
    runner(std::chrono::milliseconds(max_delay), delay_ms, i);
  }
  return 0;
  }
```

7. Create a file called `CMakeLists.txt` in the `loop` subdirectory with the following content:

```
cmake_minimum_required(VERSION 3.5.1)
project(loop)
add_executable(loop loop.cpp)

set(CMAKE_SYSTEM_NAME Linux)
set(CMAKE_SYSTEM_PROCESSOR arm)

SET(CMAKE_CXX_FLAGS "-g --std=c++11")

set(CMAKE_C_COMPILER /usr/bin/arm-linux-gnueabi-gcc)
set(CMAKE_CXX_COMPILER /usr/bin/arm-linux-gnueabi-g++)

set(CMAKE_FIND_ROOT_PATH_MODE_PROGRAM NEVER)
set(CMAKE_FIND_ROOT_PATH_MODE_LIBRARY ONLY)
set(CMAKE_FIND_ROOT_PATH_MODE_INCLUDE ONLY)
set(CMAKE_FIND_ROOT_PATH_MODE_PACKAGE ONLY)
```

8. Now, switch to the build system terminal and change the current directory to `/mnt/loop` by running the following command.

```
$ cd /mnt/loop
```

9. Build the application as follows:

```
$ cmake . && make
```

10. Switch back to your native environment, find the `loop` output file in the `loop` subdirectory, and copy it over ssh to the target system. Use the user account. Switch to the target system terminal. Log in using the user credentials if needed. Now, run the `loop` executable binary using `gdb`:

```
$ gdb ./loop
```

11. The debugger has been started and shows the command-line prompt (gdb). To run the application, type the run command:

    (gdb) run

12. You can see that the application terminated abnormally due to the runtime exception. The exception message, Time limit exceeded, gives us a clue, but does not indicate under what specific conditions it happened. Let's try to establish this. Firstly, let's check the stack trace of the crashing application:

    (gdb) bt

13. This shows seven stack frames from the top-level function, main, down to the library function, __GI_abort, which actually terminates the application. As we can see, only frames 7 and 6 belong to our application, since only they are defined in loop.cpp. Let's take a close look at frame 6, since this is the function that throws the exception:

    (gdb) frame 6

14. Run the list command to see the nearby code:

    (gdb) list

15. As we can see, the exception is thrown if the value of the delta variable exceeds the value of the limit variable. But what are what are these values?. These are the values of variable 'delta' and 'limit Run the info locals command to figure this out:

    (gdb) info locals

16. We cannot see the value of the limit variable here. Use the info args command to see it:

    (gdb) info args

17. Now, we can see that the limit is 10, and the delta 11. The crash happens when the function is called with the fn parameter set to the delay_ms function and the value of the value parameter set to 7.

How it works...

The application is intentionally created to crash under certain conditions and does not provide enough information to be able to nail down to these conditions. The application consists of two major functions – `runner` and `delay_ms`.

The `runner` function accepts three parameters—the time limit, the function of one parameter, and the function parameter value. It runs the function provided as a parameter, passing it the value, and measures the elapsed time. If the time exceeds the time limit, it throws an exception.

The `delay_ms` function performs a delay. However, it is implemented incorrectly and considers each millisecond as consisting of 1,100 microseconds instead of 1,000.

The `main` function runs the runner in the `loop` directory, providing fixing values of 10 milliseconds as a time limit and `delay_ms` as a function to run, but increasing values of the `value` parameter. At some point, the `delay_ms` function exceeds the time limit and the app crashes.

First, we build the application for the ARM platform and transfer it to the emulator to run:

```
user@dd4db343afcd: /mnt/loop -- bash
$ cd /mnt/loop
$ cmake . && make
-- The C compiler identification is GNU 7.4.0
-- The CXX compiler identification is GNU 7.4.0
-- Check for working C compiler: /usr/bin/cc
-- Check for working C compiler: /usr/bin/cc -- works
-- Detecting C compiler ABI info
-- Detecting C compiler ABI info - done
-- Detecting C compile features
-- Detecting C compile features - done
-- Check for working CXX compiler: /usr/bin/c++
-- Check for working CXX compiler: /usr/bin/c++ -- works
-- Detecting CXX compiler ABI info
-- Detecting CXX compiler ABI info - done
-- Detecting CXX compile features
-- Detecting CXX compile features - done
-- Configuring done
-- Generating done
-- Build files have been written to: /mnt/loop
Scanning dependencies of target loop
[100%] Built target loop
$
```

It is important to pass the $-g$ parameter to the compiler. This parameter instructs the compiler to add debug symbols to the resulting binary. We add it to the CMAKE_CXX_FLAGS parameter in the CMakeLists.txt file, as shown here:

```
SET(CMAKE_CXX_FLAGS "-g --std=c++11")
```

Now, we run the debugger and pass the application executable name as its parameter:

```
user@dd4db343afcd: /mnt/loop — bash
$ gdb ./loop
GNU gdb (Ubuntu 8.1-0ubuntu3) 8.1.0.20180409-git
Copyright (C) 2018 Free Software Foundation, Inc.
License GPLv3+: GNU GPL version 3 or later <http://gnu.org/licenses/gpl.html>
This is free software: you are free to change and redistribute it.
There is NO WARRANTY, to the extent permitted by law.  Type "show copying"
and "show warranty" for details.
This GDB was configured as "x86_64-linux-gnu".
Type "show configuration" for configuration details.
For bug reporting instructions, please see:
<http://www.gnu.org/software/gdb/bugs/>.
Find the GDB manual and other documentation resources online at:
<http://www.gnu.org/software/gdb/documentation/>.
For help, type "help".
Type "apropos word" to search for commands related to "word"...
Reading symbols from ./loop...done.
(gdb)
```

The application does not run immediately. We start it using the `run` GDB command and observe it crashing shortly afterward:

```
● ● ●                         user@0b277b1d08e1: ~ — bash
GNU gdb (Ubuntu 8.1-0ubuntu3) 8.1.0.20180409-git
Copyright (C) 2018 Free Software Foundation, Inc.
License GPLv3+: GNU GPL version 3 or later <http://gnu.org/licenses/gpl.html>
This is free software: you are free to change and redistribute it.
There is NO WARRANTY, to the extent permitted by law.  Type "show copying"
and "show warranty" for details.
This GDB was configured as "x86_64-linux-gnu".
Type "show configuration" for configuration details.
For bug reporting instructions, please see:
<http://www.gnu.org/software/gdb/bugs/>.
Find the GDB manual and other documentation resources online at:
<http://www.gnu.org/software/gdb/documentation/>.
For help, type "help".
Type "apropos word" to search for commands related to "word"...
Reading symbols from ./loop...done.
(gdb) run
Starting program: /mnt/loop/loop
warning: Error disabling address space randomization: Operation not permitted
terminate called after throwing an instance of 'std::runtime_error'
  what():  Time limit exceeded

Program received signal SIGABRT, Aborted.
__GI_raise (sig=sig@entry=6) at ../sysdeps/unix/sysv/linux/raise.c:51
51      ../sysdeps/unix/sysv/linux/raise.c: No such file or directory.
(gdb) 
```

Next, we use the `backtrace` command to review the stack trace:

```
● ● ●                        user@0b277b1d08e1: ~ — bash
Type "apropos word" to search for commands related to "word"...
Reading symbols from ./loop...done.
[(gdb) run
Starting program: /mnt/loop/loop
warning: Error disabling address space randomization: Operation not permitted
terminate called after throwing an instance of 'std::runtime_error'
  what():  Time limit exceeded

Program received signal SIGABRT, Aborted.
__GI_raise (sig=sig@entry=6) at ../sysdeps/unix/sysv/linux/raise.c:51
51      ../sysdeps/unix/sysv/linux/raise.c: No such file or directory.
[(gdb) bt
#0  __GI_raise (sig=sig@entry=6) at ../sysdeps/unix/sysv/linux/raise.c:51
#1  0x00007f0fd868f801 in __GI_abort () at abort.c:79
#2  0x00007f0fd8ce4957 in ?? () from /usr/lib/x86_64-linux-gnu/libstdc++.so.6
#3  0x00007f0fd8ceaab6 in ?? () from /usr/lib/x86_64-linux-gnu/libstdc++.so.6
#4  0x00007f0fd8ceaaf1 in std::terminate() ()
    from /usr/lib/x86_64-linux-gnu/libstdc++.so.6
#5  0x00007f0fd8cead24 in __cxa_throw ()
    from /usr/lib/x86_64-linux-gnu/libstdc++.so.6
#6  0x0000555a2939fe05 in runner(std::chrono::duration<long, std::ratio<1l, 1000
l> >, std::function<void (int)>, int) (limit=..., fn=..., value=7)
    at /mnt/loop/loop.cpp:15
#7  0x0000555a2939ff0f in main () at /mnt/loop/loop.cpp:29
(gdb) ▯
```

An analysis of the stack trace shows that `frame 6` should give us more information to reveal the root cause. By way of the next steps, we switch to `frame 6` and review the relevant fragment of code:

```
user@0b277b1d08e1: ~ — bash
    from /usr/lib/x86_64-linux-gnu/libstdc++.so.6
#5  0x00007f0fd8cead24 in __cxa_throw ()
    from /usr/lib/x86_64-linux-gnu/libstdc++.so.6
#6  0x0000555a2939fe05 in runner(std::chrono::duration<long, std::ratio<1l, 1000
1> >, std::function<void (int)>, int) (limit=..., fn=..., value=7)
    at /mnt/loop/loop.cpp:15
#7  0x0000555a2939ff0f in main () at /mnt/loop/loop.cpp:29
(gdb) frame 6
#6  0x0000555a2939fe05 in runner(std::chrono::duration<long, std::ratio<1l, 1000
1> >, std::function<void (int)>, int) (limit=..., fn=..., value=7)
    at /mnt/loop/loop.cpp:15
15              throw std::runtime_error("Time limit exceeded");
(gdb) list
10          fn(value);
11          auto end = std::chrono::system_clock::now();
12          std::chrono::milliseconds delta =
13              std::chrono::duration_cast<std::chrono::milliseconds>(end - start)
;
14          if (delta > limit) {
15              throw std::runtime_error("Time limit exceeded");
16          }
17      }
18
19          void delay_ms(int count) {
(gdb) 
```

Next, we analyze the values of local variables and function parameters to determine how they are related to the time limit:

```
 •  •  •                 user@0b277b1d08e1: ~ — bash
16          }
17        }
18
19      void delay_ms(int count) {
(gdb) info locals
start = {__d = {__r = 1568864598722426800}}
end = {__d = {__r = 1568864598733470400}}
delta = {__r = 11}
(gdb) info args
limit = {__r = 10}
fn = {<std::_Maybe_unary_or_binary_function<void, int>> = {<std::unary_function<
int, void>> = {<No data fields>}, <No data fields>}, <std::_Function_base> = {
    static _M_max_size = 16, static _M_max_align = 8, _M_functor = {
    _M_unused = {_M_object = 0x555a2939fe39 <delay_ms(int)>,
     _M_const_object = 0x555a2939fe39 <delay_ms(int)>,
     _M_function_pointer = 0x555a2939fe39 <delay_ms(int)>,
     _M_member_pointer = &virtual table offset 93845727084088, this adjustmen
t 93845727087629}, _M_pod_data = "9\376\071)ZU\000\000\r\f:)ZU\000"},
     _M_manager = 0x555a293a0995 <std::_Function_base::_Base_manager<void (*)(int
)>>::_M_manager(std::_Any_data&, std::_Any_data const&, std::_Manager_operation)>
},
     _M_invoker = 0x555a293a095b <std::_Function_handler<void (int), void (*)(int)>
::_M_invoke(std::_Any_data const&, int&&)>}
value = 7
(gdb) 
```

We ascertain that the crash occurs when the value passed to `delay_ms` reaches 7, not 11, as would be expected in the case of correct implementation of the delay.

There's more...

GDB commands often accept multiple parameters to fine-tune their behavior. Learn more about each command using the `help` GDB command. For example, here is the output of the `help bt` command:

```
(gdb) help bt
Print backtrace of all stack frames, or innermost COUNT frames.
With a negative argument, print outermost -COUNT frames.
Use of the 'full' qualifier also prints the values of the local variables.
Use of the 'no-filters' qualifier prohibits frame filters from executing
on this backtrace.

(gdb) 
```

This displays information on the `bt` command that is used to review and analyze stack traces. Similarly, you can get information regarding all the other commands supported by the GDB.

Working with breakpoints

In this recipe, we will learn more advanced debugging techniques when working with the GDB. We will use the same sample application and use breakpoints to find the dependency of the actual delay on the value of the `delay_ms` parameter.

Working with breakpoints in the GDB is similar to working with breakpoints in debuggers integrated into IDE, the only difference being that instead of using the built-in editor to navigate the source code, developers have to learn to use line numbers, filenames, or function names explicitly.

This is less convenient than click-and-run debuggers, but the flexibility allows developers to create powerful debugging scenarios. In this recipe, we will learn how to use breakpoints in the GDB.

How to do it...

In this recipe, we will use the same environment and the same test application as in the first recipe. Refer to steps 1 to 9 of the *Running your applications in the GDB* recipe to build the application and copy it over to the target system:

1. We want to debug our `runner` function. Let's take a look at its content. In the gdb shell, run the program as follows:

   ```
   (gdb) list runner,delay_ms
   ```

2. We want to see how the delta changes on each iteration. Let's set a breakpoint at the line:

   ```
   14 if (delta > limit) {
   ```

3. Use the `break 14` command to set a breakpoint on line 14:

   ```
   (gdb) break 14
   ```

4. Now, run the program:

   ```
   (gdb) run
   ```

5. Check the value of `delta`:

```
(gdb) print delta
$1 = {__r = 0}
```

6. Continue execution of the program by typing `continue`, or just `c`:

```
(gdb) c
```

7. Check the value of `delta` again:

```
(gdb) print delta
```

8. As we expected, the value of `delta` increases on each iteration, since `delay_ms` takes more and more time.

9. Running `print delta` each time is not convenient. Let's automate it using the command named `command`:

```
(gdb) command
```

10. Run `c` again. Now, the value of `delta` is displayed after each stop:

```
(gdb) c
```

11. However, the output is too verbose. Let's silence the GDB output by typing `command` again and writing the following instructions. Now, run the `c` or `continue` command several times to see the difference:

```
(gdb) command
Type commands for breakpoint(s) 1, one per line.
End with a line saying just "end".
>silent
>print delta
>end
(gdb) c
```

12. We can make the output even more concise by using the `printf` command, as shown here:

```
(gdb) command
Type commands for breakpoint(s) 1, one per line.
End with a line saying just "end".
>silent
>printf "delta=%d, expected=%d\n", delta.__r, value
>end
(gdb) c
```

Now, we can see two values, the calculated delay and the expected delay, and can see how they diverge over time.

How it works...

In this recipe, we want to set a breakpoint to debug the `runner` function. Since the GDB does not have a built-in editor, we need to know the line number to set the breakpoint. Though we can get it directly from a text editor, another way is to look at the relevant code snippet in the GDB. We use the `gdb` command list with two parameters – function names, to display lines of code between the first line of the function runner and the first line of the `delay_ms` function. This efficiently shows the content of the function runner:

```
user@0b277b1d08e1: ~ — bash
and "show warranty" for details.
This GDB was configured as "x86_64-linux-gnu".
Type "show configuration" for configuration details.
For bug reporting instructions, please see:
<http://www.gnu.org/software/gdb/bugs/>.
Find the GDB manual and other documentation resources online at:
<http://www.gnu.org/software/gdb/documentation/>.
For help, type "help".
Type "apropos word" to search for commands related to "word"...
Reading symbols from ./loop...done.
(gdb) list runner,delay_ms
8                    int value) {
9           auto start = std::chrono::system_clock::now();
10          fn(value);
11          auto end = std::chrono::system_clock::now();
12          std::chrono::milliseconds delta =
13              std::chrono::duration_cast<std::chrono::milliseconds>(end - start)
;
14          if (delta > limit) {
15              throw std::runtime_error("Time limit exceeded");
16          }
17      }
18
19      void delay_ms(int count) {
(gdb)
```

At *step 4*, set the breakpoint at line `14` using the `break 14` command and run the program. The execution stops at the breakpoint:

```
user@0b277b1d08e1: ~ — bash
Reading symbols from ./loop...done.
(gdb) list runner,delay_ms
8                       int value) {
9          auto start = std::chrono::system_clock::now();
10         fn(value);
11         auto end = std::chrono::system_clock::now();
12         std::chrono::milliseconds delta =
13             std::chrono::duration_cast<std::chrono::milliseconds>(end - start)
;
14         if (delta > limit) {
15             throw std::runtime_error("Time limit exceeded");
16         }
17     }
18
19     void delay_ms(int count) {
(gdb) break 14
Breakpoint 1 at 0xdb9: file /mnt/loop/loop.cpp, line 14.
(gdb) run
Starting program: /mnt/loop/loop
warning: Error disabling address space randomization: Operation not permitted

Breakpoint 1, runner(std::chrono::duration<long, std::ratio<1l, 1000l> >, std::f
unction<void (int)>, int) (limit=..., fn=..., value=0) at /mnt/loop/loop.cpp:14
14         if (delta > limit) {
(gdb)
```

We check the value of the `delta` variable using the `print` command and continue execution of the program using the `continue` command, and since the `runner` function is invoked in the loop, it stops at the same breakpoint again:

```
user@0b277b1d08e1: ~ — bash
;
14          if (delta > limit) {
15              throw std::runtime_error("Time limit exceeded");
16          }
17      }
18
19      void delay_ms(int count) {
(gdb) break 14
Breakpoint 1 at 0xdb9: file /mnt/loop/loop.cpp, line 14.
(gdb) run
Starting program: /mnt/loop/loop
warning: Error disabling address space randomization: Operation not permitted

Breakpoint 1, runner(std::chrono::duration<long, std::ratio<1l, 1000l> >, std::f
unction<void (int)>, int) (limit=..., fn=..., value=0) at /mnt/loop/loop.cpp:14
14          if (delta > limit) {
(gdb) print delta
$1 = {__r = 0}
(gdb) c
Continuing.

Breakpoint 1, runner(std::chrono::duration<long, std::ratio<1l, 1000l> >, std::f
unction<void (int)>, int) (limit=..., fn=..., value=1) at /mnt/loop/loop.cpp:14
14          if (delta > limit) {
(gdb) 
```

Next, we try a more advanced technique. We define a set of GDB commands to be executed when the breakpoint is triggered. We start with a simple `print` command. Now, every time we continue execution, we can see the value of the `delta` variable:

```
                           user@0b277b1d08e1: ~ — bash
unction<void (int)>, int) (limit=..., fn=..., value=0) at /mnt/loop/loop.cpp:14
14              if (delta > limit) {
(gdb) print delta
$1 = {__r = 0}
(gdb) c
Continuing.

Breakpoint 1, runner(std::chrono::duration<long, std::ratio<1l, 1000l> >, std::f
unction<void (int)>, int) (limit=..., fn=..., value=1) at /mnt/loop/loop.cpp:14
14              if (delta > limit) {
(gdb) print delta
$2 = {__r = 1}
(gdb) command
Type commands for breakpoint(s) 1, one per line.
End with a line saying just "end".
>print delta
>end
(gdb) c
Continuing.

Breakpoint 1, runner(std::chrono::duration<long, std::ratio<1l, 1000l> >, std::f
unction<void (int)>, int) (limit=..., fn=..., value=2) at /mnt/loop/loop.cpp:14
14              if (delta > limit) {
$3 = {__r = 2}
(gdb)
```

Next, we disable the auxiliary GDB output using the `silent` command to make the output more concise:

```
user@0b277b1d08e1: ~ — bash
>print delta
>end
(gdb) c
Continuing.

Breakpoint 1, runner(std::chrono::duration<long, std::ratio<1l, 1000l> >, std::f
unction<void (int)>, int) (limit=..., fn=..., value=2) at /mnt/loop/loop.cpp:14
14          if (delta > limit) {
$3 = {__r = 2}
(gdb) command
Type commands for breakpoint(s) 1, one per line.
End with a line saying just "end".
>silent
>print delta
>end
(gdb) c
Continuing.
$4 = {__r = 3}
(gdb) c
Continuing.
$5 = {__r = 4}
(gdb) c
Continuing.
$6 = {__r = 7}
(gdb) 
```

Finally, we use the `printf` command to format messages with the two most interesting variables:

```
●  ●  ●                          user@0b277b1d08e1: ~ — bash
(gdb) c
Continuing.
$4 = {__r = 3}
(gdb) c
Continuing.
$5 = {__r = 4}
(gdb) c
Continuing.
$6 = {__r = 7}
(gdb) command
Type commands for breakpoint(s) 1, one per line.
End with a line saying just "end".
>silent
>printf "delta=%d, expected=%d\n", delta.__r, value
>end
(gdb) c
Continuing.
delta=6, expected=6
(gdb) c
Continuing.
delta=8, expected=7
(gdb) c
Continuing.
delta=9, expected=8
(gdb)
```

As you can see, the GDB provides lots of flexibility for developers to make debugging comfortable, even lacking the graphical interface.

There's more...

It is important to remember that the optimization options, -02 and -03, may result in some lines of code being eliminated by the compiler completely. If you set breakpoints to such lines, these breakpoints are never triggered. To avoid such situations, turn off the compiler optimizations for the debug builds.

Working with core dumps

In the first recipe, we learned how to nail down the root cause of a crashing application using an interactive command-line debugger. However, there are situations when applications crash in the production environment, and it is impossible or impractical to reproduce the same issue running the application under the GDB on a test system.

Linux provides a mechanism to help with the analysis of crashing applications even when they are not run from the GDB directly. When an application is terminated abnormally, the operating system saves the image of its memory into a file named core. In this recipe, we will learn how to configure Linux to generate core dumps for crashing applications, and how to use the GDB for their analysis.

How to do it...

We are going to identify the root cause of a crash in an application that was not run in the GDB:

1. In this recipe, we will use the same environment and the same test application as in the first recipe. Refer to *steps 1* to *7* of the first recipe to build the application and copy it over to the target system.
2. Firstly, we need to enable the generation of core dumps for crashing applications. This feature is turned off by default in most Linux distribution. Run the `ulimit -c` command to check the current status:

    ```
    $ ulimit -c
    ```

3. The value reported by the preceding command is the maximum size of core dumps to generate. Zero means no core dumps. To increase the limit, we need to get superuser privileges first. Run the `su` – command. When prompted for a `Password`, type `root`:

   ```
   $ su -
   Password:
   ```

4. Run the `ulimit -c unlimited` command to allow core dumps of any size:

   ```
   # ulimit -c unlimited
   ```

5. Now, exit the root shell by pressing *Ctrl* + *D* or by running the `logout` command.

6. Preceding commands changed the core dump limit for the superuser only. To apply it to the current user, run the same command again in the user shell:

   ```
   $ ulimit -c unlimited
   ```

7. Make sure that the limit was changed:

   ```
   $ ulimit -c
   unlimited
   ```

8. Now, run the application as usual:

   ```
   $ ./loop
   ```

9. It will crash with an exception. Run the `ls` command to check whether a core file was created in the current directory:

   ```
   $ ls -l core
   -rw------- 1 dev dev 536576 May 31 00:54 core
   ```

10. Now, run `gdb`, passing the executable and the `core` files as parameters:

    ```
    $ gdb ./loop core
    ```

11. In the GDB shell, run the `bt` command to see the stack trace:

    ```
    (gdb) bt
    ```

12. You can see the same stack trace as for the application running from inside `gdb`. However, in this case, we see the stack trace of the core dump.

13. At this point, we can use the same debugging techniques as in the first recipe to narrow down the cause of the crash.

How it works...

Core dump functionality is a standard feature of Linux and other Unix-like operating systems. However, the creation of core files in every case is not practical. Since core files are snapshots of process memory, they can account for megabytes or even gigabytes on a filesystem. In many cases, this is not acceptable.

Developers need to explicitly specify the maximum size of the core files that are allowed to be generated by the operating system. This limit, among other limits, can be set using the `ulimit` command.

We run `ulimit` twice to remove the limit first for the superuser root, and then for the ordinary user/developer. The two-stage process is needed because the ordinary user limit cannot exceed the superuser limit.

After we have removed the limit for the core file size, we run our test application without the GDB. It crashes, as expected. After the crash, we can see that a new file called `core` was created in the current directory.

When we run our application, it crashes. Normally, we would not be able to track the root cause of the crash. However, since we enabled core dumps, a file named `core` was automatically created for us by the operating system:

```
user@3324138cc2c7: /mnt/loop — bash
user@3324138cc2c7:/mnt/loop$ ./loop
terminate called after throwing an instance of 'std::runtime_error'
  what():  Time limit exceeded
Aborted (core dumped)
user@3324138cc2c7:/mnt/loop$ ls -l core
-rw------- 1 user user 466944 Sep 20 21:34 core
user@3324138cc2c7:/mnt/loop$ 
```

A core file is a binary dump of all process memory, but it is difficult to analyze it without additional tools. Thankfully, the GDB provides the necessary support.

We run the GDB passing two parameters – the path to the executable, and the path to the core file. In this mode, we do not run the application from inside the GDB. We already have its state frozen at the moment of the crash in the core dump. The GDB uses the executable to bind memory addressed within the `core` file to functions and variable names:

```
                         user@3324138cc2c7: /mnt/loop — bash
Aborted (core dumped)
[user@3324138cc2c7:/mnt/loop$ ls -l core
-rw------- 1 user user 466944 Sep 20 21:34 core
[user@3324138cc2c7:/mnt/loop$ gdb ./loop core
GNU gdb (Ubuntu 8.1-0ubuntu3) 8.1.0.20180409-git
Copyright (C) 2018 Free Software Foundation, Inc.
License GPLv3+: GNU GPL version 3 or later <http://gnu.org/licenses/gpl.html>
This is free software: you are free to change and redistribute it.
There is NO WARRANTY, to the extent permitted by law.  Type "show copying"
and "show warranty" for details.
This GDB was configured as "x86_64-linux-gnu".
Type "show configuration" for configuration details.
For bug reporting instructions, please see:
<http://www.gnu.org/software/gdb/bugs/>.
Find the GDB manual and other documentation resources online at:
<http://www.gnu.org/software/gdb/documentation/>.
For help, type "help".
Type "apropos word" to search for commands related to "word"...
Reading symbols from ./loop...done.
[New LWP 39]
Core was generated by `./loop'.
Program terminated with signal SIGABRT, Aborted.
#0  __GI_raise (sig=sig@entry=6) at ../sysdeps/unix/sysv/linux/raise.c:51
51      ../sysdeps/unix/sysv/linux/raise.c: No such file or directory.
(gdb)
```

As a result, you can analyze the crashed application in an interactive debugger, even when the application was not run from the debugger. When we invoke the `bt` command, the GDB displays the stack trace at the moment of the crash:

```
user@3324138cc2c7: /mnt/loop — bash
<http://www.gnu.org/software/gdb/bugs/>.
Find the GDB manual and other documentation resources online at:
<http://www.gnu.org/software/gdb/documentation/>.
For help, type "help".
Type "apropos word" to search for commands related to "word"...
Reading symbols from ./loop...done.
[New LWP 39]
Core was generated by `./loop'.
Program terminated with signal SIGABRT, Aborted.
#0  __GI_raise (sig=sig@entry=6) at ../sysdeps/unix/sysv/linux/raise.c:51
51      ../sysdeps/unix/sysv/linux/raise.c: No such file or directory.
(gdb) bt
#0  __GI_raise (sig=sig@entry=6) at ../sysdeps/unix/sysv/linux/raise.c:51
#1  0x00007f59cf213801 in __GI_abort () at abort.c:79
#2  0x00007f59cf868957 in ?? () from /usr/lib/x86_64-linux-gnu/libstdc++.so.6
#3  0x00007f59cf86eab6 in ?? () from /usr/lib/x86_64-linux-gnu/libstdc++.so.6
#4  0x00007f59cf86eaf1 in std::terminate() ()
    from /usr/lib/x86_64-linux-gnu/libstdc++.so.6
#5  0x00007f59cf86ed24 in __cxa_throw ()
    from /usr/lib/x86_64-linux-gnu/libstdc++.so.6
#6  0x00005609a5d92e05 in runner(std::chrono::duration<long, std::ratio<1l, 1000
l> >, std::function<void (int)>, int) (limit=..., fn=..., value=8)
    at /mnt/loop/loop.cpp:15
#7  0x00005609a5d92f0f in main () at /mnt/loop/loop.cpp:29
(gdb) 
```

This way, we can nail down the root cause of an application crashing even if, initially, it was not run in a debugger.

There's more...

Analyzing core dumps using the GDB is a widely used and effective practice for embedded applications. However, to use the full capabilities of the GDB, the application should be built with debug symbol support.

In most cases, however, embedded applications are deployed and run without debug symbols to reduce the binary size. In this case, an analysis of core dumps becomes harder and may require some knowledge of assembly language for the particular architecture and of the internals of data structure implementations.

Using gdbserver for debugging

The environment for embedded development normally involves two systems— a build system and a target system, or an emulator. Although the command-line interface of the GDB makes it a good choice even for low-performance embedded systems, in many cases, interactive debugging on the target system is impractical because of the high latency of remote communication.

In such situations, developers can use remote debugging support provided by the GDB. In this setup, an embedded application is launched on the target system using gdbserver. Developers run the GDB on a build system and connect to gdbserver over the network.

In this recipe, we will learn how to start debugging an application using the GDB and gdbserver.

Getting ready...

Follow the *Connecting to the embedded system* recipe of Chapter 2, *Setting Up the Environment*, to have the `hello` application available on the target system.

How to do it...

We will use the same application we used in the preceding recipes, but now we will run the GDB and applications in different environments:

1. Switch to the target system window and type *Ctrl + D* to log out from the existing user session.
2. Log in as `user`, using the `user` password.
3. Run the `hello` application under `gdbserver`:

```
$ gdbserver 0.0.0.0:9090 ./hello
```

4. Switch to the build system terminal and change the directory to /mnt:

   ```
   # cd /mnt
   ```

5. Run gdb, passing the application binary as a parameter:

   ```
   # gdb -q hello
   ```

6. Configure a remote connection by typing the following command in the GDB command line:

   ```
   target remote X.X.X.X:9090
   ```

7. Finally, type the continue command:

   ```
   continue
   ```

   The program now runs and we can see its output and debug it as if it were run locally.

How it works...

First, we log in to our target system as root and install gdbserver, unless it is already installed. Once installation is complete, we log in again with user credentials and run gdbserver, passing the name of the application to debug, the IP address, and the port to listen to for incoming connections as its parameters.

Then, we switch to our build system and run the GDB there. However, instead of running the application in the GDB directly, we instruct the GDB to initiate a connection to a remote host using the provided IP address and port. After that, all commands you type at the GDB prompt will be transferred to gdbserver and executed there.

Adding debug logging

Logging and diagnostics are an important aspect of any embedded project. In many cases, using an interactive debugger is not possible or not practical. Hardware state can change in a few milliseconds after a program stops on a breakpoint, and a developer has insufficient time to analyze it. Collecting detailed log data and using tools for their analysis and visualization is a better approach for high-performance, multithreaded, time-sensitive embedded systems.

Logging itself introduces certain delays. Firstly, it takes time to format the log messages and put them into the log stream. Secondly, the log stream should be reliably stored in persistent storage, such as a flash card or a disk drive, or sent to the remote system.

In this recipe, we will learn how to use logging instead of interactive debugging to find the root causes of issues. We will use a system of different log levels to minimize the delays introduced by logging.

How to do it...

We will modify our application to output information that is useful for root cause analysis:

1. Go to your work directory, `~/test`, and make a copy of the `loop` project directory. Name the copy `loop2`. Change directory to `loop2`.

2. Use your text editor to open the `loop.cpp` file.

3. Add one more `include`:

```
#include <iostream>
#include <chrono>
#include <thread>
#include <functional>

#include <syslog.h>
```

4. Modify the `runner` function by adding calls to the `syslog` function, as highlighted in the following code snippet:

```
void runner(std::chrono::milliseconds limit,
            std::function<void(int)> fn,
            int value) {
  auto start = std::chrono::system_clock::now();
  fn(value);
  auto end = std::chrono::system_clock::now();
  std::chrono::milliseconds delta =
      std::chrono::duration_cast<std::chrono::milliseconds>(end -
start);
  syslog(LOG_DEBUG, "Delta is %ld",
         static_cast<long int>(delta.count()));
  if (delta > limit) {
  syslog(LOG_ERR,
  "Execution time %ld ms exceeded %ld ms limit",
  static_cast<long int>(delta.count()),
  static_cast<long int>(limit.count()));
    throw std::runtime_error("Time limit exceeded");
```

```
        }
    }
```

5. Similarly, update the `main` function to initialize and finalize `syslog`:

```
int main() {
    openlog("loop3", LOG_PERROR, LOG_USER);
    int max_delay = 10;
    for (int i = 0; i < max_delay; i++) {
        runner(std::chrono::milliseconds(max_delay), delay_ms, i);
    }
    closelog();
    return 0;
}
```

6. Switch to the build system terminal. Go to the `/mnt/loop2` directory and run the program:

   # cmake && make

7. Copy the resulting `binary` file loop to the target system and run it:

   $ ./loop

   The debug output is verbose and gives more context to find the root cause of the issue.

How it works...

In this recipe, we added logging using the standard logging tool, `syslog`. Firstly, we initialized our logging by using a call to `openlog`:

   openlog("loop3", LOG_PERROR, LOG_USER);

Next, we added logging to the `runner` function. There are different logging levels that facilitate the filtering of log messages, from most severe to least severe. We log the `delta` value, which indicates how long the function that the runner invokes actually runs for, using the `LOG_DEBUG` level:

   syslog(LOG_DEBUG, "Delta is %d", delta);

This level is used to log detailed information that is helpful for application debugging but might prove to be too verbose when running applications in production.

If the delta, however, exceeds the limit, we log this situation using the `LOG_ERR` level to indicate that this situation should not normally happen and that it is an error:

```
syslog(LOG_ERR,
        "Execution time %ld ms exceeded %ld ms limit",
        static_cast<long int>(delta.count()),
        static_cast<long int>(limit.count()));
```

Before returning from the application, we close the logging to make sure that all the log messages are properly saved:

```
closelog();
```

When we run the application on the target system, we can see our log messages on the screen:

```
pi@raspberrypi:~ — bash
[pi@raspberrypi:~$ ./loop
loop3: Delta is 0
loop3: Delta is 3
loop3: Delta is 5
loop3: Delta is 6
loop3: Delta is 11
loop3: Execution time 11 ms exceeded 0 ms limit
terminate called after throwing an instance of 'std::runtime_error'
  what():  Time limit exceeded
Aborted
pi@raspberrypi:~$ 
```

Since we use standard Linux logging, we can find the messages in the system logs as well:

```
pi@raspberrypi: ~ — bash
pi@raspberrypi:~$ tail -n 20 /var/log/syslog
Sep 20 23:38:47 raspberrypi systemd[1]: Starting OpenBSD Secure Shell server...
Sep 20 23:38:48 raspberrypi systemd[1]: Started OpenBSD Secure Shell server.
Sep 20 23:39:08 raspberrypi systemd[1]: Started Session c2 of user pi.
Sep 20 23:39:09 raspberrypi systemd[1]: session-c2.scope: Succeeded.
Sep 20 23:39:14 raspberrypi loop3: Delta is 0
Sep 20 23:39:14 raspberrypi loop3: Delta is 3
Sep 20 23:39:14 raspberrypi loop3: Delta is 6
Sep 20 23:39:14 raspberrypi loop3: Delta is 6
Sep 20 23:39:14 raspberrypi loop3: Delta is 9
Sep 20 23:39:14 raspberrypi loop3: Delta is 13
Sep 20 23:39:14 raspberrypi loop3: Execution time 13 ms exceeded 0 ms limit
Sep 20 23:39:27 raspberrypi loop3: Delta is 0
Sep 20 23:39:27 raspberrypi loop3: Delta is 3
Sep 20 23:39:28 raspberrypi loop3: Delta is 5
Sep 20 23:39:28 raspberrypi loop3: Delta is 6
Sep 20 23:39:28 raspberrypi loop3: Delta is 11
Sep 20 23:39:28 raspberrypi loop3: Execution time 11 ms exceeded 0 ms limit
Sep 20 23:49:53 raspberrypi systemd[1]: Starting Cleanup of Temporary Directorie
s...
Sep 20 23:49:53 raspberrypi systemd[1]: systemd-tmpfiles-clean.service: Succeede
d.
Sep 20 23:49:53 raspberrypi systemd[1]: Started Cleanup of Temporary Directories
.
pi@raspberrypi:~$ ▯
```

As you can see, logging is not hard to implement, but it is extremely helpful in finding the root causes of various issues in your application during debugging and normal operation.

There's more...

There are a number of logging libraries and frameworks that may be more suitable for particular tasks than the standard logger; for example, *Boost.Log*, at https://theboostcpplibraries.com/boost.log, and *spdlog*, at https://github.com/gabime/spdlog. They provide a more convenient C++ interface compared to the generic C interface of syslog. When starting work on your project, check existing logging libraries and pick the one that best suits your requirements.

Working with debug and release builds

As we learned in the preceding recipe, logging has costs associated with it. It introduces delays to format log messages and writes them to persistent storage or a remote system.

Using log levels helps to reduce the overhead by skipping the writing of some messages to the log file. However, the message is usually being formatted before passing to a `log` function. For example, in the case of a system error, a developer wants to add an error code reported by the system to the log message. Although string formatting is generally less expensive than writing data to a file, it might still be an issue for highly-loaded systems or systems with limited resources.

Debug symbols added by a compiler do not add runtime overhead. However, they increase the size of the resulting binary. Moreover, performance optimizations made by the compiler can make interactive debugging difficult.

In this recipe, we will learn how to avoid runtime overheads by separating debug and release builds and using the C pre-processor macros.

How to do it...

We are going to modify build rules of the application we used in the preceding recipes to have two build targets—debug and release:

1. Go to your work directory, `~/test`, and make a copy of the `loop2` project directory. Name the copy `loop3`. Change directory to `loop3`.
2. Use your text editor to open the `CMakeLists.txt` file. Replace the following line:

   ```
   SET(CMAKE_CXX_FLAGS "-g --std=c++11")
   ```

3. The preceding line needs to be replaced with the following lines:

   ```
   SET(CMAKE_CXX_FLAGS_RELEASE "--std=c++11")
   SET(CMAKE_CXX_FLAGS_DEBUG "${CMAKE_CXX_FLAGS_RELEASE} -g -DDEBUG")
   ```

4. Use your text editor to open the `loop.cpp` file. Modify the file by adding the highlighted lines:

   ```
   #include <iostream>
   #include <chrono>
   #include <thread>
   #include <functional>
   ```

```
#include <cstdarg>

#ifdef DEBUG
#define LOG_DEBUG(fmt, args...) fprintf(stderr, fmt, args)
#else
#define LOG_DEBUG(fmt, args...)
#endif

void runner(std::chrono::milliseconds limit,
            std::function<void(int)> fn,
            int value) {
  auto start = std::chrono::system_clock::now();
  fn(value);
  auto end = std::chrono::system_clock::now();
  std::chrono::milliseconds delta =
      std::chrono::duration_cast<std::chrono::milliseconds>(end -
start);
    LOG_DEBUG("Delay: %ld ms, max: %ld ms\n",
            static_cast<long int>(delta.count()),
            static_cast<long int>(limit.count()));
  if (delta > limit) {
    throw std::runtime_error("Time limit exceeded");
  }
}
```

5. Switch to the build system terminal. Go to the /mnt/loop3 directory and run the following code:

```
# cmake -DCMAKE_BUILD_TYPE=Release . && make
```

6. Copy the resulting loop binary file to the target system and run it:

```
$ ./loop
```

7. As you can see, the application does not generate any debug output. Let's now check its size using the ls -l command:

```
$ ls -l loop
-rwxr-xr-x 1 dev dev 24880 Jun 1 00:50 loop
```

8. The size of the resulting binary is 24 KB. Now, let's build the Debug build and effect a comparison as shown here:

```
$ cmake -DCMAKE_BUILD_TYPE=Debug && make clean && make
```

9. Check the size of the executable file:

```
$ ls -l ./loop
-rwxr-xr-x 1 dev dev 80008 Jun 1 00:51 ./loop
```

10. The size of the executable is now 80 KB. It is more than three times bigger than the release build. Run it the same way as before:

```
$ ./loop
```

As you can see, the output is now different.

How it works...

We start with the copy of the project we used for the *Adding debug logging* recipe and create two distinct build configurations:

- **Debug**: A configuration with interactive debugging and debug logging support
- **Release**: A highly optimized configuration that has all debug support disabled at compile time

To implement it, we utilize the functionality provided by CMake. It supports different built types out of the box. We only need to define compile options for release and debug builds separately.

The only build flag we define for the release build is the C++ standard to use. We explicitly require the code to conform to the C++11 standard:

```
SET(CMAKE_CXX_FLAGS_RELEASE "--std=c++11")
```

For the debug build, we reuse the same flags as for the release build, referencing them as ${CMAKE_CXX_FLAGS_RELEASE}, and adding two more options. -g instructs the compiler to add debug symbols to the target executable binary, and -DDEBUG defines a pre-processor macro, DEBUG.

We use the DEBUG macro in the code of loop.cpp to select between two different implementations of the LOG_DEBUG macro.

If DEBUG is defined, LOG_DEBUG is expanded to the call of the fprintf function, which performs actual logging in the standard error channel. If, however, DEBUG is not defined, LOG_DEBUG is expanded to the empty string. This means that in this case, LOG_DEBUG does not produce any code, and hence does not add any runtime overhead.

We use LOG_DEBUG in the body of the runner function to log values of the actual delay and the limit. Note that there is no if around LOG_DEBUG – the decision to format and log data or do nothing is done not by our program when it runs, but by the code pre-processor when we build the application.

To select a build type, we invoke cmake, passing the name of the build type as a command-line parameter:

```
cmake -DCMAKE_BUILD_TYPE=Debug
```

CMake only generates a Make file to actually build the application we require in order to invoke make. We can combine these two commands in a single command line:

```
cmake -DCMAKE_BUILD_TYPE=Release && make
```

When we build and run our application for the first time, we select the release build. As a result, we do not see any debug output:

```
user@3324138cc2c7: /mnt/loop3 — bash
$ cmake -DCMAKE_BUILD_TYPE=Release . && make
-- Configuring done
-- Generating done
-- Build files have been written to: /mnt/loop3
[100%] Built target loop
$ ./loop
terminate called after throwing an instance of 'std::runtime_error'
  what():  Time limit exceeded
Aborted (core dumped)
$ 
```

After that, we rebuild our application using the debug build type and see a different result when running it:

```
user@3324138cc2c7: /mnt/loop3 — bash
$ cmake -DCMAKE_BUILD_TYPE=Debug . && make
-- Configuring done
-- Generating done
-- Build files have been written to: /mnt/loop3
[100%] Built target loop
$ ./loop
Delay: 0 ms, max: 10 ms
Delay: 1 ms, max: 10 ms
Delay: 2 ms, max: 10 ms
Delay: 3 ms, max: 10 ms
Delay: 5 ms, max: 10 ms
Delay: 7 ms, max: 10 ms
Delay: 9 ms, max: 10 ms
Delay: 10 ms, max: 10 ms
Delay: 11 ms, max: 10 ms
terminate called after throwing an instance of 'std::runtime_error'
  what():  Time limit exceeded
Aborted (core dumped)
$
```

With debug and release builds, you can have sufficient information for comfortable debugging, but be sure that the production build won't have any unnecessary overhead.

There's more...

When switching between release and debug builds in a complex project, make sure that all the files were rebuilt properly. The easiest way to do this is by removing all the previous build files. When using make, this can be done by invoking the make clean command.

It can be added as part of the command line along with cmake and make:

```
cmake -DCMAKE_BUILD_TYPE=Debug && make clean && make
```

Combining all three commands into one line makes this more convenient for developers.

Memory Management

6

Memory efficiency is one of the major requirements for embedded applications. Since target embedded platforms often have limited performance and memory capabilities, developers need to know how to use available memory in the most efficient way.

Surprisingly, the most efficient way does not necessarily mean that the least amount of memory is used. Since embedded systems are specialized, developers know in advance which applications or components will be executed on the system. Saving memory in one application does not result in any gain unless another application running in the same system can use the extra memory. That is why the most important characteristic of memory management in embedded systems is determinism, or predictability. It is much more important to know that an application can use two megabytes of memory under any load than knowing an application can use one megabyte of memory most of the time, but can occasionally require three megabytes.

Similarly, predictability also applies to memory allocation and deallocation time. In many situations, embedded applications favor spending more memory to achieve deterministic timing.

In this chapter, we will learn several of memory management techniques that are widely used in embedded applications. The recipes covered in this chapter are as follows:

- Using dynamic memory allocation
- Exploring object pools
- Using ring buffers
- Using shared memory
- Using specialized memory

These recipes will help you understand memory management best practices and can be used as building blocks when working with memory allocation in your applications.

Using dynamic memory allocation

Dynamic memory allocation is a common practice among C++ developers, and it is widely utilized in the C++ standard library; however, in the context of embedded systems, it often becomes a source of issues that are hard to discover and hard to avoid.

The most notable issue is timing. The worst-case time for memory allocation is not-bound; however, embedded systems, especially those controlling real-world processes or equipment, are often required to respond within a specific amount of time.

Another problem is fragmentation. When memory blocks of different sizes are allocated and deallocated, memory regions appear that are technically free but cannot be allotted because they are too small to fulfill an application request. Memory fragmentation grows over time and can lead to the situation where a memory allocation request fails despite a substantial total amount of free memory.

A simple yet powerful strategy to avoid these types of issue is to allocate all the memory that an application might need in advance at compile time or at startup time. Then the application uses this memory as needed. This memory, once allocated, is never freed until the application terminates.

A disadvantage of this approach is that the application allocates more memory than it really uses at this point in time instead of letting other applications use it. In practice, this is not an issue for embedded applications, since they are running within a controlled environment, where all applications and their memory needs are known in advance.

How to do it...

In this recipe, we will learn how to preallocate memory and use it later in your application:

1. In your working ~/test directory, create a subdirectory called `prealloc`.
2. Use your favorite text editor to create a file called `prealloc.cpp` in the `prealloc` subdirectory. Copy the following code snippet into the `prealloc.cpp` file to define a `SerialDevice` class:

```
#include <cstdint>
#include <string.h>

constexpr size_t kMaxFileNameSize = 256;
constexpr size_t kBufferSize = 4096;
constexpr size_t kMaxDevices = 16;
```

```
class SerialDevice {
    char device_file_name[256];
    uint8_t input_buffer[kBufferSize];
    uint8_t output_buffer[kBufferSize];
    int file_descriptor;
    size_t input_length;
    size_t output_length;

  public:
    SerialDevice():
      file_descriptor(-1), input_length(0), output_length(0) {}

    bool Init(const char* name) {
      strncpy(device_file_name, name, sizeof(device_file_name));
    }

    bool Write(const uint8_t* data, size_t size) {
      if (size > sizeof(output_buffer)) {
        throw "Data size exceeds the limit";
      }
      memcpy(output_buffer, data, size);
    }

    size_t Read(uint8_t* data, size_t size) {
      if (size < input_length) {
        throw "Read buffer is too small";
      }
      memcpy(data, input_buffer, input_length);
      return input_length;
    }
};
```

3. Add the `main` function that uses the `SerialDevice` class:

```
int main() {
  SerialDevice devices[kMaxDevices];
  size_t number_of_devices = 0;

  uint8_t data[] = "Hello";
  devices[0].Init("test");
  devices[0].Write(data, sizeof(data));
  number_of_devices = 1;

  return 0;
}
```

4. Create a file called `CMakeLists.txt` in the `loop` subdirectory with the following content:

```
cmake_minimum_required(VERSION 3.5.1)
project(prealloc)
add_executable(prealloc prealloc.cpp)

set(CMAKE_SYSTEM_NAME Linux)
set(CMAKE_SYSTEM_PROCESSOR arm)

SET(CMAKE_CXX_FLAGS "--std=c++17")
set(CMAKE_CXX_COMPILER /usr/bin/arm-linux-gnueabi-g++)
```

You can now build and run the application. It does not output any data since its purpose is to demonstrate how we preallocate memory in advance without knowing the number of devices and the size of the messages we exchange with devices.

How it works...

In this recipe, we define objects that encapsulate data exchange with serial devices. A device is identified by a device file name string of variable length. We can send and receive messages of variable length to and from devices.

Since we can only discover the number of devices connected to the system at runtime, we might be tempted to create a device object when it is discovered. Similarly, since we do not know the sizes of the messages we send and receive, it is natural to allocate memory for message dynamically.

Instead, we preallocate arrays of uninitialized device objects:

```
SerialDevice devices[kMaxDevices];
```

In turn, each object preallocates a sufficient amount of memory to store messages and the device filename:

```
char device_file_name[kMaxFileNameSize];
uint8_t input_buffer[kBufferSize];
uint8_t output_buffer[kBufferSize];
```

We use local variables to track the actual size of data in the input and output buffers. There is no need to track the size of the file name since it is expected to be zero-terminated:

```
size_t input_length;
size_t output_length;
```

Similarly, we track the actual amount of devices discovered:

```
size_t number_of_devices = 0;
```

This way, we avoid dynamic memory allocation. It has its costs, though: we artificially limit the maximum number of devices and the maximum size of messages we support. Secondly, a substantial amount of allocated memory is never used. For example, if we support up to 16 devices and only 1 is present in the system, we actually use only 1/16 of allocated memory. As mentioned before, this is not a problem for embedded systems, since all applications and their requirements are predefined. There is no application that can benefit from the extra memory it can allocate.

Exploring object pools

As we discussed in the first recipe in this chapter, preallocation of all memory used by the application is an efficient strategy that helps embedded applications avoid various pitfalls related to memory fragmentation and allocation time.

One disadvantage of ad-hoc memory preallocation is that the application is now responsible for the tracking of preallocated object usage.

Object pools aim to hide the burden of object tracking by providing a generalized and convenient interface, similar to dynamic memory allocation but working with objects in the preallocated arrays.

How to do it...

In this recipe, we will create a simple implementation of an object pool and learn how to use it in your applications:

1. In your working ~/test directory, create a subdirectory called objpool.
2. Use your favorite text editor to create a objpool.cpp file in the objpool subdirectory. Let's define a templated ObjectPool class. We start with the private data members and a constructor:

```
#include <iostream>

template<class T, size_t N>
class ObjectPool {
  private:
    T objects[N];
```

```
      size_t available[N];
      size_t top = 0;
   public:
      ObjectPool(): top(0) {
         for (size_t i = 0; i < N; i++) {
            available[i] = i;
         }
      }
```

3. Now let's add a method to get elements from the pool:

```
T& get() {
   if (top < N) {
      size_t idx = available[top++];
      return objects[idx];
   } else {
      throw std::runtime_error("All objects are in use");
   }
}
```

4. Next, we add a method that returns an element to the pool:

```
void free(const T& obj) {
   const T* ptr = &obj;
   size_t idx = (ptr - objects) / sizeof(T);
   if (idx < N) {
      if (top) {
         top--;
         available[top] = idx;
      } else {
         throw std::runtime_error("Some object was freed more than once");
      }
   } else {
      throw std::runtime_error("Freeing object that does not belong to
      the pool");
   }
}
```

5. Then, wrap up the class definition with a small function that returns the number of elements that are requested from the pool:

```
size_t requested() const { return top; }
};
```

6. Define a data type to be stored in the object pool as shown in the following code:

```
struct Point {
   int x, y;
};
```

7. Then add code that works with the object pool:

```
int main() {
  ObjectPool<Point, 10> points;

  Point& a = points.get();
  a.x = 10; a.y=20;
  std::cout << "Point a (" << a.x << ", " << a.y << ") initialized,
requested "             <<
    points.requested() << std::endl;

  Point& b = points.get();
  std::cout << "Point b (" << b.x << ", " << b.y << ") not
initialized, requested " <<
    points.requested() << std::endl;

  points.free(a);
  std::cout << "Point a(" << a.x << ", " << a.y << ") returned,
requested " <<
    points.requested() << std::endl;

  Point& c = points.get();
  std::cout << "Point c(" << c.x << ", " << c.y << ") not
intialized, requested " <<
    points.requested() << std::endl;

  Point local;
  try {
    points.free(local);
  } catch (std::runtime_error e) {
    std::cout << "Exception caught: " << e.what() << std::endl;
  }
}
```

8. Create a file called CMakeLists.txt in the loop subdirectory with the following content:

```
cmake_minimum_required(VERSION 3.5.1)
project(objpool)
add_executable(objpool objpool.cpp)

set(CMAKE_SYSTEM_NAME Linux)
```

```
set(CMAKE_SYSTEM_PROCESSOR arm)

SET(CMAKE_CXX_FLAGS "--std=c++11")
set(CMAKE_CXX_COMPILER /usr/bin/arm-linux-gnueabi-g++)
```

9. Build the application and copy the resulting executable binary to the target system. Use recipes from `Chapter 2,`*Setting Up the Environment,* to do it.
10. Switch to the target system terminal. Log in using user credentials, if needed.
11. Run the binary.

How it works...

In this application, we use the same idea (static arrays of preallocated objects) that we used in the first recipe; however, we wrap it into a templated `ObjectPool` class to provide a generic interface for handling objects of different types.

Our template has two parameters—a class or a data type of objects stored in an instance of the `ObjectPool` class, and the pool size. These parameters are used to define two private data fields of the class—an array of objects and an array of free indices:

```
T objects[N];
size_t available[N];
```

Since template parameters are being resolved at compile time, these arrays are allocated statically. Additionally, the class has a private data member called `top` that acts as an index in the `available` array and points to the next available object.

The available array contains indices of all objects in the `objects` array that are currently available for use. At the very beginning, all objects are free, and the available array is populated with indices of all elements in the objects array:

```
for (size_t i = 0; i < N; i++) {
  available[i] = i;
}
```

When the application needs to get an element from the pool, it invokes the `get` method. This method uses the top variable to get the index of the next available element in the pool:

```
size_t idx = available[top++];
return objects[idx];
```

When the `top` index reaches the size of the array, it means that no more elements can be allocated, and so the method throws an exception to indicate the error condition:

```
throw std::runtime_error("All objects are in use");
```

Objects can be returned into the pool using `free`. First, it detects an index of the element based on its address. The index is calculated as a difference between the object address and the pool start address. Since pool objects are stored in memory contiguously, we can easily filter out objects of the same type, but not those that originate from this pool:

```
const T* ptr = &obj;
size_t idx = (ptr - objects) / sizeof(T);
```

Note that, since the `size_t` type is unsigned, we do not need to check that the resulting index is less than zero—it is not possible. If we try to return an object to the pool that does not belong to it and has an address less than the pool's start address, it will be treated as a positive index anyway.

If the object we return belongs to the pool, we update the top counter and put the resulting index into the available array for further use:

```
top--;
available[top] = idx;
```

Otherwise, we throw an exception indicating that we tried to return an object that was not taken from this pool:

```
throw std::runtime_error("Freeing object that does not belong to the
pool");
```

The method requested is used to track pool object usage. It returns the top variable, which efficiently tracks the number of objects that were claimed but have not yet been returned to the pool.

```
size_t requested() const { return top; }
```

Let's define a data type and try to work with objects from the pool. We declare a struct called `Point` that holds two `int` fields, as shown in the following code:

```
struct Point {
  int x, y;
};
```

Now we create a pool of `Point` objects of size `10`:

```
ObjectPool<Point, 10> points;
```

We get one object from the pool and populate its data fields:

```
Point& a = points.get();
a.x = 10; a.y=20;
```

The program produces the following output:

```
user@feb23236b84c: /mnt/test/objpool — bash
user@feb23236b84c:/mnt/test/objpool$ ./objpool
Point a (10, 20) initialized, requested 1
Point b (0, 0) not initialized, requested 2
Hello 10, 20
Point a(10, 20) returned, requested 1
Point c(10, 20) not intialized, requested 2
Exception caught: Freeing object that does not belong to the pool
user@feb23236b84c:/mnt/test/objpool$
```

The first line of the output reports one object as requested.

We request one more object and print its data fields as-is, without any initialization. The pool reports that two objects were requested, as expected.

Now we return our first object back to the pool and make sure that the count of requested objects decreases. We can also note that, even after returning the object to the pool, we can read data from it.

Let's claim one more object from the pool. The requested count increases, but the requested object is the same as the one we returned on the preceding step.

We can see that Point c was not initialized after it was taken from the pool, but its fields contain the same values as Point a. In fact, now a and c are references to the same object in the pool, and so the modification of variable a will affect variable c. This is one of the limitations of our implementation of the object pool.

Finally, we create a local Point object and try to return it into the pool:

```
Point local;
try {
  points.free(local);
} catch (std::runtime_error e) {
  std::cout << "Exception caught: " << e.what() << std::endl;
}
```

It is expected to fail with an exception, and it does. In the program output, you can see an Exception caught: Freeing object that does not belong to the pool message.

There's more...

Even though the implementation of the object pool simplifies working with preallocated objects, it has a number of limitations.

Firstly, all objects are created at the very beginning. As a result, calling the `get` method of our pool does not trigger an object constructor, and calling the `free` method does not call a destructor. Developers need to use various workarounds for the initialization and deinitialization of objects.

One possible workaround is to define special methods of the target object, such as `initialize` and `deinitialize`, which will be invoked respectively by the `get` and `free` methods of the `ObjectPool` class. This approach, however, couples the implementation of the classes to the `ObjectPool` implementation. Later in the chapter, we will look at more advanced techniques to overcome this limitation.

Our implementation of the pool does not detect whether the `free` method was called more than once for an object. It is a mistake, but it is common and leads to issues that are hard to debug. While technically feasible, it adds extra complexity to the implementation that is not necessary for this example.

Using ring buffers

A ring buffer, or circular buffer, is a widely used data structure in the embedded world. It works as a queue placed on top of a fixed-size memory array. The buffer can contain a fixed number of elements. A function that generates these elements puts them into the buffer sequentially, one by one. When the end of the buffer is reached, it switches to the start of the buffer, as if its first element follows the last element.

This design has proven to be remarkably efficient when it comes to organizing data exchange between data producers and consumers that are independent and cannot wait for each other, which is a common scenario in embedded development. For example, an interrupt service routine should quickly queue data coming from a device for further processing, while interrupts are disabled. It cannot wait for the function that processes the data if it lags behind. At the same time, the processing function does not need to be completely in sync with the **Interrupt Service Routine (ISR)**; it can process several elements at once and catch up with the ISR later.

This, along with the fact that ring they can be preallocated statically, makes ring buffers the best choice in many cases.

How to do it...

In this recipe, we will learn how to create and use a ring buffer on top of a C++ array:

1. In your working ~/test directory, create a subdirectory called ringbuf.
2. Use your favorite text editor to create a ringbuf.cpp file in the ringbuf subdirectory.
3. Define the RingBuffer class, starting from the private data fields:

```cpp
#include <iostream>
template<class T, size_t N>
class RingBuffer {
  private:
    T objects[N];
    size_t read;
    size_t write;
    size_t queued;
  public:
    RingBuffer(): read(0), write(0), queued(0) {}
```

4. Now we add a method to push data to the buffer:

```cpp
T& push() {
  T& current = objects[write];
  write = (write + 1) % N;
  queued++;
  if (queued > N) {
    queued = N;
    read = write;
  }
  return current;
}
```

5. Next, we add a method to pull data from the buffer:

```cpp
const T& pull() {
  if (!queued) {
    throw std::runtime_error("No data in the ring buffer");
  }
  T& current = objects[read];
  read = (read + 1) % N;
  queued--;
  return current;
}
```

6. Let's add a small method to check whether the buffer contains any data and wrap up the class definition:

```
bool has_data() {
  return queued != 0;
}
};
```

7. With `RingBuffer` defined, we can now add code that uses it. Firstly, let's define the data type we are going to use:

```
struct Frame {
  uint32_t index;
  uint8_t data[1024];
};
```

8. Secondly, add the `main` function and define an instance of `RingBuffer` as its variable, along with code that tries to work with an empty buffer:

```
int main() {
  RingBuffer<Frame, 10> frames;

  std::cout << "Frames " << (frames.has_data() ? "" : "do not ")
      << "contain data" << std::endl;
  try {
    const Frame& frame = frames.pull();
  } catch (std::runtime_error e) {
    std::cout << "Exception caught: " << e.what() << std::endl;
  }
```

9. Next, add code that works with five elements in the buffer:

```
for (size_t i = 0; i < 5; i++) {
Frame& out = frames.push();
out.index = i;
out.data[0] = 'a' + i;
out.data[1] = '\0';
  }
std::cout << "Frames " << (frames.has_data() ? "" : "do not ")
<< "contain data" << std::endl;
while (frames.has_data()) {
const Frame& in = frames.pull();
    std::cout << "Frame " << in.index << ": " << in.data <<
std::endl;
  }
```

10. After that, add similar code that deals with a larger number of elements that can be added:

```
for (size_t i = 0; i < 26; i++) {
Frame& out = frames.push();
out.index = i;
out.data[0] = 'a' + i;
out.data[1] = '\0';
}
std::cout << "Frames " << (frames.has_data() ? "" : "do not ")
  << "contain data" << std::endl;
while (frames.has_data()) {
const Frame& in = frames.pull();
std::cout << "Frame " << in.index << ": " << in.data << std::endl;
}
}
```

11. Create a file called CMakeLists.txt in the loop subdirectory with the following content:

```
cmake_minimum_required(VERSION 3.5.1)
project(ringbuf)
add_executable(ringbuf ringbuf.cpp)

set(CMAKE_SYSTEM_NAME Linux)
set(CMAKE_SYSTEM_PROCESSOR arm)

SET(CMAKE_CXX_FLAGS "--std=c++11")
set(CMAKE_CXX_COMPILER /usr/bin/arm-linux-gnueabi-g++)
```

12. Build the application and copy the resulting executable binary to the target system. Use recipes from Chapter 2, *Setting Up the Environment*, to do it.

13. Switch to the target system terminal. Log in using user credentials, if needed.

14. Run the binary.

How it works...

We implement our ring buffer as a templated C++ class that has three private data fields:

- objects: A static array of N elements of type T
- read: An index to read elements from
- write: An index to write elements to

The RingBuffer class exposes three public methods:

- push(): To write data into the buffer
- pull(): To read data from the buffer
- has_data(): To check whether the buffer contains data

Let's take a close look at how they work.

The push() method is intended to be used by a function to store data in the buffer. Unlike the similar push() method for a dynamic queue or dynamic stack, which accepts a value to store as a parameter, our implementation does not accept any parameters. Since all elements are preallocated at compile time, it returns a reference to a value in the buffer to be updated.

The implementation of the push() method is straightforward; it gets a pointer to the element via the write index, then advances the write index and increments the number of elements stored in the buffer. Note how the division remainder operator is used to wrap the write index to the beginning of the array once it reaches the size limit:

```
T& current = objects[write];
write = (write + 1) % N;
queued++;
```

What happens if we try to push more elements than the capacity of the objects array can handle? That depends on the nature of the data we plan to store in the buffer. In our implementation, we assume that the receiver is interested in the most recent data and can tolerate the loss of intermediate data if it cannot catch up with the sender. If the receiver is too slow, it does not matter how many laps the sender runs before the receiver read data: all data more than N steps behind is overwritten at this point. That is why, as soon as the number of stored elements exceeds N, we start advancing the read index along with the write index to keep them exactly N steps apart:

```
if (queued > N) {
  queued = N;
  read = write;
}
```

The `pull()` method is used by functions that read data from the buffer. Similarly to the `push()` method, it does not accept any parameters and returns a reference to an element in the buffer. Unlike the `push()` method, though, it returns a constant reference (as shown in the following code) to indicate the fact that it is not supposed to modify data in the buffer:

```
const T& pull() {
```

Firstly, it checks whether there is data in the buffer and throws an exception if the buffer does not contain elements:

```
if (!queued) {
  throw std::runtime_error("No data in the ring buffer");
}
```

It gets a reference to an element by the read index, then advances the `read` index, applying the same division remainder operator that the `push()` method does for the `write` index:

```
read = (read + 1) % N;
queued--;
```

The implementation of the `has_data()` method is trivial. It returns `false` if the object counter is zero and `true` otherwise:

```
bool has_data() {
return queued != 0;
}
```

Now, let's try it in action. We declare a simple data structure, `Frame`, that mimics data generated by a device. It contains a frame index and an opaque data buffer:

```
uint32_t index;
uint8_t data[1024];
};
```

We define a ring buffer with a capacity of `10` elements of the `frame` type:

```
RingBuffer<Frame, 10> frames;
```

Let's take a look at the program output:

```
                        user@feb23236b84c: /mnt/test/ringbuf — bash
user@feb23236b84c:/mnt/test/ringbuf$ ./ringbuf
Frames do not contain data
Exception caught: No data in the ring buffer
Frames contain data
Frame 0: a
Frame 1: b
Frame 2: c
Frame 3: d
Frame 4: e
Frames contain data
Frame 16: q
Frame 17: r
Frame 18: s
Frame 19: t
Frame 20: u
Frame 21: v
Frame 22: w
Frame 23: x
Frame 24: y
Frame 25: z
user@feb23236b84c:/mnt/test/ringbuf$ 
```

Firstly, we try to read from the empty buffer and get an exception, as expected.

Then, we write five elements to the buffer, using characters of the Latin alphabet as the data payload:

```
for (size_t i = 0; i < 5; i++) {
  Frame& out = frames.push();
  out.index = i;
  out.data[0] = 'a' + i;
  out.data[1] = '\0';
}
```

Note how we get the reference to an element and then update it in-place rather than push a local copy of frame into the ring buffer. Then we read all the data in the buffer and print it on the screen:

```
while (frames.has_data()) {
  const Frame& in = frames.pull();
  std::cout << "Frame " << in.index << ": " << in.data << std::endl;
}
```

The program output indicates that we can successfully read all five elements. Now we try to write all 26 letters of the Latin alphabet to the array, way more than its capacity.

```
for (size_t i = 0; i < 26; i++) {
  Frame& out = frames.push();
  out.index = i;
  out.data[0] = 'a' + i;
  out.data[1] = '\0';
}
```

Then we read the data in the same way that we did for the five elements. The read is successful, but we receive only the last 10 elements written; all other frames were lost and overwritten by this point. It is not critical for our sample application, but maybe this isn't acceptable for many other applications. The best way to ensure that data is not being lost is to guarantee that the receiver is activated more frequently than the sender. Sometimes the receiver will be activated if no data is available in the buffer, but this is an acceptable price to pay to avoid data loss.

Using shared memory

In modern operating systems running on hardware that supports an **MMU** (short for **memory management unit**), each application runs as a process and has its memory isolated from other applications.

Such isolation brings important reliability benefits. An application cannot accidentally corrupt the memory of another application. Similarly, an application that accidentally corrupts its own memory and crashes can be shut down by the operating system without affecting other applications in the system. Decoupling the functionality of the embedded system into several isolated applications that communicate with each other over a well-defined API significantly decreases the complexity of the implementation, resulting in improved stability.

The isolation, however, incurs costs. Since each process has its own isolated address space, data exchange between two applications implies data copying, context switching, and the use of operating system kernel synchronization mechanisms that can be relatively expensive.

Shared memory is a mechanism provided by many operating systems to declare certain memory regions as shared. This way, applications can exchange data without copying. This is especially important for the exchange of large data objects, such as video frames or audio samples.

How to do it...

In this recipe, we will learn how to use a Linux shared memory API for data exchange between two or more applications:

1. In your working ~/test directory, create a subdirectory called shmem.

2. Use your favorite text editor to create a shmem.cpp file in the shmem subdirectory. Define the SharedMem class, starting with common headers and constants:

```cpp
#include <algorithm>
#include <iostream>
#include <chrono>
#include <thread>

#include <sys/mman.h>
#include <fcntl.h>
#include <unistd.h>

const char* kSharedMemPath = "/sample_point";
const size_t kPayloadSize = 16;

using namespace std::literals;

template<class T>
class SharedMem {
    int fd;
    T* ptr;
    const char* name;

    public:
```

3. Then, define a constructor that does most of the work:

```cpp
SharedMem(const char* name, bool owner=false) {
fd = shm_open(name, O_RDWR | O_CREAT, 0600);
if (fd == -1) {
throw std::runtime_error("Failed to open a shared memory region");
}
if (ftruncate(fd, sizeof(T)) < 0) {
close(fd);
throw std::runtime_error("Failed to set size of a shared memory
region");
};
ptr = (T*)mmap(nullptr, sizeof(T), PROT_READ | PROT_WRITE,
MAP_SHARED, fd, 0);
if (!ptr) {
```

```
close(fd);
    throw std::runtime_error("Failed to mmap a shared memory
region");
}
    this->name = owner ? name : nullptr;
    std::cout << "Opened shared mem instance " << name <<
std::endl;
}
```

4. Add the definition of the destructor:

```
~SharedMem() {
  munmap(ptr, sizeof(T));
  close(fd);
  if (name) {
    std::cout << "Remove shared mem instance " << name << std::endl;
    shm_unlink(name);
  }
}
```

5. Finalize the class definition with a small method that returns a reference to the shared object:

```
        T& get() const {
          return *ptr;
        }
        };
```

6. Our `SharedMem` class can work with different data types. Let's declare a custom data structure that we want to use:

```
struct Payload {
  uint32_t index;
  uint8_t raw[kPayloadSize];
};
```

7. Now add code that writes data to the shared memory:

```
void producer() {
  SharedMem<Payload> writer(kSharedMemPath);
  Payload& pw = writer.get();
  for (int i = 0; i < 5; i++) {
    pw.index = i;
    std::fill_n(pw.raw, sizeof(pw.raw) - 1, 'a' + i);
    pw.raw[sizeof(pw.raw) - 1] = '\0';
    std::this_thread::sleep_for(150ms);
  }
}
```

8. Also, add code that reads data from the shared memory:

```
void consumer() {
  SharedMem<Payload> point_reader(kSharedMemPath, true);
  Payload& pr = point_reader.get();
  for (int i = 0; i < 10; i++) {
    std::cout << "Read data frame " << pr.index << ": " << pr.raw
<< std::endl;
    std::this_thread::sleep_for(100ms);
  }
}
```

9. Add the `main` function to tie everything together, as shown in the following code:

```
int main() {

  if (fork()) {
    consumer();
  } else {
    producer();
  }
}
```

10. Create a file called `CMakeLists.txt` in the `loop` subdirectory with the following content:

```
cmake_minimum_required(VERSION 3.5.1)
project(shmem)
add_executable(shmem shmem.cpp)
target_link_libraries(shmem rt)

set(CMAKE_SYSTEM_NAME Linux)
set(CMAKE_SYSTEM_PROCESSOR arm)

SET(CMAKE_CXX_FLAGS "--std=c++14")
set(CMAKE_CXX_COMPILER /usr/bin/arm-linux-gnueabi-g++)
```

11. Build the application and copy the resulting executable binary to the target system. Use recipes from Chapter 2, *Setting Up the Environment,* to do it.

12. Switch to the target system terminal. Log in using user credentials, if needed.

13. Run the binary.

How it works...

In this recipe, we use the **POSIX** (short for **Portable Operating System Interface**) API to work with shared memory. This is a flexible and fine-grained C API, with lots of parameters that can be tuned or configured. Our goal is to hide the complexity of this low-level API by implementing a more convenient and type-safe C++ wrapper on top of it. We are going to use the **RAII** (short for **resource acquisition is initialization**) idiom to make sure all allocated resources are properly deallocated and we do not have memory or file descriptor leaks in our application.

We define a templated `SharedMem` class. The template argument defines a data type that is stored in our shared memory instance. This way, we make instances of the `SharedMem` class type safe. Instead of our working with void pointers and casting types in the application code, the C++ compiler does it for us automatically:

```
template<class T>
class SharedMem {
```

All shared memory allocation and initialization is implemented in the `SharedMem` constructor. It accepts two parameters:

- A shared memory object name
- An ownership flag

POSIX defines a `shm_open` API, where shared memory objects are identified by names, similar to filenames. This way, two independent processes that use the same name can reference the same shared memory object. What is the lifetime of the shared object? The shared object is destroyed when the `shm_unlink` function is invoked for the same object name. If the object is used by multiple processes, the first one that calls `shm_open` will create it, and the others will reuse the same object. But which of them is responsible for its deletion? This is what the ownership flag is used for. When set to `true`, it indicates that the `SharedMem` instance is responsible for the shared object cleanup when it is destroyed.

The constructor sequentially calls three POSIX API functions. Firstly, it creates a shared object using `shm_open`. Though the function accepts access flags and file permissions as its parameters, we always use the read–write access mode and read and write access for the current user:

```
fd = shm_open(name, O_RDWR | O_CREAT, 0600);
```

Next, we define the size of the shared region using the `ftruncate` call. We use the size of the template data type for this purpose:

```
if (ftruncate(fd, sizeof(T)) < 0) {
```

Finally, we map the shared region into our process memory address space using the `mmap` function. It returns a pointer that we can use to reference our data instance:

```
ptr = (T*)mmap(nullptr, sizeof(T), PROT_READ | PROT_WRITE, MAP_SHARED, fd,
0);
```

The object holds the file descriptor for the shared memory block and the pointer to the memory region as its private members. The destructor deallocates them when the object is being destroyed. If the owner flag is set, we also keep the object name so that we can remove it:

```
int fd;
T* ptr;
const char* name;
```

The `SharedMem` destructor unmaps the shared memory object from the address space:

```
munmap(ptr, sizeof(T));
```

In the event that the object is the owner, we can remove it using a `shm_unlink` call. Note that we do not need the owner flag anymore since the name is set to `nullptr`, unless the object is the owner:

```
if (name) {
  std::cout << "Remove shared mem instance " << name << std::endl;
  shm_unlink(name);
}
```

To access shared data, the class provides a simple `get` method. It returns a reference to the object stored in the shared memory:

```
T& get() const {
    return *ptr;
}
```

Let's create two independent processes that use the shared memory API we created. We use a POSIX `fork` function to spawn a child process. The child process will be a data producer and the parent process will be a data consumer:

```
if (fork()) {
  consumer();
} else {
```

```
    producer();
}
```

We define a `Payload` data type, used by both the producer and the consumer for data exchange:

```
struct Payload {
uint32_t index;
uint8_t raw[kPayloadSize];
};
```

The data producer creates a `SharedMem` instance:

```
SharedMem<Payload> writer(kSharedMemPath);
```

It updates the shared object every 150 milliseconds using the reference it received using the `get` method. Each time, it increments the index field of the payload and fills its data with letters of the Latin alphabet that match the index.

The consumer is as simple as the producer. It creates a `SharedMem` instance with the same name as the producer, but it claims the ownership of the object. This means that it will be responsible for its deletion, as shown in the following code:

```
SharedMem<Payload> point_reader(kSharedMemPath, true);
```

Run the application and observe the following output:

```
user@feb23236b84c: /mnt/test/shmem — bash
user@feb23236b84c:/mnt/test/shmem$ ./shmem
Opened shared mem instance /sample_point
Read data frame 0:
Opened shared mem instance /sample_point
Read data frame 0: aaaaaaaaaaaaaaaa
Read data frame 1: bbbbbbbbbbbbbbbb
Read data frame 2: cccccccccccccccc
Read data frame 2: cccccccccccccccc
Read data frame 3: dddddddddddddddd
Read data frame 4: eeeeeeeeeeeeeeee
Read data frame 4: eeeeeeeeeeeeeeee
Read data frame 4: eeeeeeeeeeeeeeee
Read data frame 4: eeeeeeeeeeeeeeee
Remove shared mem instance /sample_point
user@feb23236b84c:/mnt/test/shmem$
```

Every 100 milliseconds, the application reads data from the shared object and prints it to the screen. In the consumer output, we can see that it receives data written by the producer. Since the duration of the consumer and the producer cycles does not match, we can see that sometimes the same data is being read twice

An important part of the logic that was intentionally omitted in this example is the synchronization of the producer and the consumer. Since they run as independent projects, there is no guarantee that the producer has updated any data by the time the consumer tries to read it. The following is what we see in the resulting output:

```
Opened shared mem instance /sample_point
Read data frame 0:
Opened shared mem instance /sample_point
```

We can see that the consumer opened the shared memory object and read some data before the producer opened the same object.

Similarly, there is no guarantee that data fields are updated completely by the producer when the consumer tries to read them. We will discuss this topic in more detail in the next chapter.

There's more...

Shared memory is a fast and efficient mechanism for inter-process communication by itself, but it really shines when combined with ring buffers. By placing a ring buffer into shared memory, developers allow independent data producers and data consumers to exchange data asynchronously, and with minimal overhead for synchronization.

Using specialized memory

Embedded systems often provide access to their peripheral devices over specific ranges of memory addresses. When a program accesses an address in such a region, it does not read or write a value in memory. Instead, data is sent to a device or read from a device mapped to this address.

This technique is commonly named **MMIO** (short for **memory-mapped input/output**). In this recipe, we will learn how to access peripheral devices of the Raspberry PI using MMIO from userspace Linux applications.

How to do it...

The Raspberry PI has a number of peripheral devices that are accessible over MMIO. To demonstrate how MMIO works, our application will access the system timer:

1. In your working ~/test directory, create a subdirectory called timer.
2. Use your favorite text editor to create a file named timer.cpp in the timer subdirectory.
3. Put the required headers, constants, and declarations of types into timer.cpp:

```cpp
#include <iostream>
#include <chrono>
#include <system_error>
#include <thread>

#include <fcntl.h>
#include <sys/mman.h>


constexpr uint32_t kTimerBase = 0x3F003000;

struct SystemTimer {
  uint32_t CS;
  uint32_t counter_lo;
  uint32_t counter_hi;
};
```

4. Add the main function, which contains all the logic of the program:

```cpp
int main() {

  int memfd = open("/dev/mem", O_RDWR | O_SYNC);
  if (memfd < 0) {
  throw std::system_error(errno, std::generic_category(),
  "Failed to open /dev/mem. Make sure you run as root.");
  }

  SystemTimer *timer = (SystemTimer*)mmap(NULL,
sizeof(SystemTimer),
  PROT_READ|PROT_WRITE, MAP_SHARED,
  memfd, kTimerBase);
  if (timer == MAP_FAILED) {
  throw std::system_error(errno, std::generic_category(),
  "Memory mapping failed");
  }
```

```
  uint64_t prev = 0;
  for (int i = 0; i < 10; i++) {
   uint64_t time = ((uint64_t)timer->counter_hi << 32) +
timer->counter_lo;
    std::cout << "System timer: " << time;
    if (i > 0) {
    std::cout << ", diff " << time - prev;
     }
    prev = time;
    std::cout << std::endl;
    std::this_thread::sleep_for(std::chrono::milliseconds(10));
  }
  return 0;
  }
```

5. Create a file called `CMakeLists.txt` in the `timer` subdirectory with the following content:

    ```
    cmake_minimum_required(VERSION 3.5.1)
    project(timer)
    add_executable(timer timer.cpp)

    set(CMAKE_SYSTEM_NAME Linux)
    set(CMAKE_SYSTEM_PROCESSOR arm)

    SET(CMAKE_CXX_FLAGS "--std=c++11")

    set(CMAKE_CXX_COMPILER /usr/bin/arm-linux-gnueabi-g++)
    ```

6. You can now build and run the application.

Please note that it should be run under `root` on a real Raspberry PI 3 device.

How it works...

The system timer is a peripheral device that is connected to the processor using an MMIO interface. This means it has a dedicated range of physical addresses, each of them with a specific format and purpose.

Our application works with a timer counter represented as two 32-bit values. Combined, they form a 64-bit read-only counter always incrementing when the system is running.

For the Raspberry PI 3, a physical memory address range allocated for the system timer has offset the following —0x3F003000 (it may be different depending on the Raspberry PI hardware revision). We define it as a constant.

```
constexpr uint32_t kTimerBase = 0x3F003000;
```

To access individual fields within the region, we define a `SystemTimer` struct:

```
struct SystemTimer {
  uint32_t CS;
  uint32_t counter_lo;
  uint32_t counter_hi;
};
```

Now, we need to get the pointer to the timer address range and convert it to a pointer to `SystemTimer`. This way, we can access the addresses of the counter by reading the `SystemTimer` data fields.

There is, however, a problem we need to solve. We know the offset in the physical address space, but our Linux application works within the virtual address space. We need to find a way to map physical addresses to virtual addresses.

Linux provides access to physical memory addresses using the special `/proc/mem` file. Since it contains a snapshot of all physical memory, it is accessible only by `root`.

We open it as a regular file using the `open` function:

```
int memfd = open("/dev/mem", O_RDWR | O_SYNC);
```

Once the file is open and we know its descriptor, we can map it into our virtual address space. We do not need to map the whole physical memory. A region related to the timer is sufficient; that is why we pass the system timer range start as an offset parameter and the size of the `SystemTimer` structure as the size parameter:

```
SystemTimer *timer = (SystemTimer*)mmap(NULL, sizeof(SystemTimer),
PROT_READ|PROT_WRITE, MAP_SHARED, memfd, kTimerBase);
```

Now we can access the timer fields. We read the timer counter in the loop and display its current value and its variance from the preceding value. When we run our application as `root`, we get the following output:

```
●  ●  ●                    ⇧ ~ — igor@raspberrypi: ~ — ssh pi
igor@raspberrypi:~ $ ./timer
terminate called after throwing an instance of 'std::system_error'
  what():  Failed to open /dev/mem. Make sure you run as root.: Permission d
d
Aborted
igor@raspberrypi:~ $ sudo ./timer
System timer: 620354537923
System timer: 620354548340, diff 10417
System timer: 620354558477, diff 10137
System timer: 620354568600, diff 10123
System timer: 620354578720, diff 10120
System timer: 620354588837, diff 10117
System timer: 620354598967, diff 10130
System timer: 620354609096, diff 10129
System timer: 620354619255, diff 10159
System timer: 620354629388, diff 10133
igor@raspberrypi:~ $ ▌
```

As we can see, reading from this memory address returns increasing values. The value of the difference is around 10,000 and pretty constant. Since we added a 10-millisecond delay into the counter read loop, we can infer that the memory address is associated with the timer, not regular memory, and the timer counter granularity is 1 microsecond.

There's more...

The Raspberry Pi has a number of peripheral devices that are accessible over MMIO. You can find detailed information about their address ranges and access semantics in the *BCM2835 ARM Peripherals manual*, available at `https://www.raspberrypi.org/documentation/hardware/raspberrypi/bcm2835/BCM2835-ARM-Peripherals.pdf`

Please note that developers have to be extremely careful when working with memory that can be accessed by multiple devices simultaneously. When memory is accessible by multiple processors or multiple cores of the same processor, you may need to use advanced synchronization techniques such as memory barriers to avoid synchronization issues. We will discuss some of them in the next chapter. Things become even more complicated if you use **direct memory access** (**DMA**), or MMIO. Since the CPU may be unaware that memory is changed by external hardware, its cache may be out of sync, leading to data-coherency issues.

7
Multithreading and Synchronization

Embedded platforms span a vast landscape of computing power. There are microcontrollers with just a few kilobytes of memory; there are powerful **systems-on-chip** (**SoCs**) with gigabytes of memory; there are multi-core CPUs capable of running many applications at the same time.

With more computational resources available for embedded developers, and more complex applications they can build on top of them, multithreading support has become very important. Developers need to know how to parallelize their applications to efficiently utilize all CPU cores. We will learn how to write applications that can utilize all available CPU cores in an efficient and safe way.

In this chapter, we will cover the following topics:

- Exploring thread support in C++
- Exploring data synchronization
- Using condition variables
- Using atomic variables
- Using the C++ memory model
- Exploring lock-free synchronization
- Using atomic variables in shared memory
- Exploring async functions and futures

These recipes can be used as examples of building your own efficient multithreading and multiprocessing synchronization code.

Exploring thread support in C++

Prior to C++11, threads were completely out of the scope of C++ as a language. Developers could use platform-specific libraries, such as pthreads or the Win32 **application programming interface** (**API**). Since each library has its own behavior, porting applications to another platform required significant development and testing efforts.

C++11 introduced threads as part of the C++ standard and defined a set of classes to create multithreaded applications in its standard library.

In this recipe, we will learn how to use C++ to spawn multiple concurrent threads in a single application.

How to do it...

In this recipe, we will learn how to create two worker threads that run concurrently.

1. In your ~/test working directory, create a subdirectory called threads.
2. Use your favorite text editor to create a threads.cpp file in the threads subdirectory. Copy the code snippet into the threads.cpp file:

```cpp
#include <chrono>
#include <iostream>
#include <thread>

void worker(int index) {
  for (int i = 0; i < 10; i++) {
    std::cout << "Worker " << index << " begins" << std::endl;
    std::this_thread::sleep_for(std::chrono::milliseconds(50));
    std::cout << "Worker " << index << " ends" << std::endl;
    std::this_thread::sleep_for(std::chrono::milliseconds(1));
  }
}

int main() {
  std::thread worker1(worker, 1);
  std::thread worker2(worker, 2);
  worker1.join();
  worker2.join();
  std::cout << "Done" << std::endl;
}
```

3. Create a file called `CMakeLists.txt` in the `loop` subdirectory, with the following content:

```
cmake_minimum_required(VERSION 3.5.1)
project(threads)
add_executable(threads threads.cpp)

set(CMAKE_SYSTEM_NAME Linux)
set(CMAKE_SYSTEM_PROCESSOR arm)

SET(CMAKE_CXX_FLAGS "--std=c++11")
target_link_libraries(threads pthread)

set(CMAKE_CXX_COMPILER /usr/bin/arm-linux-gnueabi-g++)
```

You can build and run the application.

How it works...

In this application, we defined a function called `worker`. To keep the code simple, it does not do much useful work, only printing `Worker X starts` and `Worker X ends` 10 times, with 50 milliseconds' delay between the messages.

In the `main` function, we create two worker threads, `worker1` and `worker2`:

```
std::thread worker1(worker, 1);
std::thread worker2(worker, 2);
```

We pass two parameters into the thread constructors:

- A function that runs in the thread.
- A parameter for the function. Since we pass the previously defined `worker` function as a thread function, the parameter should match its type—in our case, it is `int`.

This way, we defined two worker thread that do the same job but have different indices—1 and 2.

The threads start running immediately as soon as they are created; there is no need to call any additional methods to start them. They are executed completely concurrently, as we can see from the program output:

```
● ● ●              root@3324138cc2c7: /mnt/threads — bash
root@3324138cc2c7:/mnt/threads# ./threads
Worker 1 begins
Worker 2 begins
Worker Worker 21 ends ends
Worker 1 begins

Worker 2 begins
Worker Worker 2 ends1 ends
Worker 2 begins

Worker 1 begins
Worker 1 ends
Worker 1 begins
Worker 2 ends
Worker 2 begins
Worker 1 ends
Worker 1 begins
Worker 2 ends
Worker 2 begins
Worker Worker 1 ends2 ends
Worker 2 begins

Worker 1 begins
Worker 1 ends
Worker 1 begins
```

The output from our worker thread is mixed, and sometimes garbled, such as `Worker Worker 1 ends2 ends`. This happens because output to the Terminal is also working concurrently.

Since worker threads are executed independently, the main thread has nothing to do after creating the worker thread. However, if the execution of the main thread reaches the end of the `main` function, the program terminates. To avoid this, we added calls to the `join` method for each of our worker threads. This method blocks until the thread terminates. This way, we exit the main program only after both of the worker threads complete their work.

Exploring data synchronization

Data synchronization is an important aspect of any application that deals with multiple execution threads. Different threads often need to access the same variables or memory regions. Writing to the same memory at the same time by two or more independent threads can result in data corruption. Even reading the variable at the same time when it is being updated by another thread is dangerous, since it can be only partially updated at the moment of the read.

To avoid these issues, concurrent threads can use so-called synchronization primitives, the API that makes access to the shared memory deterministic and predictable.

Similar to the case with thread support, the C++ language did not provide any synchronization primitives prior to the C++11 standard. Starting with C++11, a number of synchronization primitives were added into the C++ standard library as part of the standard.

In this recipe, we will learn how to synchronize access to a variable, using a mutex and a lock guard.

How to do it...

In the preceding recipe, we learned how to run two worker threads completely concurrently and noticed that it can lead to garbled output to the Terminal. We are going to modify the code from the preceding recipe to add synchronization, using a mutex and a lock guard, and see the difference.

1. In your ~/test working directory, create a subdirectory called mutex.
2. Use your favorite text editor to create a mutex.cpp file in the mutex subdirectory. Copy the code snippet into the mutex.cpp file:

```
#include <chrono>
#include <iostream>
#include <mutex>
#include <thread>

std::mutex m;

void worker(int index) {
  for (int i = 0; i < 10; i++) {
    {
      std::lock_guard<std::mutex> g(m);
      std::cout << "Worker " << index << " begins" << std::endl;
```

```
        std::this_thread::sleep_for(std::chrono::milliseconds(50));
        std::cout << "Worker " << index << " ends" << std::endl;
    }
    std::this_thread::sleep_for(std::chrono::milliseconds(1));
  }
}

int main() {
  std::thread worker1(worker, 1);
  std::thread worker2(worker, 2);
  worker1.join();
  worker2.join();
  std::cout << "Done" << std::endl;
}
```

3. Create a file called `CMakeLists.txt` in the `loop` subdirectory, with the following content:

```
cmake_minimum_required(VERSION 3.5.1)
project(mutex)
add_executable(mutex mutex.cpp)

set(CMAKE_SYSTEM_NAME Linux)
set(CMAKE_SYSTEM_PROCESSOR arm)

SET(CMAKE_CXX_FLAGS "--std=c++11")
target_link_libraries(mutex pthread)

set(CMAKE_CXX_COMPILER /usr/bin/arm-linux-gnueabi-g++)
```

You can build and run the application.

How it works...

After we build and run our application, we can see that its output is similar to the output of the thread application. However, there are also noticeable differences:

Firstly, the output is not garbled. Secondly, we can see a clear order—no worker is interrupted by another worker, and each begin is followed by the corresponding end. The difference lies in the highlighted fragments of the source code. We create a global mutex m:

```
std::mutex m;
```

Then, we use lock_guard to protect our critical section of code, which starts from the line that prints Worker X begins and ends at the line that prints Worker X ends.

lock_guard is a wrapper on top of a mutex that uses an **RAII** (short for **Resource Acquisition Is Initialization**) technique to automatically lock the corresponding mutex in the constructor when the lock object is defined, and unlock it in the destructor after reaching the end of its scope. That is why we add extra curly braces to define the scope of our critical section:

```
{
    std::lock_guard<std::mutex> g(m);
    std::cout << "Worker " << index << " begins" << std::endl;
    std::this_thread::sleep_for(std::chrono::milliseconds(50));
    std::cout << "Worker " << index << " ends" << std::endl;
}
```

Though it is possible to lock and unlock the mutex explicitly, by calling its lock and unlock methods, it is not recommended. Forgetting to unlock a locked mutex leads to multithreading synchronization issues that are hard to detect and hard to debug. The RAII approach unlocks mutexes automatically, making code safer, easier to read, and easier to understand.

There's more...

Proper implementation of thread synchronization requires a lot of attention to detail and thorough analysis. A very common problem in multithreaded applications is a deadlock. This is a situation whereby a thread is blocked because it is waiting for another thread that, in turn, is blocked because it is waiting for the first thread. As a result, two threads are blocked infinitely.

A deadlock occurs if two or more mutexes are required for synchronization. C++17 introduced *std::scoped_lock*, available at `https://en.cppreference.com/w/cpp/thread/scoped_lock` an RAII wrapper for multiple mutexes that helps to avoid deadlocks.

Using condition variables

We learned how to synchronize simultaneous access to the same variable from two or more threads. The particular order in which threads accessed the variable was not important; we only prevented simultaneous reads and writes to the variable.

A thread waiting for another thread to start processing data is a common scenario. In this case, the second thread should be notified by the first thread when the data is available. It can be done using condition variables, supported by C++, starting from the C++11 standard.

In this recipe, we will learn how to use condition variables to activate data processing in a separate thread as soon as the data is available.

How to do it...

We are going to implement an application with two worker threads, similar to the application we created in the *Exploring data synchronization* recipe.

1. In your ~/test working directory, create a subdirectory called condvar.
2. Use your favorite text editor to create a condv.cpp file in the condvar subdirectory.

3. Now, we put the required headers and define global variables in `condvar.cpp`:

```cpp
#include <condition_variable>
#include <iostream>
#include <mutex>
#include <thread>
#include <vector>

std::mutex m;
std::condition_variable cv;
std::vector<int> result;
int next = 0;
```

4. After the global variables are defined, we add our `worker` function, which is similar to the `worker` function from the preceding recipes:

```cpp
void worker(int index) {
  for (int i = 0; i < 10; i++) {
    std::unique_lock<std::mutex> l(m);
    cv.wait(l, [=]{return next == index; });
    std::cout << "worker " << index << "\n";
    result.push_back(index);
    next = next + 1;
    if (next > 2) { next = 1; };
    cv.notify_all();
  }
}
```

5. Finally, we define our entry point—the `main` function:

```cpp
int main() {
  std::thread worker1(worker, 1);
  std::thread worker2(worker, 2);
  {
    std::lock_guard<std::mutex> l(m);
    next = 1;
  }
  std::cout << "Start\n";
  cv.notify_all();
  worker1.join();
  worker2.join();
  for (int e : result) {
    std::cout << e << ' ';
  }
  std::cout << std::endl;
}
```

6. Create a file called `CMakeLists.txt` in the `loop` subdirectory, with the following content:

```
cmake_minimum_required(VERSION 3.5.1)
cmake_minimum_required(VERSION 3.5.1)
project(condvar)
add_executable(condvar condvar.cpp)

set(CMAKE_SYSTEM_NAME Linux)
set(CMAKE_SYSTEM_PROCESSOR arm)

SET(CMAKE_CXX_FLAGS "--std=c++11")
target_link_libraries(condvar pthread)

set(CMAKE_CXX_COMPILER /usr/bin/arm-linux-gnueabi-g++)
```

You can build and run the application.

How it works...

Similarly to the application that we created in the *Exploring data synchronization* recipe, we create two worker threads, `worker1` and `worker2`, that use the same `worker` function thread and differ only by the `index` parameter.

Besides printing messages to the console, the worker thread update a global vector result. Each worker just adds its index into the `result` variable in its loop, as shown in the following command:

```
std::vector<int> result;
```

We want each worker to add its index to the result only on its turn— `worker 1`, then `worker 2`, then `worker 1` again, and so on. It is not possible to do this without synchronization; however, simple synchronization using mutexes is not sufficient. It can guarantee that two concurrent threads will not access the same critical section of the code at the same time, but cannot guarantee the order. It is possible that `worker 1` will lock the mutex again before `worker 2` locks it.

To solve the ordering problem, we define a `cv` condition variable and a `next` integer variable:

```
std::condition_variable cv;
int next = 0;
```

The `next` variable contains an index of the worker. It is initialized with 0 and set to a specific worker index in the `main` function. Since this variable is accessed from multiple threads, we do it under the protection of the lock guard:

```
{
    std::lock_guard<std::mutex> l(m);
    next = 1;
}
```

Though the worker threads start executing after their creation, both of them are immediately blocked on the condition variables, waiting until the value of the `next` variable matches their index. Condition variables need `std::unique_lock` for waiting. We create it right before calling the `wait` method:

```
std::unique_lock<std::mutex> l(m);
cv.wait(l, [=]{return next == index; });
```

Though the condition variable `cv` was set to 1 in the `main` function, it is not enough. We need to explicitly notify threads waiting on the condition variable. We do this using the `notify_all` method:

```
cv.notify_all();
```

This wakes up all waiting threads, and they compare their index against the `next` variable. The matching thread unblocks, and all other threads go to sleep again.

The active thread writes a message to the console and updates the `result` variable. Then, it updates the `next` variable to choose a thread that will be activated next. We increment the index until it reaches the maximum value, then reset it to 1:

```
next = next + 1;
if (next > 2) { next = 1; };
```

Similar to the case with the code in the `main` function, after the index of the `next` thread is decided, we need to invoke `notify_all` to wake all threads up and let them decide whose turn it is to work:

```
cv.notify_all();
```

While the worker threads work, the `main` function waits for their completion:

```
worker1.join();
worker2.join();
```

When all worker threads complete, the value of the `result` variable is printed:

```
for (int e : result) {
  std::cout << e << ' ';
}
```

After we build and run our program, we get the following output:

```
user@3324138cc2c7: /mnt/condvar — bash
user@3324138cc2c7:/mnt/condvar$ ./condvar
Start
worker 1
worker 2
worker 1
worker 2
worker 1
worker 2
worker 1
worker 2
worker 1
worker 2
worker 1
worker 2
worker 1
worker 2
worker 1
worker 2
worker 1
worker 2
worker 1
worker 2
1 2 1 2 1 2 1 2 1 2 1 2 1 2 1 2 1 2 1 2
user@3324138cc2c7:/mnt/condvar$ []
```

As we can see, all threads were activated in the expected order.

There's more...

In this recipe, we only used a few methods provided by the condition variable object. Besides the simple `wait` function, there are functions for waiting for a specific time or waiting until a specified time point is reached. Learn more about the *C++ condition variable class* at its `https://en.cppreference.com/w/cpp/thread/condition_variable` reference page.

Using atomic variables

Atomic variables are named as such because they cannot be read or written partially. Compare, for example, the `Point` and `int` data types:

```
struct Point {
   int x, y;
};

Point p{0, 0};
int b = 0;

p = {10, 10};
b = 10;
```

In this example, modification of the `p` variable is equivalent to two assignments:

```
p.x = 10;
p.y = 10;
```

This means that any concurrent thread reading the `p` variable can get partially modified data, such as x=10, y=0, which can lead to incorrect calculations that are hard to detect and hard to reproduce. That is why access to such data types should be synchronized.

How about the `b` variable? Can it be modified partially? The answer is: yes, depending on the platform. However, C++ provides a set of data types and templates to ensure that a variable changes all at once, as a whole, atomically.

In this recipe, we will learn how to use atomic variables for the synchronization of multiple threads. Since atomic variables cannot be modified partially, there is no need to use mutexes or other expensive synchronization primitives.

How to do it...

We will create an application that spawns two worker threads to concurrently update an array of data. Instead of mutexes, we will use atomic variables to make sure the concurrent updates are safe.

1. In your ~/test working directory, create a subdirectory called `atomic`.
2. Use your favorite text editor to create an `atomic.cpp` file in the `atomic` subdirectory.

3. Now, we put the required headers, and define global variables in `atomic.cpp`:

```
#include <atomic>
#include <chrono>
#include <iostream>
#include <thread>
#include <vector>

std::atomic<size_t> shared_index{0};
std::vector<int> data;
```

4. After global variables are defined, we add our `worker` function. It resembles the `worker` function from the preceding recipes, but besides an `index`, it has an additional parameter—`timeout`:

```
void worker(int index, int timeout) {
    while(true) {
    size_t worker_index = shared_index.fetch_add(1);
    if (worker_index >= data.size()) {
        break;
    }
    std::cout << "Worker " << index << " handles "
                << worker_index << std::endl;
    data[worker_index] = data[worker_index] * 2;
    std::this_thread::sleep_for(std::chrono::milliseconds(timeout));
    }
    }
```

5. Finally, we define our entry point— the `main` function:

```
int main() {
    for (int i = 0; i < 10; i++) {
      data.emplace_back(i);
    }
    std::thread worker1(worker, 1, 50);
    std::thread worker2(worker, 2, 20);
    worker1.join();
    worker2.join();
    std::cout << "Result: ";
    for (auto& v : data) {
      std::cout << v << ' ';
    }
    std::cout << std::endl;
}
```

6. Create a file called `CMakeLists.txt` in the `loop` subdirectory, with the following content:

```
cmake_minimum_required(VERSION 3.5.1)
project(atomic)
add_executable(atomic atomic.cpp)

set(CMAKE_SYSTEM_NAME Linux)
set(CMAKE_SYSTEM_PROCESSOR arm)

SET(CMAKE_CXX_FLAGS "--std=c++11")
target_link_libraries(atomic pthread)

set(CMAKE_CXX_COMPILER /usr/bin/arm-linux-gnueabi-g++)
```

You can build and run the application.

How it works...

We are creating an application that updates all elements of an array using multiple worker threads. For expensive update operations, this approach can result in substantial performance gains on a multi-core platform.

The difficulty is sharing the work between multiple worker threads, given that each of them may require a different amount of time to process a data element.

We use a `shared_index` atomic variable to store an index of the next element that has not yet been claimed by any of the worker threads. This variable, along with the array to be processed, is declared as a global variable:

```
std::atomic<size_t> shared_index{0};
std::vector<int> data;
```

Our `worker` function resembles the `worker` function from earlier recipes but has important differences. Firstly, it has an additional parameter, `timeout`. This is used to simulate differences in the time required to process each element.

Secondly, instead of a fixed number of iterations, our worker threads run in a loop until the `shared_index` variable reaches the maximum value. This indicates that all elements were processed, and the worker can terminate.

On each iteration, a worker reads the value of `shared_index`. If there are elements to process, it stores the value of the `shared_index` variable in a local `worker_index` variable and increments the `shared_index` variable at the same time.

Though it is possible to use an atomic variable in the same way as a regular variable—first, get its current value, and then increment the variable—it can lead to a race condition. Both worker threads can read the variable at almost the same time. In this case, both of them get the same value, then start processing the same element, interfering with each other. That is why we use a special method, `fetch_add`, which increments the variable and returns the value it had before the increment as a single, non-interruptible action:

```
size_t worker_index = shared_index.fetch_add(1);
```

If the `worker_index` variable reaches the size of the array, it means that all elements were processed, and the worker can terminate:

```
if (worker_index >= data.size()) {
    break;
}
```

If the `worker_index` variable is valid, it is used by the worker to update the value of the array element by this index. In our case, we just multiply it by 2:

```
data[worker_index] = data[worker_index] * 2;
```

To simulate expensive data operation, we use a custom delay. The duration of the delay is determined by the `timeout` parameter:

```
std::this_thread::sleep_for(std::chrono::milliseconds(timeout));
```

In the `main` function, we add elements to process into the data vector. We use a loop to populate the vector with numbers from zero to nine:

```
for (int i = 0; i < 10; i++) {
    data.emplace_back(i);
}
```

After the initial dataset is ready, we create two worker threads, providing the `index` and the `timeout` parameters. Different timeouts of the worker thread are used to simulate different performances:

```
std::thread worker1(worker, 1, 50);
std::thread worker2(worker, 2, 20);
```

Then, we wait till both worker threads complete their jobs, and print the result to the console. When we build and run our application, we get the following output:

```
• ● ●                user@3324138cc2c7: /mnt/atomic — bash
user@3324138cc2c7:/mnt/atomic$ ./atomic
Worker 1 handles 0
Worker 2 handles 1
Worker 2 handles 2
Worker 2 handles 3
Worker 1 handles 4
Worker 2 handles 5
Worker 2 handles 6
Worker 1 handles 7
Worker 2 handles 8
Worker 2 handles 9
Result: 0 2 4 6 8 10 12 14 16 18
user@3324138cc2c7:/mnt/atomic$
```

As we can see, `Worker 2` has processed more elements than `Worker 1` because its timeout was 20 milliseconds, compared to the 50 milliseconds of `Worker 1`. Also, all elements were processed without omissions and repetitions, as intended.

There's more...

We learned how to work with integer atomic variables. Though this type of atomic variable is the most commonly used, C++ allows atomic variables of other types to be defined as well, including non-integral types, given that they are trivially copyable, copy constructible, and copy assignable.

Besides the `fetch_add` method we used in our example, atomic variables have other similar methods that help developers to query the value and modify the variable in a single operation. Consider using these methods to avoid race conditions or expensive synchronization using mutexes.

In C++20, atomic variables receive `wait`, `notify_all`, and `notify_one` methods, similar to the methods of condition variables. They allow implementation of the logic that previously required condition variables by using much more efficient and lightweight atomic variables.

More information about atomic variables can be found at `https://en.cppreference.com/w/cpp/atomic/atomic`.

Using the C++ memory model

Beginning with the C++11 standard, C++ defined an API and primitives for threads and synchronization as part of the language. Memory synchronization in a system that has multiple processor cores is complicated because modern processors can optimize code execution by reordering instructions. Even when using atomic variables, there is no guarantee that the data is modified or accessed in the desired order, since the order can be changed by a compiler.

To avoid ambiguity, C++11 introduced the memory model, defining the behavior of the concurrent access to the memory region. As part of the memory model, C++ defined the std::memory_order enum, which gives hints to a compiler regarding the intended model of access. This helps the compiler to optimize the code in a way that does not interfere with the intended code behavior.

In this recipe, we will learn how to use the simplest form of the std::memory_order enum to implement a shared counter variable.

How to do it...

We are implementing an application that has a shared counter that is incremented by two concurrent worker threads.

1. In your ~/test working directory, create a subdirectory called memorder.
2. Use your favorite text editor to create a memorder.cpp file in the atomic subdirectory.
3. Now, we put the required headers and define global variables in memorder.cpp:

```cpp
#include <atomic>
#include <chrono>
#include <iostream>
#include <thread>
#include <vector>

std::atomic<bool> running{true};
std::atomic<int> counter{0};
```

4. After global variables are defined, we add our `worker` function. The function only increments a counter, and then sleeps for a specific time interval:

```
void worker() {
 while(running) {
 counter.fetch_add(1, std::memory_order_relaxed);
 }
 }
```

5. Then, we define our `main` function:

```
int main() {
    std::thread worker1(worker);
    std::thread worker2(worker);
    std::this_thread::sleep_for(std::chrono::seconds(1));
    running = false;
    worker1.join();
    worker2.join();
    std::cout << "Counter: " << counter << std::endl;
}
```

6. Create a file called `CMakeLists.txt` in the `loop` subdirectory, with the following content:

```
cmake_minimum_required(VERSION 3.5.1)
project(memorder)
add_executable(memorder memorder.cpp)

set(CMAKE_SYSTEM_NAME Linux)
set(CMAKE_SYSTEM_PROCESSOR arm)

SET(CMAKE_CXX_FLAGS "--std=c++11")
target_link_libraries(memorder pthread)

set(CMAKE_CXX_COMPILER /usr/bin/arm-linux-gnueabi-g++)
```

You can build and run the application.

How it works...

In our application, we are going to create two worker threads that will increment a shared counter, and let them run for a specific amount of time.

As a first step, we define two global atomic variables, `running` and `counter`:

```
std::atomic<bool> running{true};
std::atomic<int> counter{0};
```

The `running` variable is a binary flag. When it is set to `true`, the worker threads should keep running. After it changes to `false`, the worker threads should terminate.

The `counter` variable is our shared counter. The worker threads will concurrently increment it. We use the `fetch_add` method that we already used in the *Using atomic variables* recipe. It is used to increment a variable atomically. In this recipe, we pass an additional argument, `std::memory_order_relaxed`, to this method:

```
counter.fetch_add(1, std::memory_order_relaxed);
```

This argument is a hint. While consistency in atomicity and modification is important and should be guaranteed for an implementation of a counter, the order among concurrent memory accesses is not that important. `std::memory_order_relaxed` defines this kind of memory access for atomic variables. Passing it into the `fetch_add` method allows us to fine-tune it for a particular target platform, to avoid unneeded synchronization delays that can affect performance.

In the `main` function, we create two worker threads:

```
std::thread worker1(worker);
std::thread worker2(worker);
```

Then, the main thread is paused for 1 second. After the pause, the main thread sets the value of the `running` variable to `false`, indicating that the worker threads should terminate:

```
running = false;
```

After the worker threads terminate, we print the value of the counter:

```
user@3324138cc2c7: /mnt/memorder — bash
user@3324138cc2c7:/mnt/memorder$ ./memorder
Counter: 50174381
user@3324138cc2c7:/mnt/memorder$
```

The resulting counter value is determined by the timeout intervals passed to the `worker` functions. Changing the type of memory order in the `fetch_add` method does not result in a noticeable change in the resulting value in our example. However, it can result in the better performance of highly concurrent applications that use atomic variables, because a compiler can reorder operations in concurrent threads without breaking the application logic. This kind of optimization is highly dependent on a developer's intents, and cannot be inferred automatically without hints from the developer.

There's more...

The C++ memory model and memory ordering types are complex topics that require a deep understanding of how modern CPUs access memory and optimize their code execution. *C++ Memory Model reference* , `https://en.cppreference.com/w/cpp/language/memory_model` provides lots of information and is a good starting point to learn advanced techniques for the optimization of multithreaded applications.

Exploring lock-free synchronization

In the preceding recipes, we learned how to synchronize access of multiple threads to shared data, using mutexes and locks. If several threads try to run critical sections of the code protected by a lock, only one thread at a time can do it. All other threads have to wait until that thread leaves the critical section.

In some cases, however, it is possible to synchronize access to shared data without mutexes and explicit locks. The idea is to use a local copy of data for modification, and then update the shared copy in a single, uninterruptible, and undividable operation.

This type of synchronization depends on the hardware. Target processors should provide some form of **Compare And Swap** (**CAS**) instruction. This checks whether the value in a memory location matches a given value, and replaces it with a new given value only if they match. Since it is a single-processor instruction, it cannot be interrupted by a context switch. This makes it a basic building block for more complex atomic operations.

In this recipe, we will learn how to check whether an atomic variable is lock-free or implemented using mutexes or other locking operations. We will also implement a lock-free push operation for a custom stack, based on the example for the atomic compare-exchange family of functions for C++11, available at `https://en.cppreference.com/w/cpp/atomic/atomic_compare_exchange`

How to do it...

We are implementing a simple `Stack` class that provides a constructor and a function named `Push`.

1. In your ~/`test` working directory, create a subdirectory called `lockfree`.
2. Use your favorite text editor to create a `lockfree.cpp` file in the `lockfree` subdirectory.
3. Now, we put in the required headers, and define a `Node` helper data type in the `lockfree.cpp` file:

```
#include <atomic>
#include <iostream>

struct Node {
    int data;
    Node* next;
};
```

4. Next, we define a simple `Stack` class. This uses the `Node` data type to organize data storage:

```
class Stack {
    std::atomic<Node*> head;

  public:
    Stack() {
      std::cout << "Stack is " <<
      (head.is_lock_free() ? "" : "not ")
      << "lock-free" << std::endl;
    }

    void Push(int data) {
       Node* new_node = new Node{data, nullptr};
       new_node->next = head.load();
       while(!std::atomic_compare_exchange_weak(
               &head,
               &new_node->next,
               new_node));
    }
};
```

5. Finally, we define a simple `main` function that creates an instance of `Stack` and pushes an element into it:

```
int main() {
    Stack s;
    s.Push(1);
}
```

6. Create a file called `CMakeLists.txt` in the `loop` subdirectory, with the following content:

```
cmake_minimum_required(VERSION 3.5.1)
project(lockfree)
add_executable(lockfree lockfree.cpp)

set(CMAKE_SYSTEM_NAME Linux)
set(CMAKE_SYSTEM_PROCESSOR arm)

SET(CMAKE_CXX_FLAGS "--std=c++11")
target_link_libraries(lockfree pthread)

set(CMAKE_CXX_COMPILER /usr/bin/arm-linux-gnueabi-g++)
```

You can build and run the application.

How it works...

We created a simple application that implements a simple stack of integer values. We store elements of the stack in dynamic memory, and for each element, we should be able to determine the elements that follow it.

For this purpose, we define a `Node` helper structure that has two data fields. The `data` field stores the actual value of an element, while the `next` field is a pointer to the next element in the stack:

```
int data;
Node* next;
```

Then, we define the `Stack` class. Normally, a stack implies two operations:

- `Push`: to place an element on top of the stack
- `Pull`: to fetch an element from the top of the stack

To track the top of the stack, we create a `top` variable that holds a pointer to the `Node` object. It will be the top of our stack:

```
std::atomic<Node*> head;
```

We also define a simple constructor that initializes the value of our `top` variable and checks whether it is lock-free or not. In C++, atomic variables can be implemented using atomic **Consistency, Availability, and Partition tolerance (CAP)** operations or using regular mutexes. It depends on the target CPU:

```
(head.is_lock_free() ? "" : "not ")
```

In our application, we implement only the `Push` method, to demonstrate how it can be done in a lock-free way.

The `Push` method accepts a value to put on top of the stack. To do this, we create a new instance of the `Node` object:

```
Node* new_node = new Node{data, nullptr};
```

Since we put the element on the top of the stack, the pointer to the newly created instance should be assigned to the `top` variable, and the old value of the `top` variable should be assigned to the `next` pointer of our new `Node` object.

However, doing it directly is not thread-safe. Two or more threads can modify the `top` variable simultaneously, causing data corruption. We need some kind of data synchronization. We can do this using locks and mutexes, but it is also possible to do it in a lock-free way.

That is why we initially update only the next pointer. Since our new `Node` object is not yet part of the stack, we can do it without synchronization, since other threads do not have access to it:

```
new_node->next = head.load();
```

Now, we need to add it as a new `top` variable of the stack. We do this using a loop over the `std::atomic_compare_exchange_weak` function:

```
while(!std::atomic_compare_exchange_weak(
        &head,
        &new_node->next,
        new_node));
```

This function compares the value of the `top` variable to the value stored in the `next` pointer of the new element. If they match, it replaces the value of the `top` variable with the pointer to the new node and returns `true`. Otherwise, it writes the value of the `top` variable into the `next` pointer of the new element and returns `false`. Since we updated the `next` pointer to match the `top` variable on the next step, this can only happen if another thread modified it before the `std::atomic_compare_exchange_weak` function was invoked. Eventually, the function will return `true`, indicating that the `top` header is updated with the pointer to our element.

The `main` function creates an instance of stack and pushes one element to it. In the output, we can see if the underlying implementation is lock-free or not:

For our target, the implementation is lock-free.

There's more...

Lock-free synchronization is an extremely complex topic. The development of lock-free data structures and algorithms requires lots of effort. Even the implementation of simple `Push` logic using lock-free operations is not easy to understand. An even larger effort is needed for proper analysis and debugging of your code. Often, it can lead to subtle issues that are hard to notice and hard to implement.

Though the implementation of a lock-free algorithm can improve the performance of your application, consider using one of the existing libraries of lock-free data structures instead of writing of your own. For example, `Boost.Lockfree` provides a collection of lock-free data types for you to use.

Using atomic variables in shared memory

We learned how to use atomic variables for the synchronization of two or more threads in a multithreaded application. However, atomic variables can also be used to synchronize independent applications that run as separate processes.

We already know how to use shared memory for exchanging data between two applications. Now, we can combine these two techniques—shared memory and atomic variables—to implement both the data exchange and synchronization of two independent applications.

How to do it...

In this recipe, we will modify an application we created in Chapter 6, *Memory Management*, for exchanging data between two processors using a shared memory region.

1. In your ~/test working directory, create a subdirectory called shmatomic.
2. Use your favorite text editor to create a shmatomic.cpp file in the shmatomic subdirectory.
3. We reuse the shared memory data structure we created in the shmem application. Put the common headers and constants into the shmatomic.cpp file:

```
#include <atomic>
#include <iostream>
#include <chrono>
#include <thread>

#include <sys/mman.h>
#include <fcntl.h>
#include <unistd.h>

const char* kSharedMemPath = "/sample_point";
```

4. Next, start defining the templated SharedMem class:

```
template<class T>
class SharedMem {
    int fd;
    T* ptr;
    const char* name;

    public:
```

5. The class will have a constructor, a destructor, and a getter method. Let's add the constructor:

```
SharedMem(const char* name, bool owner=false) {
    fd = shm_open(name, O_RDWR | O_CREAT, 0600);
    if (fd == -1) {
        throw std::runtime_error("Failed to open a shared
```

```
  memory region");
}
if (ftruncate(fd, sizeof(T)) < 0) {
  close(fd);
  throw std::runtime_error("Failed to set size of a shared
  memory region");
};
ptr = (T*)mmap(nullptr, sizeof(T), PROT_READ | PROT_WRITE,
MAP_SHARED, fd, 0);
if (!ptr) {
  close(fd);
  throw std::runtime_error("Failed to mmap a shared memory
  region");
}
this->name = owner ? name : nullptr;
}
```

6. The simple destructor and the getter follow:

```
~SharedMem() {
munmap(ptr, sizeof(T));
close(fd);
if (name) {
std::cout << "Remove shared mem instance " << name << std::endl;
shm_unlink(name);
}
}

T& get() const {
return *ptr;
}
};
```

7. Now, we define the data type we will use for data exchange and synchronization:

```
struct Payload {
std::atomic_bool data_ready;
std::atomic_bool data_processed;
int index;
};
```

8. Next, we define a function that will generate data:

```
void producer() {
   SharedMem<Payload> writer(kSharedMemPath);
   Payload& pw = writer.get();
if (!pw.data_ready.is_lock_free()) {
throw std::runtime_error("Flag is not lock-free");
   }
for (int i = 0; i < 10; i++) {
pw.data_processed.store(false);
pw.index = i;
     pw.data_ready.store(true);
while(!pw.data_processed.load());
}
}
```

9. It is followed by the function that consumes the data:

```
void consumer() {
SharedMem<Payload> point_reader(kSharedMemPath, true);
Payload& pr = point_reader.get();
if (!pr.data_ready.is_lock_free()) {
throw std::runtime_error("Flag is not lock-free");
}
for (int i = 0; i < 10; i++) {
 while(!pr.data_ready.load());
     pr.data_ready.store(false);
std::cout << "Processing data chunk " << pr.index << std::endl;
     pr.data_processed.store(true);
}
}
```

10. Finally, we add our `main` function, which ties everything together:

```
int main() {

if (fork()) {
     consumer();
} else {
     producer();
}
}
```

11. Create a file called `CMakeLists.txt` in the `loop` subdirectory, with the following content:

```
cmake_minimum_required(VERSION 3.5.1)
project(shmatomic)
```

```
add_executable(shmatomic shmatomic.cpp)

set(CMAKE_SYSTEM_NAME Linux)
set(CMAKE_SYSTEM_PROCESSOR arm)

SET(CMAKE_CXX_FLAGS "--std=c++11")
target_link_libraries(shmatomic pthread rt)

set(CMAKE_CXX_COMPILER /usr/bin/arm-linux-gnueabi-g++)
```

You can build and run the application.

How it works...

In our application, we reuse the templated `SharedMem` class we introduced in Chapter 6, *Memory Management*. This class is used to store an element of a specific type in a shared memory region. Let's quickly recap how it works.

The `SharedMem` class is a wrapper on top of the **Portable Operating System Interface** (**POSIX**) shared memory API. It defines three private data fields to hold system-specific handlers and pointers, and exposes a public interface consisting of two functions:

- A constructor function that accepts the name of a shared region and the ownership flag
- A `get` method that returns a reference to the object stored in shared memory

The class also defines a destructor that performs all operations needed to properly close the shared object. As a result, the `SharedMem` class can be used for safe resource management using the C++ RAII idiom.

The `SharedMem` class is a templated class. It is parameterized by the data type we want to store in the shared memory. For this purpose, we define a structure called `Payload`:

```
struct Payload {
  std::atomic_bool data_ready;
  std::atomic_bool data_processed;
  int index;
};
```

It has an `index` integer variable that we are going to use as a data exchange field, and two atomic Boolean flags, `data_ready` and `data_processed`, that are used for data synchronization.

We also define two functions, `producer` and `consumer`, that will work in separate processes and exchange data between each other using a shared memory region.

The `producer` function is producing data chunks. Firstly, it creates an instance of the `SharedMem` class, parametrized by the `Payload` data type. It passes a path to the shared memory region to the `SharedMem` constructor:

```
SharedMem<Payload> writer(kSharedMemPath);
```

After the shared memory instance is created, it gets the reference to the payload data stored there and checks whether any of the atomic flags we defined in the `Payload` data type are lock-free:

```
if (!pw.data_ready.is_lock_free()) {
    throw std::runtime_error("Flag is not lock-free");
}
```

The function produces 10 chunks of data in a loop. An index of the chunk is put into the `index` field of the payload:

```
pw.index = i;
```

However, besides putting the data into shared memory, we need to synchronize access to this data. This is when we use our atomic flags.

For each iteration, before updating the `index` field, we reset the `data_processed` flag. After the index is updated, we set the `data ready` flag, which is an indicator to the consumer that a new chunk of data is ready, and wait till the data is processed by the consumer. We loop until the `data_processed` flag becomes `true`, and then go to the next iteration:

```
pw.data_ready.store(true);
while(!pw.data_processed.load());
```

The `consumer` function works in a similar way. Since it works in a separate process, it opens the same shared memory region by creating an instance of the `SharedMem` class using the same path. We also make the `consumer` function the owner of the shared memory instance. It means it is responsible for removing the shared memory region after its instance of `SharedMem` is destroyed:

```
SharedMem<Payload> point_reader(kSharedMemPath, true);
```

Similarly to the `producer` function, the `consumer` function checks whether an atomic flag is lock-free, and enters the loop of data consumption.

For each iteration, it waits in a tight loop until the data is ready:

```
while(!pr.data_ready.load());
```

After the `producer` function sets the `data_ready` flag to `true`, the `consumer` function can safely read and process data. In our implementation, it only prints the `index` field to the console. After the data is processed, the `consumer` function indicates this by setting the `data_processed` flag to `true`:

```
pr.data_processed.store(true);
```

This triggers the next iteration of data production on the `producer` function side:

As a result, we can see a deterministic output of processed data chunks, with no omissions or duplications; this is common in cases where data access is not synchronized.

Exploring async functions and futures

Dealing with data synchronization in multithreaded applications is hard, error-prone, and requires developers to write a lot of code to properly align data exchange and data notifications. In order to simplify development, C++11 introduced a standard API for writing asynchronous code in a way that resembles regular synchronous function calls and hides lots of the synchronization complexities under the hood.

In this recipe, we will learn how to use asynchronous function invocations and futures to run our code in multiple threads with virtually no extra effort, for data synchronization.

How to do it...

We will implement a simple application that invokes a long-running function in a separate thread and waits for its result. While the function is running, the application can keep working on other calculations.

1. In your ~/test working directory, create a subdirectory called async.
2. Use your favorite text editor to create an async.cpp file in the async subdirectory.
3. Put the code of our application into the async.cpp file, starting from the common headers and our long-running function:

```cpp
#include <chrono>
#include <future>
#include <iostream>

int calculate (int x) {
    auto start = std::chrono::system_clock::now();
    std::cout << "Start calculation\n";
    std::this_thread::sleep_for(std::chrono::seconds(1));
    auto delta = std::chrono::system_clock::now() - start;
    auto ms =
std::chrono::duration_cast<std::chrono::milliseconds>(delta);
    std::cout << "Done in " << ms.count() << " ms\n";
    return x*x;
}
```

4. Next, add the test function, which invokes the long-running function:

```cpp
void test(int value, int worktime) {
    std::cout << "Request result of calculations for " << value <<
std::endl;
    std::future<int> fut = std::async (calculate, value);
    std::cout << "Keep working for " << worktime << " ms" <<
std::endl;
    std::this_thread::sleep_for(std::chrono::milliseconds(worktime));
    auto start = std::chrono::system_clock::now();
    std::cout << "Waiting for result" << std::endl;
    int result = fut.get();
    auto delta = std::chrono::system_clock::now() - start;
    auto ms =
```

```
std::chrono::duration_cast<std::chrono::milliseconds>(delta);

    std::cout << "Result is " << result
            << ", waited for " << ms.count() << " ms"
            << std::endl << std::endl;
}
```

5. Finally, add a `main` minimalistic function:

```
int main ()
{
  test(5, 400);
  test(8, 1200);
  return 0;
}
```

6. Create a file called `CMakeLists.txt` in the `loop` subdirectory, with the following content:

```
cmake_minimum_required(VERSION 3.5.1)
project(async)
add_executable(async async.cpp)

set(CMAKE_SYSTEM_NAME Linux)
set(CMAKE_SYSTEM_PROCESSOR arm)

SET(CMAKE_CXX_FLAGS "--std=c++14")
target_link_libraries(async pthread -static-libstdc++)

set(CMAKE_CXX_COMPILER /usr/bin/arm-linux-gnueabi-g++)
```

You can build and run the application.

How it works...

In our application, we defined a `calculate` function that should take a long time to run. Technically, our function calculates the square of an integer argument, but we added an artificial delay to make it run for 1 second. We use a `sleep_for` standard library function to add a delay to the application:

```
std::this_thread::sleep_for(std::chrono::seconds(1));
```

Besides calculations, the function logs to the console when it started working, when it completed, and how much time it took.

Next, we defined a `test` function that invokes the `calculate` function, to demonstrate how asynchronous invocation works.

The function has two parameters. The first parameter is a value that is passed to the `calculate` function. The second parameter is the amount of time the `test` function is going to spend after running the `calculate` function and before requesting the result. This way, we model the useful work the function can perform in parallel to the calculations it requested.

The `test` function starts working by running the `calculate` function in asynchronous mode and passing it the first parameter, `value`:

```
std::future<int> fut = std::async (calculate, value);
```

The `async` function implicitly spawns a thread and starts the execution of the `calculate` function.

Since we run the function asynchronously, the result is not yet ready. Instead, the `async` function returns an instance of `std::future`, an object that will hold the result when it is available.

Next, we simulate the useful work. In our case, it is the pause for the specified interval of time. After the work that can be done in parallel is completed, we need to get the result of the `calculate` function to proceed. To request the result, we use the `get` method of our `std::future` object, as shown:

```
int result = fut.get();
```

The `get` method blocks until the result is available. Then, we can calculate the amount of time we have spent waiting for the result, and output the result—along with the wait time—to the console.

In the `main` function, we run the `test` function to evaluate two scenarios:

- The useful work takes less time than the calculation of the result.
- The useful work takes more time than the calculation of the result.

Running the application produces the following output.

In the first scenario, we can see that we are starting the calculations, and then started waiting for the result before the calculation has been completed. As a result, the `get` method blocked for 600 milliseconds until the result was ready:

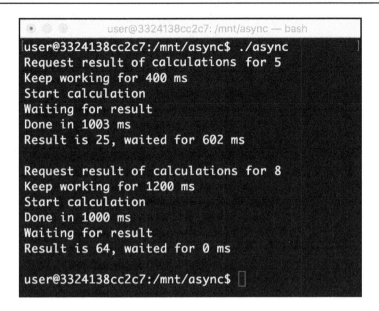

In the second scenario, the useful work took `1200` milliseconds. As we can see, the calculation has been done before the result was requested, and because of that, the `get` method did not block, and immediately returned the result.

There's more...

Futures and async functions provide a powerful mechanism for writing parallel and understandable code. Async functions are flexible and support different execution policies. Promises are another mechanism that enables developers to overcome the complexities of asynchronous programming. More information can be found in the reference pages for `std::future` at [https://en.cppreference.com/w/cpp/thread/future], `std::promise` at [https://en.cppreference.com/w/cpp/thread/promise], and `std::async` at [https://en.cppreference.com/w/cpp/thread/async].

8
Communication and Serialization

Complex embedded systems are rarely composed of a single application. Having all the logic in the same application is brittle, error-prone, and sometimes hardly feasible because different functions of the system may be developed by different teams and even different vendors. That is why isolating the logic of the functions in standalone applications and communicating with each other using a well-defined protocol is a common approach used to scale embedded software. In addition, this kind of isolation can be used with minimal modifications to communicate with applications hosted on remote systems, making it even more scalable. We will learn how to build robust and scalable applications by splitting their logic into independent components that communicate with each other.

In this chapter, we will cover the following topics:

- Using inter-process communication in applications
- Exploring the mechanisms of inter-process communication
- Learning about message queue and publisher-subscriber models
- Using C++ lambdas for callbacks
- Exploring data serialization
- Using the FlatBuffers library

The recipes in this chapter will help you understand the basic concepts of scalable and platform-independent data exchange. They can be used to implement data transfer from an embedded system to the cloud or to a remote backend, or to design an embedded system using microservice architecture.

Using inter-process communication in applications

Most modern operating systems use memory virtualization support provided by the underlying hardware platform to isolate application processes from each other.

Each process has its own virtual address space that is completely independent of the address spaces of other applications. This provides huge benefits to developers. Since the address processes of applications are independent, an application cannot accidentally corrupt the memory of another application. As a result, a failure in one application does not affect the whole system. Since all the other applications keep working, the system can recover by restarting the failing application.

The benefits of memory isolation come at a cost. Since one process cannot access the memory of another, it needs to use a dedicated **Application Program Interface (API)** for data exchange, or **inter-process communication (IPC)**, which is provided by the operating system.

In this recipe, we will learn how to exchange information between two processes using shared files. It may not be the most performance-efficient mechanism, but it is ubiquitous, easy to use, and good enough for various practical use cases.

How to do it...

In this recipe, we will create a sample application that creates two processes. One process generates data while another reads the data and prints it to the console:

1. In your working directory (~/test), create a subdirectory called ipc1.
2. Use your favorite text editor to create an ipc1.cpp file in the ipc1 subdirectory.
3. We are going to define two templated classes to organize our data exchange. The first class, Writer, is used to write data into a file. Let's put its definition in the ipc1.cpp file:

```
#include <fstream>
#include <iostream>
#include <thread>
#include <vector>

#include <unistd.h>

std::string kSharedFile = "/tmp/test.bin";
```

```
template<class T>
class Writer {
  private:
    std::ofstream out;
  public:
    Writer(std::string& name):
      out(name, std::ofstream::binary) {}

    void Write(const T& data) {
      out.write(reinterpret_cast<const char*>(&data), sizeof(T));
    }
};
```

4. This is followed by the definition of the `Reader` class, which is responsible for reading data from a file:

```
template<class T>
class Reader {
  private:
    std::ifstream in;
  public:
    Reader(std::string& name) {
      for(int count=10; count && !in.is_open(); count--) {
        in.open(name, std::ifstream::binary);
        std::this_thread::sleep_for(std::chrono::milliseconds(10));
      }
    }

    T Read() {
      int count = 10;
      for (;count && in.eof(); count--) {
        std::this_thread::sleep_for(std::chrono::milliseconds(10));
      }

      T data;
      in.read(reinterpret_cast<char*>(&data), sizeof(data));
      if (!in) {
        throw std::runtime_error("Failed to read a message");
      }
      return data;
    }
};
```

5. Next, we define the data type that we will use for our data:

```
struct Message {
  int x, y;
};

std::ostream& operator<<(std::ostream& o, const Message& m) {
  o << "(x=" << m.x << ", y=" << m.y << ")";
}
```

6. To wrap everything together, we define the DoWrites and DoReads functions, as well as the main function that invokes them:

```
void DoWrites() {
  std::vector<Message> messages {{1, 0}, {0, 1}, {1, 1}, {0, 0}};
  Writer<Message> writer(kSharedFile);
  for (const auto& m : messages) {
    std::cout << "Write " << m << std::endl;
    writer.Write(m);
  }
}

void DoReads() {
  Reader<Message> reader(kSharedFile);
  try {
    while(true) {
      std::cout << "Read " << reader.Read() << std::endl;
    }
  } catch (const std::runtime_error& e) {
    std::cout << e.what() << std::endl;
  }
}

int main(int argc, char** argv) {
  if (fork()) {
    DoWrites();
  } else {
    DoReads();
  }
}
```

7. Finally, create a CMakeLists.txt file containing the build rules for our program:

```
cmake_minimum_required(VERSION 3.5.1)
project(ipc1)
add_executable(ipc1 ipc1.cpp)
```

```
set(CMAKE_SYSTEM_NAME Linux)
set(CMAKE_SYSTEM_PROCESSOR arm)

SET(CMAKE_CXX_FLAGS "--std=c++11")

set(CMAKE_CXX_COMPILER /usr/bin/arm-linux-gnueabi-g++)
```

You can now build and run the application.

How it works...

In our application, we explore data exchange between two independent processes using a shared file in a filesystem. One process writes data to a file, another reads data from the same file.

Files can store any unstructured sequences of bytes. In our application, we utilize the C++ templates' capabilities to work with strictly typed C++ values rather than raw byte streams. This approach helps in writing clean and error-free code.

We start with a definition of the `Write` class. It is a simple wrapper on top of the standard C++ `fstream` class used for file input/output. The constructor of the class only opens a file stream to write the following:

```
Writer(std::string& name):
    out(name, std::ofstream::binary) {}
```

Besides the constructor, the class contains only one method, `Write`, which is responsible for writing data to a file. Since the file API operates with byte streams, we first need to convert our templated data type into a raw character buffer. We can do this using the C++ `reinterpret_cast`:

```
out.write(reinterpret_cast<const char*>(&data), sizeof(T));
```

The `Reader` class does the opposite job—it reads data written by the `Writer` class. Its constructor is a bit more complicated. Since the data file might not be ready by the time the instance of the `Reader` class is created, the constructor tries to open it in a loop until an open attempt succeeds. It makes 10 attempts with 10-millisecond pauses between each:

```
for(int count=10; count && !in.is_open(); count--) {
    in.open(name, std::ifstream::binary);
    std::this_thread::sleep_for(std::chrono::milliseconds(10));
}
```

The `Read` method reads data from the input stream into a temporary value and returns it to the caller. Similar to the `Write` method, we use `reinterpret_cast` to access the memory of our data objects as raw character buffers:

```
in.read(reinterpret_cast<char*>(&data), sizeof(data));
```

We also add a wait loop into the `Read` method to wait for data being written by `Write`. If we reach the end of the file, we wait for up to 1 second for new data:

```
for (;count && in.eof(); count--) {
  std::this_thread::sleep_for(std::chrono::milliseconds(10));
}
```

If data is not available in the file at this point, or in the case of an I/O error, we throw an exception to indicate it:

```
if (!in) {
  throw std::runtime_error("Failed to read a message");
}
```

 Please note that we do not need to add any code to handle a situation where a file cannot be opened within 1 second, or data is not ready within one second. Both of these cases are handled by the same preceding code.

Now that the `Writer` and `Reader` classes are implemented, we can define a data type for our data exchange. In our application, we will exchange coordinates, represented as the `x` and `y` integer values. Our data message looks like this:

```
struct Message {
  int x, y;
};
```

For convenience, we override the << operator for our `Message` structure. Any time an instance of `Message` is written to an output stream, it is formatted as `(x, y)`:

```
std::ostream& operator<<(std::ostream& o, const Message& m) {
  o << "(x=" << m.x << ", y=" << m.y << ")";
}
```

With all the preparations in place, let's write the functions for data exchange. The `DoWrites` function defines a vector of four coordinates and creates a `Writer` object:

```
std::vector<Message> messages {{1, 0}, {0, 1}, {1, 1}, {0, 0}};
Writer<Message> writer(kSharedFile);
```

Then, it writes all the coordinates in a loop:

```
for (const auto& m : messages) {
  std::cout << "Write " << m << std::endl;
  writer.Write(m);
}
```

The `DoReads` function, in turn, creates an instance of the `Reader` class using the same filename as the `Writer` instance before it. It enters an endless loop, trying to read all the messages in the file:

```
while(true) {
  std::cout << "Read " << reader.Read() << std::endl;
}
```

When no more messages are available, the `Read` method throws an exception that breaks the loop:

```
} catch (const std::runtime_error& e) {
  std::cout << e.what() << std::endl;
}
```

The `main` function creates two independent processes, running `DoWrites` in one of them and `DoReads` in another. After running the application, we get the following output:

```
user@3324138cc2c7:/mnt/ipc1 — bash
user@3324138cc2c7:/mnt/ipc1$ ./ipc1
Write (x=1, y=0)
Write (x=0, y=1)
Write (x=1, y=1)
Write (x=0, y=0)
user@3324138cc2c7:/mnt/ipc1$ Read (x=1, y=0)
Read (x=0, y=1)
Read (x=1, y=1)
Read (x=0, y=0)
Read Failed to read a message
```

As we can see, the writer did write four coordinates and the reader was able to read the same four coordinates using a shared file.

There's more...

We created our application to be as simple as possible, focusing on strictly typed data exchange and leaving data synchronization and data serialization out of the scope. We are going to use this application as a foundation for more advanced techniques, which will be described in the recipes that follow.

Exploring the mechanisms of inter-process communication

Modern operating systems provide a number of IPC mechanisms beyond the shared files we have already learned about, namely the following:

- Pipes
- Named pipes
- Local sockets
- Network sockets
- Shared memory

It is interesting that many of them provide exactly the same API that we use when working with regular files. As a result, switching between these types of IPC is trivial and the same code that we used to read and write to local files can be used to communicate with applications running on a remote network host.

In this recipe, we will learn how to use Portable Operating System Interface (**POSIX**) named pipes to communicate between two applications that reside on the same computer.

Getting ready

We are going to use the source code of the application we created as part of the *Using inter-process communication in applications* recipe as a starting point for this recipe.

How to do it...

In this recipe, we will start with the source code that uses regular files for IPC. We will modify it to use an IPC mechanism called **named pipes**:

1. Copy the contents of the `ipc1` directory into a new directory called `ipc2`.

2. Open the `ipc1.cpp` file and add two more `include` instance after `#include <unistd.h>`:

    ```
    #include <unistd.h>
    #include <sys/types.h>
    #include <sys/stat.h>
    ```

3. Modify the `Write` method of the `Writer` class by adding one more line:

    ```
    void Write(const T& data) {
      out.write(reinterpret_cast<const char*>(&data), sizeof(T));
      out.flush();
    }
    ```

4. Modifications in the `Reader` class are more substantial. Both the constructor and the `Read` method are affected:

    ```
    template<class T>
    class Reader {
      private:
        std::ifstream in;
      public:
        Reader(std::string& name):
          in(name, std::ofstream::binary) {}
        T Read() {
          T data;
          in.read(reinterpret_cast<char*>(&data), sizeof(data));
          if (!in) {
            throw std::runtime_error("Failed to read a message");
          }
          return data;
        }
    };
    ```

5. Add a small change to the `DoWrites` function. The only difference is we add a 10 millisecond delay after sending each message:

    ```
    void DoWrites() {
      std::vector<Message> messages {{1, 0}, {0, 1}, {1, 1}, {0, 0}};
      Writer<Message> writer(kSharedFile);
      for (const auto& m : messages) {
    ```

```
        std::cout << "Write " << m << std::endl;
        writer.Write(m);
        std::this_thread::sleep_for(std::chrono::milliseconds(10));
    }
}
```

6. Finally, modify our `main` function to create a named pipe instead of a regular file:

```
int main(int argc, char** argv) {
    int ret = mkfifo(kSharedFile.c_str(), 0600);
    if (!ret) {
        throw std::runtime_error("Failed to create named pipe");
    }
    if (fork()) {
        DoWrites();
    } else {
        DoReads();
    }
}
```

You can now build and run the application.

How it works...

As you can see, we introduced a minimal number of changes to the code of our application. All the mechanisms and the API for reading and writing data remain the same. The crucial difference hides behind a single line of code:

```
int ret = mkfifo(kSharedFile.c_str(), 0600);
```

This line creates a special type of file called `named pipe`. It looks like a regular file—it has a name, permission attributes, and a modification time. However, it does not store any real data. Everything written to this file is immediately delivered to the processes that read from this file.

This difference has a number of consequences. Since no real data is stored in the file, all reading attempts are blocked until any data is written. Similarly, writes are blocked until previous data is read by the readers.

As a result, there is no further need for external data synchronization. Take a look at the `Reader` class implementation. It does not have a retry loop in the constructor or in the `Read` method.

To test that we really do not need to use any additional synchronization, we added an artificial delay after writing each of the messages:

```
std::this_thread::sleep_for(std::chrono::milliseconds(10));
```

When we build and run the application, we can see the following output:

```
user@3324138cc2c7: /mnt/ipc2 — bash
user@3324138cc2c7:/mnt/ipc2$ ./ipc2
Write (x=1, y=0)
Read (x=1, y=0)
Write (x=0, y=1)
Read (x=0, y=1)
Write (x=1, y=1)
Read (x=1, y=1)
Write (x=0, y=0)
Read (x=0, y=0)
Read Failed to read a message
user@3324138cc2c7:/mnt/ipc2$
```

Each `Write` method is followed by the proper `Read` method, despite the fact that we did not add any delays or checks anywhere in the `Reader` code. The IPC mechanisms of the operating system take care of data synchronization transparently for us, leading to cleaner and more readable code.

There's more...

As you can see, working with named pipes is as simple as working with regular functions. A socket API is another widely used mechanism of IPC. It is a little bit more complex but provides more flexibility. By choosing different transport layers, developers can use the same socket APIs for both local data exchange and for network connectivity with remote hosts.

More information about socket APIs can be found at `http://man7.org/linux/man-pages/man7/socket.7.html`.

Learning about message queue and publisher-subscriber models

Most of the IPC mechanisms provided by POSIX operating systems are quite basic. Their APIs are built using file descriptors and they treat input and output channels as raw sequences of bytes.

Applications, however, tend to use data fragments of specific lengths and purposes for data interchange messages. Despite API mechanisms of operating systems being flexible and generic, they are not always convenient for message exchange. That is why dedicated libraries and components were built on top of default IPC mechanisms to simplify the message exchange mode.

In this recipe, we will learn how to implement an asynchronous data exchange between two applications using the **publisher-subscriber (pub-sub)** model.

The model is easy to understand and widely used for the development of software systems designed as collections of independent, loosely coupled components communicating with each other. The isolation of functions and asynchronous data exchange allows us to build flexible, scalable, and robust solutions.

In the pub-sub model, applications act as publishers, subscribers, or both. Instead of sending requests to particular applications and expecting them to respond, an application can publish a message to a specific topic or subscribe to receive messages on a topic it is interested in. When publishing a message, the application does not care how many subscribers are listening to the topic. Similarly, a subscriber does not know which application is going to send a message on a particular topic or when to expect it.

How to do it...

The application we created as part of the *Exploring the mechanisms of IPC* recipe already contains a number of building blocks we can reuse to implement the pub/sub communication.

The `Writer` class can act as a publisher and the `Reader` class as a subscriber. We implemented them to handle the strictly defined data types that will define our messages. The named pipes mechanism we used in the preceding recipe works on a byte level and does not guarantee that messages are delivered automatically.

To overcome this limitation, we will use the POSIX message queue API instead of the named pipes. A name used to identify a message queue that both `Reader` and `Writer` will accept in their constructors will be used as a topic:

1. Copy the contents of the `ipc2` directory that we created in the previous recipe into a new directory: `ipc3`.

2. Let's create a C++ wrapper for the POSIX message queue API. Open `ipc1.cpp` in your editor and add the required header files and constant definition:

```
#include <unistd.h>
#include <signal.h>
#include <fcntl.h>
#include <sys/stat.h>
#include <mqueue.h>

std::string kQueueName = "/test";
```

3. Then, define a `MessageQueue` class. This holds a message queue handle as its private data member. We can use constructors and destructors to manage the opening and closing of the handle in a safe manner using the C++ RAII idiom:

```
class MessageQueue {
  private:
    mqd_t handle;
  public:
    MessageQueue(const std::string& name, int flags) {
      handle = mq_open(name.c_str(), flags);
      if (handle < 0) {
        throw std::runtime_error("Failed to open a queue for
          writing");
      }
    }

    MessageQueue(const std::string& name, int flags, int max_count,
      int max_size) {
      struct mq_attr attrs = { 0, max_count, max_size, 0 };
      handle = mq_open(name.c_str(), flags | O_CREAT, 0666,
        &attrs);
      if (handle < 0) {
        throw std::runtime_error("Failed to create a queue");
      }
    }

    ~MessageQueue() {
      mq_close(handle);
    }
```

4. Then, we define two simple methods to write messages into and read messages from the queue:

```
void Send(const char* data, size_t len) {
    if (mq_send(handle, data, len, 0) < 0) {
        throw std::runtime_error("Failed to send a message");
    }
}

void Receive(char* data, size_t len) {
    if (mq_receive(handle, data, len, 0) < len) {
        throw std::runtime_error("Failed to receive a message");
    }
}
};
```

5. We now modify our `Writer` and `Reader` classes to work with the new API. Our `MessageQueue` wrapper does most of the heavy lifting and the code changes are minimal. The `Writer` class now looks like this:

```
template<class T>
class Writer {
  private:
    MessageQueue queue;
  public:
    Writer(std::string& name):
      queue(name, O_WRONLY) {}

    void Write(const T& data) {
        queue.Send(reinterpret_cast<const char*>(&data),
sizeof(data));
    }
};
```

6. Modifications in the `Reader` class are more substantial. We make it act as a subscriber and we encapsulate the logic that fetches and handles messages from the queue directly into the class:

```
template<class T>
class Reader {
  private:
    MessageQueue queue;
  public:
    Reader(std::string& name):
      queue(name, O_RDONLY) {}

    void Run() {
```

```
      T data;
      while(true) {
        queue.Receive(reinterpret_cast<char*>(&data),
          sizeof(data));
        Callback(data);
      }
    }

  protected:
    virtual void Callback(const T& data) = 0;
};
```

7. Since we still want to keep the `Reader` class as generic as possible, we will define a new class (`CoordLogger`), which is derived from `Reader`, to define the specific handling of our messages:

```
class CoordLogger : public Reader<Message> {
  using Reader<Message>::Reader;

  protected:
    void Callback(const Message& data) override {
      std::cout << "Received coordinate " << data << std::endl;
    }
};
```

8. The `DoWrites` code remains mostly the same; the only change is that we use a different constant to identify our queue:

```
void DoWrites() {
  std::vector<Message> messages {{1, 0}, {0, 1}, {1, 1}, {0, 0}};
  Writer<Message> writer(kQueueName);
  for (const auto& m : messages) {
    std::cout << "Write " << m << std::endl;
    writer.Write(m);
    std::this_thread::sleep_for(std::chrono::milliseconds(10));
  }
}
```

9. Since the message handling logic was moved to the `Reader` and `CoordLogger` classes, `DoReads` is now as simple as this:

```
void DoReads() {
  CoordLogger logger(kQueueName);
  logger.Run();
}
```

10. The updated `main` function follows:

```
int main(int argc, char** argv) {
  MessageQueue q(kQueueName, O_WRONLY, 10, sizeof(Message));
  pid_t pid = fork();
  if (pid) {
    DoWrites();
    std::this_thread::sleep_for(std::chrono::milliseconds(100));
    kill(pid, SIGTERM);
  } else {
    DoReads();
  }
}
```

11. Finally, our application needs to be linked with the `rt` library. We do this by adding one line into our `CMakeLists.txt` file:

```
target_link_libraries(ipc3 rt)
```

You can now build and run the application.

How it works...

In our application, we reused a lot of the code from the application we created in the preceding recipe, *Exploring the mechanisms of IPC*. To implement the pub-sub model, we need to make two important changes:

- Make our IPC message-based. We should be able to send and receive messages automatically. Messages sent by one publisher should not break messages sent by other publishers and subscribers should be able to read messages as a whole.
- Let subscribers define the callbacks that are invoked as soon as a new message is available.

To make message-based communication, we switch from the named pipes to the POSIX message queue API. The message queue API differs from the regular file-based API of named pipes, which is why we implement a C++ wrapper on top of the plain C interface provided by the Linux standard library.

The main goal of the wrapper is to provide safe resource management using the **Resource Acquisition Is Initialization (RAII)** idiom. We do this by defining the constructors that acquire the queue handler by calling `mq_open` and the destructor that releases it using `mq_close`. This way, the queue is automatically closed when the corresponding instance of the `MessageQueue` class is destroyed.

The wrapper class has two constructors. One constructor is used to open an existing queue. It accepts two parameters—a queue name and access flags. The second constructor is used to create a new queue. It accepts two additional parameters—a message length and the maximal size of a message in the queue.

In our application, we create a queue in the `main` function, passing `10` as the number of messages that can be stored in the queue. The size of the `Message` structure is the maximum size of the message in our queue:

```
MessageQueue q(kQueueName, O_WRONLY, 10, sizeof(Message));
```

Then, the `DoWrites` and `DoReads` functions open the queue already created with the same name.

Since the public API for our `MessageQueue` class is similar to the `fstream` interface we used for IPC using named pipes, it requires only minimal changes in the writer and reader to make them work with another IPC mechanism. We use an instance of `MessageQueue` instead of `fstream` as a data member, keeping other logic unchanged.

To let subscribers define their callback methods, we need to modify the `Reader` class. Instead of a `Read` method that reads and returns a single method, we introduce the `Run` method. It loops over all the messages available in the queue. For each method being read, it invokes a callback method:

```
while(true) {
  queue.Receive(reinterpret_cast<char*>(&data), sizeof(data));
  Callback(data);
}
```

Our goal is to keep the `Reader` class generic and reusable for different types of messages. However, there is no such thing as a generic callback. Each callback is specific and should be defined by users of the `Reader` class.

One way to resolve this contradiction is by making `Reader` an abstract class. We define our `Callback` method as a `virtual` function:

```
protected:
  virtual void Callback(const T& data) = 0;
```

Now, since `Reader` is abstract, we cannot create instances of this class. We have to inherit it and provide a definition of the `Callback` method in a derived class named `CoordLogger`:

```
protected:
  void Callback(const Message& data) override {
    std::cout << "Received coordinate " << data << std::endl;
  }
```

Please note that since the `Reader` constructor accepts a parameter, we need to define constructors in the inherited class as well. We'll use the inheriting constructors that were added in the C++11 standard:

```
using Reader<Message>::Reader;
```

Now, having a `CoordLogger` class that is capable of handling the messages of the `Message` type, we can use it in our `DoReads` implementation. We only need to create an instance of this class and invoke its `Run` method:

```
CoordLogger logger(kQueueName);
logger.Run();
```

When we run the application, we get the following output:

This output is not that different from the output from the preceding recipe, but now the implementation is much more scalable. The `DoReads` method does not do anything specific to messages. Its only task is to create and run subscribers. All data handling is encapsulated in specific classes. You can add, replace, and combine publishers and subscribers without changing the architecture of the application.

There's more...

The POSIX message queue API provides basic functionality for message queues but it also has a number of limitations. It is not possible to send a message to multiple subscribers using one message queue. You have to create a separate queue for each subscriber, otherwise only one of the subscribers reading from a queue will receive the message.

There are a number of elaborated message queues and pub-sub middleware available in the form of external libraries. ZeroMQ is a powerful, flexible and—at the same time—lightweight transport library. This makes it an ideal choice for embedded applications that are built using the pub-sub model of data exchange.

Using C++ lambdas for callbacks

In the pub-sub model, a subscriber usually registers a callback that is being invoked when a message from a publisher is delivered to the subscriber.

In the preceding recipe, we created a mechanism to register callbacks using inheritance and abstract classes. It is not the only mechanism available in C++. Lambda functions available in C++, starting from the C++11 standard, can be used as an alternative solution. This eliminates lots of boilerplate code needed to define derived classes and, in most cases, allows developers to express their intent in a clearer way.

In this recipe, we will learn how to use C++ lambda functions to define callbacks.

How to do it...

We are going to use most of the code from the preceding recipe, *Learning about message queue and publisher-subscriber models*. We will modify the `Reader` class to accept a callback as a parameter. With this modification, we can use `Reader` directly and do not need to rely on inheritance to define a callback:

1. Copy the contents of the `ipc3` directory that we created in the preceding recipe into a new directory: `ipc4`.
2. Keep all the code unchanged, except for the `Reader` class. Let's replace that with the following code snippet:

```
template<class T>
class Reader {
  private:
```

```
        MessageQueue queue;
        void (*func)(const T&);
    public:
        Reader(std::string& name, void (*func)(const T&)):
          queue(name, O_RDONLY), func(func) {}

        void Run() {
          T data;
          while(true) {
            queue.Receive(reinterpret_cast<char*>(&data),
             sizeof(data));
            func(data);
          }
        }
    };
```

3. Now that our `Reader` class is changed, we can update the `DoReads` method. We can use a lambda function to define a callback handler and pass it to the `Reader` constructor:

```
void DoReads() {
  Reader<Message> logger(kQueueName, [](const Message& data) {
    std::cout << "Received coordinate " << data << std::endl;
  });
  logger.Run();
}
```

4. The `CoordLogger` class is not needed anymore, so we can safely remove it from our code entirely.
5. You can build and run the application.

How it works...

In this recipe, we modified the preceding defined `Reader` class to accept an additional parameter in its constructor. This parameter has a specific data type—a pointer to a function, which will be used as a callback:

```
Reader(std::string& name, void (*func)(const T&)):
```

The handler is stored in the data field for future use:

```
void (*func)(const T&);
```

Now, every time the `Run` method reads a message, it invokes the function stored in the `func` field, rather than the `Callback` method that we need to override:

```
queue.Receive(reinterpret_cast<char*>(&data), sizeof(data));
func(data);
```

Getting rid of the `Callback` function makes `Reader` a concrete class and we can create its instance directly. However, now we need to provide a handler as a parameter of its constructor.

With plain C, we would have to define a `named` function and pass its name as a parameter. With C++, this approach is also possible, but C++ also provides the mechanism of anonymous functions or lambda functions, which can be defined right in-place.

In the `DoReads` method, we create a lambda function and pass it directly to the `Reader` constructor:

```
Reader<Message> logger(kQueueName, [](const Message& data) {
    std::cout << "Received coordinate " << data << std::endl;
});
```

Building and running the application produces the following output:

```
user@3324138cc2c7: /mnt/ipc4 — bash
user@3324138cc2c7:/mnt/ipc4$ ./ipc4
Write (x=1, y=0)
Received coordinate (x=1, y=0)
Write (x=0, y=1)
Received coordinate (x=0, y=1)
Write (x=1, y=1)
Received coordinate (x=1, y=1)
Write (x=0, y=0)
Received coordinate (x=0, y=0)
user@3324138cc2c7:/mnt/ipc4$
```

As we can see, it is identical to the output of the application we created in the preceding recipe. However, we do it with less code and in a more readable way.

Lambda functions should be used wisely. They make the code more readable if kept minimal. If a function grows bigger than five lines, consider using a named function instead.

There's more...

C++ provides flexible mechanisms for working with function-like objects and binds them with parameters. These mechanisms are widely used to forward calls and build function adapters. The *Function objects* page at `https://en.cppreference.com/w/cpp/utility/functional` is a good starting point to get a deeper understanding of these topics.

Exploring data serialization

We already briefly touched on some aspects of serialization in Chapter 3, *Working with Different Architectures*. When it comes to data exchange, serialization is crucial. The task of serialization is to represent all data being sent by the sender application in a way that can be unambiguously read by the receiver application. This task is not that straightforward, given that the sender and the receiver may be running on different hardware platforms and connected over a variety of transport links—a **Transmission Control Protocol/Internet Protocol** (**TCP/IP**) network, a **Serial Peripheral Interface** (**SPI**) bus, or a serial link.

There are many different ways of implementing serialization depending on requirements, which is why the C++ standard library does not provide it out of the box.

In this recipe, we will learn how to implement simple generic serialization and deserialization in a C++ application.

How to do it...

The goal of serialization is to encode any data in a way that can be properly decoded on another system or in another application. The typical obstacles for developers are as follows:

- Platform-specific differences, such as data alignment and endianness.
- Data scattered across memory; for example, elements of a linked list can be located far away from each other. The representation of disconnected blocks linked by pointers is natural for memory but cannot be automatically translated into a sequence of bytes when transferring it to another process.

A generic approach to this problem is letting a class define the functions to convert its content into a serialized form and restore an instance of a class from the serialized form.

In our application, we will overload `operator<<` of the output stream and `operator>>` of the input stream to serialize and deserialize data respectively:

1. In your `~/test` working directory, create a subdirectory called `stream`.
2. Use your favorite text editor to create a `stream.cpp` file in the `stream` subdirectory.
3. Start with the definition of the data structures that you want to serialize:

    ```cpp
    #include <iostream>
    #include <sstream>
    #include <list>

    struct Point {
        int x, y;
    };

    struct Paths {
        Point source;
        std::list<Point> destinations;
    };
    ```

4. Next, we overload the `<<` and `>>` operators that are responsible for writing and reading the `Point` objects into and from a stream respectively. For the `Point` data type enter the following:

    ```cpp
    std::ostream& operator<<(std::ostream& o, const Point& p) {
        o << p.x << " " << p.y << " ";
        return o;
    }

    std::istream& operator>>(std::istream& is, Point& p) {
        is >> p.x;
        is >> p.y;
        return is;
    }
    ```

5. They are followed by the << and >> overloaded operators for the `Paths` objects:

```cpp
std::ostream& operator<<(std::ostream& o, const Paths& paths) {
  o << paths.source << paths.destinations.size() << " ";
  for (const auto& x : paths.destinations) {
    o << x;
  }
  return o;
}

std::istream& operator>>(std::istream& is, Paths& paths) {
  size_t size;
  is >> paths.source;
  is >> size;
  for (;size;size--) {
    Point tmp;
    is >> tmp;
    paths.destinations.push_back(tmp);
  }
  return is;
}
```

6. Now, let's wrap everything up in the `main` function:

```cpp
int main(int argc, char** argv) {
  Paths paths = {{0, 0}, {{1, 1}, {0, 1}, {1, 0}}};

  std::stringstream in;
  in << paths;
  std::string serialized = in.str();
  std::cout << "Serialized paths into the string: ["
            << serialized << "]" << std::endl;

  std::stringstream out(serialized);
  Paths paths2;
  out >> paths2;
  std::cout << "Original: " << paths.destinations.size()
            << " destinations" << std::endl;
  std::cout << "Restored: " << paths2.destinations.size()
            << " destinations" << std::endl;

  return 0;
}
```

7. Finally, create a CMakeLists.txt file containing the build rules for our program:

```
cmake_minimum_required(VERSION 3.5.1)
project(stream)
add_executable(stream stream.cpp)

set(CMAKE_SYSTEM_NAME Linux)
set(CMAKE_SYSTEM_PROCESSOR arm)

SET(CMAKE_CXX_FLAGS "--std=c++11")

set(CMAKE_CXX_COMPILER /usr/bin/arm-linux-gnueabi-g++)
```

You can now build and run the application.

How it works...

In our test application, we defined a data type to represent paths from a source point to multiple destination points. We intentionally used hierarchical structures scattered in memory to demonstrate how to approach this problem in a generic way.

If we do not have specific requirements for performance, one of the possible approaches to serialization is storing data in text format. Besides its simplicity, it has two major advantages:

- Text encoding automatically resolves all issues related to endianness, alignment, and the size of integer data types.
- It is readable by humans. Developers can use serialized data for debugging without any additional tools.

To work with text representation, we can use the input and output streams provided by the standard library. They already define functions to write and read formatted numbers.

The Point structure is defined as two integer values: x and y. We override operator<< for this data type to write the x and y values followed by spaces. This way, we can read them sequentially in the overridden operator>> operation.

The Path data type is a bit trickier. It contains a linked list of destinations. Since the size of the list may vary, we need to write the actual size of the list before serializing its content to be able to recover it properly during deserialization:

```
o << paths.source << paths.destinations.size() << " ";
```

Since we have the `Point` methods for the `<<` and `>>` operators already overridden, we can use them in the `Paths` methods. This way, we write the `Point` objects to a stream or read them from a stream without knowing the contents of their data fields. Hierarchical data structures are handled recursively:

```
for (const auto& x : paths.destinations) {
  o << x;
}
```

Finally, we test our implementation of serialization and deserialization. We create a sample instance of the `Paths` object:

```
Paths paths = {{0, 0}, {{1, 1}, {0, 1}, {1, 0}}};
```

Then, we serialize its content into a string using the `std::stringstream` data type:

```
std::stringstream in;
in << paths;
std::string serialized = in.str();
```

Next, we create an empty `Path` object and deserialize the content of the string into it:

```
Paths paths2;
out >> paths2;
```

Finally, we check whether they match. When we run the application, we can use the following output to do this:

```
user@3324138cc2c7: /mnt/stream — bash
user@3324138cc2c7:/mnt/stream$ ./stream
Serialized paths into the string: [0 0 3 1 1 0 1 1 0 ]
Original: 3 destinations
Restored: 3 destinations
user@3324138cc2c7:/mnt/stream$
```

The size of the `destinations` list of the restored object matches the size of the `destinations` list of the original object. We can also see the content of the serialized data.

This example shows how to build custom serialization for any data type. It can be done without any external libraries. However, in cases where performance and memory efficiency matter, using third-party serialization libraries would be a more practical approach.

There's more...

Implementing serialization from scratch is difficult. The cereal library at `https://uscilab.github.io/cereal/` and the boost library at `https://www.boost.org/doc/libs/1_71_0/libs/serialization/doc/index.html` provide a foundation that helps you to add serialization to applications much faster and more easily.

Using the FlatBuffers library

Serialization and deserialization is a complex topic. While ad hoc serialization may look simple and straightforward, it is difficult to make it generic, easy to use, and fast. Thankfully, there are libraries that handle all of these complexities.

In this recipe, we will learn how to use one of the serialization libraries: FlatBuffers. It was designed with embedded programming in mind, making serialization and deserialization memory efficient and fast.

FlatBuffers uses an **Interface Definition Language** (IDL) to define a data schema. The schema describes all the fields of data structures that we need to serialize. When the schema is designed, we use a special tool called **flatc** to generate the code for a particular programming language, which is C++ in our case.

The generated code stores all data in serialized form and provides developers with so-called **getter** and **setter** methods to access the data fields. The getters perform deserialization on the fly. Storing data in its serialized form makes FlatBuffers really memory efficient. There is no need for extra memory to store serialized data and, in most cases, the overhead of deserialization is low.

In this recipe, we will learn how to start using FlatBuffers for data serialization in our applications.

How to do it...

FlatBuffers is a set of tools and libraries. Before using it, we need to download and build it:

1. Download the most recent archive of FlatBuffers, available at `https://codeload.github.com/google/flatbuffers/zip/master`, and extract it in the `test` directory. This will create a new directory called `flatbuffers-master`.

2. Switch to the build console, change the directory to `flatbuffers-master`, and run the following commands to build and install the library and tools. Make sure you run as root. If not, press *Ctrl + C* to exit the user shell:

```
# cmake .
# make
# make install
```

Now, we are ready to use FlatBuffers in our application. Let's reuse an application we created in one of the previous recipes:

3. Copy the contents of the `ipc4` directory into the newly created directory named `flat`.

4. Create a file named `message.fbs`, open it in an editor, and put in the following code:

```
struct Message {
x: int;
y: int;
}
```

5. Generate the C++ source code from `message.fbs` by running the following:

```
$ flatc --cpp message.fbs
```

This will create a new file called `message_generated.h`.

6. Open `ipc1.cpp` in your editor. Add an `include` directive for the generated `message_generated.h` file after the `mqueue.h` include:

```
#include <mqueue.h>

#include "message_generated.h"
```

7. Now, get rid of the `Message` struct declared in our code. We are going to use the structure generated in the FlatBuffers schema file instead.

8. Since FlatBuffers uses getter methods instead of direct access to the structure fields, we need to modify the body of the redefined `operator<<` operation we used to print point data to the console. The changes are minimal—we only add parentheses to each data field:

```
std::ostream& operator<<(std::ostream& o, const Message& m) {
  o << "(x=" << m.x() << ", y=" << m.y() << ")";
}
```

9. The code modifications are done. Now, we need to update the build rules to link with the FlatBuffers library. Open `CMakeLists.txt` and put in the following lines:

```
cmake_minimum_required(VERSION 3.5.1)
project(flat)
add_executable(flat ipc1.cpp)

set(CMAKE_SYSTEM_NAME Linux)
set(CMAKE_SYSTEM_PROCESSOR arm)

SET(CMAKE_CXX_FLAGS_RELEASE "--std=c++11")
SET(CMAKE_CXX_FLAGS_DEBUG "${CMAKE_CXX_FLAGS_RELEASE} -g -DDEBUG")
target_link_libraries(flat rt flatbuffers)

set(CMAKE_C_COMPILER /usr/bin/arm-linux-gnueabi-gcc)
set(CMAKE_CXX_COMPILER /usr/bin/arm-linux-gnueabi-g++)

set(CMAKE_FIND_ROOT_PATH_MODE_PROGRAM NEVER)
set(CMAKE_FIND_ROOT_PATH_MODE_LIBRARY ONLY)
set(CMAKE_FIND_ROOT_PATH_MODE_INCLUDE ONLY)
set(CMAKE_FIND_ROOT_PATH_MODE_PACKAGE ONLY)
```

10. Switch to the build console, then change to the user shell:

```
# su - user
$
```

11. Build and run the application.

How it works...

FlatBuffers is an external library that is not available in the Ubuntu repository of packages, which is why we need to download, build, and install it first. After the installation is done, we can use it in our application.

We use an existing application we created for the *Using C++ lambdas for callbacks* recipe as a starting point. In that application, we defined a structure, called Message, to represent a type of data we use for IPC. We are going to replace it with a new data type provided by FlatBuffers. This new data type will perform all the necessary serialization and deserialization transparently for us.

We remove the definition of the Message struct from our code completely. Instead, we generate a new header file, called message_generated.h. This file is generated from the message.fbs FlatBuffers schema file. This schema file defines a structure with two integer fields—x and y:

```
x: int;
y: int;
```

This definition is identical to our preceding definition; the only difference is the syntax—FlatBuffers' schema uses a colon to separate field names from the field types.

Once message_generated.h is created by the flatc command invocation, we can use it in our code. We add the proper include as follows:

```
#include "message_generated.h"
```

The generated message is identical to the message structure we used before but as we discussed earlier, FlatBuffers stores data in serialized form and needs to deserialize it on the fly. That is why, instead of direct access to the data fields, we have to use the x() accessor method instead of just x and the y() accessor method instead of just y.

The only place we use direct access to the message data field is in the overridden operator<< operation. We add parentheses to turn direct field access into the invocation of the FlatBuffers getter methods:

```
o << "(x=" << m.x() << ", y=" << m.y() << ")";
```

Let's build and run the application. We will see the following output:

```
user@3324138cc2c7: /mnt/flat — bash
user@3324138cc2c7:/mnt/flat$ ./flat
Write (x=1, y=0)
Received coordinate (x=1, y=0)
Write (x=0, y=1)
Received coordinate (x=0, y=1)
Write (x=1, y=1)
Received coordinate (x=1, y=1)
Write (x=0, y=0)
Received coordinate (x=0, y=0)
user@3324138cc2c7:/mnt/flat$
```

The output is the same as for our custom message data type. With only a few modifications in our code, we migrated our messages to FlatBuffers. Now, we can run our publishers and subscribers on multiple computers—which can have different architectures—and be sure that each of them interprets messages correctly.

There's more...

Besides FlatBuffers, there are a number of other serialization libraries and techniques, each having its own pros and cons. Refer to the *C++ Serialization FAQ* at https://isocpp.org/wiki/faq/serialization for a better understanding of how to design serialization in your applications.

9
Peripherals

Communication with peripheral devices is an essential part of any embedded application. Applications need to check the availability and status and send data to and receive data from a variety of devices.

Each target platform is different and many ways of connecting peripheral devices to the computing unit exist. There are, however, several hardware and software interfaces that have become industry standard for communication with peripheral devices. In this chapter, we will learn how to work with peripheral devices connected directly to processor pins or over serial interfaces. This chapter covers the following topics:

- Controlling devices connected via GPIO
- Exploring pulse-width modulation
- Using ioctl to access a real-time clock in Linux
- Using libgpiod to control GPIO pins
- Controlling I2C peripheral devices

The recipes in this chapter involve interaction with real hardware and are intended to be run on a real Raspberry Pi board.

Controlling devices connected via GPIO

General Purpose Input-Output (GPIO) is the simplest way of connecting peripheral devices to the CPU. Every processor usually has some number of pins reserved for general purposes. These pins can be electrically connected directly to the pins of a peripheral device. An embedded application can control the device by changing the signal level of the pins configured for output or by reading the signal level of the input pins.

The interpretation of the signal levels does not follow any protocol and is determined by the peripheral device. Developers need to consult the device datasheet to be able to program the communication properly.

This type of communication is usually done on the kernel side using a dedicated device driver. This is, however, not always a requirement. In this recipe, we will learn how to use the GPIO interface on a Raspberry Pi board from a user-space application.

How to do it...

We are going to create a simple application that controls a **Light Emitting Diode** (LED) connected to a general-purpose pin on a Raspberry Pi board:

1. In your ~/test working directory, create a subdirectory called gpio.
2. Use your favorite text editor to create a gpio.cpp file in the gpio subdirectory.
3. Put the following code snippet into the file:

```cpp
#include <chrono>
#include <iostream>
#include <thread>
#include <wiringPi.h>

using namespace std::literals::chrono_literals;
const int kLedPin = 0;

int main (void)
{
  if (wiringPiSetup () <0) {
    throw std::runtime_error("Failed to initialize wiringPi");
  }

  pinMode (kLedPin, OUTPUT);
  while (true) {
    digitalWrite (kLedPin, HIGH);
    std::cout << "LED on" << std::endl;
    std::this_thread::sleep_for(500ms) ;
    digitalWrite (kLedPin, LOW);
    std::cout << "LED off" << std::endl;
    std::this_thread::sleep_for(500ms) ;
  }
  return 0 ;
}
```

4. Create a CMakeLists.txt file containing the build rules for our program:

```cmake
cmake_minimum_required(VERSION 3.5.1)
project(gpio)
add_executable(gpio gpio.cpp)
target_link_libraries(gpio wiringPi)
```

5. Connect an LED to your Raspberry Pi board using the instructions from the *WiringPI example* section at `http://wiringpi.com/examples/blink/`.

6. Set up an SSH connection to your Raspberry Pi board. Follow the instructions from the *Raspberry Pi documentation* section at `https://www.raspberrypi.org/documentation/remote-access/ssh/`.

7. Copy the contents of the `gpio` folder to the Raspberry Pi board over SSH.

8. Log in to the board over SSH, then build and run the application:

```
$ cd gpio && cmake . && make && sudo ./gpio
```

Your application should run and you should be able to observe the LED blinking.

How it works...

Raspberry Pi boards have 40 pins (26 in the first models) that can be programmed using a **Memory-Mapped Input-Output** (**MMIO**) mechanism. MMIO allows developers to query or set the state of pins by reading or writing specific addresses in the physical memory of the system.

In the *Using specialized memory* recipe in `Chapter 6`, *Memory Management*, we learned how to access MMIO registers. In this recipe, we are going to offload the MMIO address's manipulations to the specialized library, `wiringPi`. It hides all the complexities of memory mapping and finding proper offsets under the hood, exposing a clean API instead.

This library is pre-installed on Raspberry Pi boards, so to simplify the build process, we are going to build the code directly on the board instead of using cross-compilation. Unlike other recipes, our build rules do not mention a cross compiler—we are going to use the native ARM compiler on the board. We only add a dependency to the `wiringPi` library:

```
target_link_libraries(gpio wiringPi)
```

The code of this example is a modification of the `wiringPi` example for blinking an LED. Firstly, we initialize the `wiringPi` library:

```
if (wiringPiSetup () < 0) {
    throw std::runtime_error("Failed to initialize wiringPi");
}
```

Next, we enter the endless loop. On each iteration, we set the pin to the `HIGH` state:

```
digitalWrite (kLedPin, HIGH);
```

After the `500 ms` delay, we set the same pit to the `LOW` state and add another delay:

```
digitalWrite (kLedPin, LOW);
std::cout << "LED off" << std::endl;
std::this_thread::sleep_for(500ms) ;
```

We configured our program to use pin 0, which corresponds to `GPIO.0` or pin 17 of the `BCM2835` chip of Raspberry Pi:

```
const int kLedPin = 0;
```

If an LED is connected to this pin, it will blink, turning on for 0.5 seconds and then off for another 0.5 seconds. By tweaking the delays in the loop, you can change the blinking pattern.

Since the program enters an endless loop, we can terminate it at any time by pressing *Ctrl + C* in the SSH console; otherwise, it will run forever.

When we run the application, we only see the following output:

```
igor@raspberrypi:~/gpio $ ./gpio
wiringPiSetup: Unable to open /dev/mem or /dev/gpiomem: Permission denied.
  Aborting your program because if it can not access the GPIO
  hardware then it most certianly won't work
  Try running with sudo?
igor@raspberrypi:~/gpio $ sudo ./gpio
LED on
LED off
LED on
LED off
LED on
LED off
LED on
LED off
LED on
LED off
LED on
LED off
LED on
LED off
^C
igor@raspberrypi:~/gpio $
```

We log when we turn the LED on or off, but to check that the program actually works, we need to look at the LED connected to the pin. If we follow the wiring instructions, we can see how it works. While the program is running, the LED on the boards blinks synchronously with the program output:

We are able to control simple devices connected directly to the CPU pins without writing complicated device drivers.

Exploring pulse-width modulation

Digital pins can only be in one of two states: either HIGH or LOW. An LED connected to a digital pin can also only be in one of two states: on or off, correspondingly. But is there a way to control the brightness of this LED? Yes, we can use a method called **Pulse-width Modulation (PWM)**.

The idea behind PWM is simple. We limit the amount of power delivered by the electrical signal by turning it on or off periodically. This makes the signal pulse with some frequency and the amount of power is proportional to the width of the pulse—the time when the signal was HIGH.

For example, if we turn a pin to HIGH for 10 microseconds and then LOW for another 90 microseconds in a loop, a device connected to that pin receives 10% of the power that would be delivered if the pin were always HIGH.

In this recipe, we will learn how to use PWM to control the brightness of an LED connected to a digital GPIO pin on the Raspberry Pi board.

How to do it...

We are going to create a simple application that gradually changes the brightness of an LED connected to a general-purpose pin on a Raspberry Pi board:

1. In your ~/test working directory, create a subdirectory called pwm.

2. Use your favorite text editor to create a pwm.cpp file in the pwm subdirectory.

3. Let's put in the required include functions and define a function called Blink:

```cpp
#include <chrono>
#include <thread>

#include <wiringPi.h>

using namespace std::literals::chrono_literals;

const int kLedPin = 0;

void Blink(std::chrono::microseconds duration, int percent_on) {
    digitalWrite (kLedPin, HIGH);
    std::this_thread::sleep_for(
            duration * percent_on / 100) ;
    digitalWrite (kLedPin, LOW);
    std::this_thread::sleep_for(
            duration * (100 - percent_on) / 100) ;
}
```

4. This is followed by a main function:

```cpp
int main (void)
{
  if (wiringPiSetup () <0) {
    throw std::runtime_error("Failed to initialize wiringPi");
  }

  pinMode (kLedPin, OUTPUT);

  int count = 0;
  int delta = 1;
  while (true) {
    Blink(10ms, count);
    count = count + delta;
    if (count == 101) {
      delta = -1;
    } else if (count == 0) {
      delta = 1;
    }
```

```
      }
      return 0 ;
  }
```

5. Create a `CMakeLists.txt` file containing the build rules for our program:

```
cmake_minimum_required(VERSION 3.5.1)
project(pwm)
add_executable(pwm pwm.cpp)
target_link_libraries(pwm wiringPi)
```

6. Connect an LED to your Raspberry Pi board using the instructions from the *WiringPI example* section at `http://wiringpi.com/examples/blink/`.

7. Set up an SSH connection to your Raspberry Pi board. Follow instructions from the *Raspberry PI documentation* section at `https://www.raspberrypi.org/documentation/remote-access/ssh/`.

8. Copy the contents of the `pwm` folder to the Raspberry Pi board over SSH.

9. Log in to the board over SSH, then build and run the application:

```
$ cd pwm && cmake . && make && sudo ./pwm
```

Your application should now run and you can observe the LED blinking.

How it works...

This recipe reuses the code to blink an LED and the schematics from the preceding recipe. We moved this code from the `main` function to a new function, `Blink`.

The `Blink` function accepts two parameters—`duration` and `percent_on`:

```
void Blink(std::chrono::microseconds duration, int percent_on)
```

`duration` determines the total width of the pulse in microseconds. `percent_on` defines a ratio of the time when the signal is `HIGH` to the total duration of the pulse.

The implementation is straightforward. When `Blink` is invoked, it turns the pin to `HIGH` and waits for the amount of time proportional to `percent_on`:

```
digitalWrite (kLedPin, HIGH);
std::this_thread::sleep_for(
        duration * percent_on / 100);
```

After that, it turns the pin to LOW and waits for the remaining time:

```
digitalWrite (kLedPin, LOW);
std::this_thread::sleep_for(
        duration * (100 - percent_on) / 100);
```

Blink is the main building block for implementing PWM. We can control the brightness by changing percent_on from 0 to 100, and if we pick duration short enough, we will not see any flickering.

A duration that is equal to or shorter than the refresh rate of a TV or monitor is good enough. For 60 Hz, the duration is 16.6 milliseconds. We use 10 milliseconds for simplicity.

Next, we wrap everything up in another endless loop, but now it has another parameter, count:

```
int count = 0;
```

It is updated with each iteration and bounces between 0 and 100. The delta variable defines the direction of change—either a decrease or increase—as well as the amount of change, which is always 1 in our case:

```
int delta = 1;
```

When the count reaches 101 or 0, the direction changes:

```
if (count == 101) {
   delta = -1;
} else if (count == 0) {
   delta = 1;
}
```

On each iteration, we invoke Blink, passing 10ms as a pulse and count as a ratio that defines the amount of time when LED is on, hence its brightness (as shown in the following image):

```
Blink(10ms, count);
```

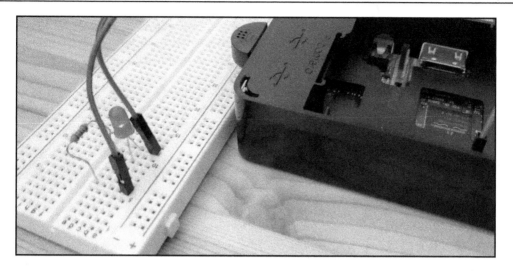

Due to the high frequency of updates, we cannot tell when the LED turns from on to off.

When we wire everything up and run the program, we can see that the LED gets brighter or dimmer smoothly.

There's more...

PWM is widely used in embedded systems for a variety of purposes. It is a common mechanism for servo control and voltage regulation. Use the *Pulse-width modulation* Wikipedia page, available at `https://en.wikipedia.org/wiki/Pulse-width_modulation`, as a starting point to learn more about this technique.

Using ioctl to access a real-time clock in Linux

In our preceding recipes, we used MMIO to access peripheral devices from user-space Linux applications. This interface, however, is not the recommended way of communication between user-space applications and device drivers.

In Unix-like operating systems such as Linux, most of the peripheral devices can be accessed in the same way as regular files using so-called device files. When an application opens a device file, it can read from it, fetching data from the corresponding device, or write to it, sending data to the device.

In many cases, device drivers cannot work with unstructured data streams. They expect data exchange organized in the form of requests and responses, where each request and response has a specific and fixed format.

This kind of communication is covered by the `ioctl` system call. It accepts a device-dependant request code as its parameter. It may also contain other parameters that encode the request data or provide storage for the output data. These parameters are specific to a particular device and request code.

In this recipe, we will learn how to use `ioctl` in user-space applications for data exchange with device drivers.

How to do it...

We will create an application that reads the current time from the **Real-Time Clock (RTC)** connected to the Raspberry Pi board:

1. In your ~/test working directory, create a subdirectory called `rtc`.
2. Use your favorite text editor to create a `rtc.cpp` file in the `rtc` subdirectory.
3. Let's put the required `include` functions into the `rtc.cpp` file:

```
#include <iostream>
#include <system_error>

#include <time.h>
#include <unistd.h>
#include <fcntl.h>
#include <sys/ioctl.h>
#include <linux/rtc.h>
```

4. Now, we define a class called `Rtc` that encapsulates the communication to the real-clock device:

```
class Rtc {
    int fd;
    public:
        Rtc() {
            fd = open("/dev/rtc", O_RDWR);
            if (fd < 0) {
                throw std::system_error(errno,
                    std::system_category(),
                    "Failed to open RTC device");
            }
        }
}
```

```
    ~Rtc() {
      close(fd);
    }

    time_t GetTime(void) {
      union {
        struct rtc_time rtc;
        struct tm tm;
      } tm;
      int ret = ioctl(fd, RTC_RD_TIME, &tm.rtc);
      if (ret < 0) {
        throw std::system_error(errno,
            std::system_category(),
            "ioctl failed");
      }
      return mktime(&tm.tm);
    }
};
```

5. Once the class is defined, we put a simple usage example into the `main` function:

```
int main (void)
{
  Rtc rtc;
  time_t t = rtc.GetTime();
  std::cout << "Current time is " << ctime(&t)
            << std::endl;

  return 0 ;
}
```

6. Create a `CMakeLists.txt` file containing the build rules for our program:

```
cmake_minimum_required(VERSION 3.5.1)
project(rtc)
add_executable(rtc rtc.cpp)

set(CMAKE_SYSTEM_NAME Linux)
set(CMAKE_SYSTEM_PROCESSOR arm)

set(CMAKE_CXX_COMPILER /usr/bin/arm-linux-gnueabi-g++)
```

7. Build your application and copy the resulting `rtc` binary to our Raspberry Pi emulator.

How it works...

We are implementing an application that talks directly to the hardware RTC connected to the system. There is a difference between the system clock and the RTC. The system clock is active and maintained only when the system is running. When the system is powered off or goes into sleep mode, the system clock becomes invalid. The RTC is active even when the system is off. It maintains the actual time that is used to configure the system clock when the system is up. Moreover, it can be programmed to wake up the system at a specific time when in sleep mode.

We encapsulate all communication with the RTC driver into a class called Rtc. All data exchange with the driver goes through the /dev/rtc special device file. In the Rtc class constructor, we open the device file and store the resulting file descriptor in the fd instance variable:

```
fd = open("/dev/rtc", O_RDWR);
```

Similarly, a destructor is used to close the file:

```
~Rtc() {
  close(fd);
}
```

Since the device is closed in the destructor as soon as the Rtc instance is destroyed, we can use the **Resource Acquisition is Initialization** (RAII) idiom to throw exceptions when something goes wrong without leaking the file descriptors:

```
if (fd < 0) {
  throw std::system_error(errno,
      std::system_category(),
      "Failed to open RTC device");
}
```

Our class defines only one member function—GetTime. It is a wrapper on top of the RTC_RD_TIME ioctl call. This call expects a rtc_time structure to return the current time. It is almost identical to the tm structure that we are going to use to convert the time returned by the RTC driver into a POSIX timestamp format, so we place both of them into the same memory location as a union data type:

```
union {
  struct rtc_time rtc;
  struct tm tm;
} tm;
```

This way, we avoid copying identical fields from one structure to another.

Once the data structure is ready, we invoke the `ioctl` call, passing the `RTC_RD_TIME` constant as a request ID and a pointer to our structure as an address to store data to:

```
int ret = ioctl(fd, RTC_RD_TIME, &tm.rtc);
```

Once successful, `ioctl` returns 0. In this case, we convert the resulting data structure into the `time_t` POSIX timestamp format using the `mktime` function:

```
return mktime(&tm.tm);
```

In the `main` function, we create an instance of the `Rtc` class and then invoke the `GetTime` method:

```
Rtc rtc;
time_t t = rtc.GetTime();
```

Since the POSIX timestamp represents the number of seconds since January 1, 1970, we convert it into a human-friendly representation using the `ctime` function and output the result to the console:

```
std::cout << "Current time is " << ctime(&t)
```

When we run our application, we can see the following output:

```
                              QEMU
pi@raspberrypi:~/rtc $ ./rtc
terminate called after throwing an instance of 'std::system_error'
  what():  Failed to open RTC device: Permission denied
Aborted
pi@raspberrypi:~/rtc $ sudo ./rtc
Current time is Tue Feb 25 21:31:22 2020

pi@raspberrypi:~/rtc $
```

We were able to read the current time directly from the hardware clock using `ioctl`. The `ioctl` API is widely used in Linux embedded applications to communicate with devices.

There's more

In our simple example, we learned how to use only one `ioctl` request. RTC devices support many other requests that can be used to set the alarm, update the time, and control RTC interrupts. More details can be found in the *RTC ioctl documentation* section available at https://linux.die.net/man/4/rtc.

Using libgpiod to control GPIO pins

In the preceding recipe, we learned how to access the RTC using the `ioctl` API. Can we use it to control GPIO pins as well? The answer is yes. Recently, a generic GPIO driver was added to Linux, along with a user-space library, `libgpiod`, to simplify access to devices connected to GPIO by adding a convenience layer on top of the generic `ioctl` API. This interface allows embedded developers to manage their devices on any Linux-based platform without writing device drivers. Additionally, it provides bindings for C++ out of the box.

As a result, the `wiringPi` library has been deprecated, despite still being widely used because of its easy-to-use interface.

In this recipe, we will learn how to use the `libgpiod` C++ bindings. We are going to use the same LED blinking example to see the differences and similarities in the `wiringPi` and `libgpiod` approaches.

How to do it...

We will create an application that blinks an LED connected to the Raspberry Pi board using a new `libgpiod` API:

1. In your ~/`test` working directory, create a subdirectory called `gpiod`.
2. Use your favorite text editor to create a `gpiod.cpp` file in the `gpiod` subdirectory.
3. Put the code for the application into the `rtc.cpp` file:

```
#include <chrono>
#include <iostream>
#include <thread>

#include <gpiod.h>
#include <gpiod.hpp>
```

```
using namespace std::literals::chrono_literals;

const int kLedPin = 17;

int main (void)
{

  gpiod::chip chip("gpiochip0");
  auto line = chip.get_line(kLedPin);
  line.request({"test",
                gpiod::line_request::DIRECTION_OUTPUT,
                0}, 0);

  while (true) {
    line.set_value(1);
    std::cout << "ON" << std::endl;
    std::this_thread::sleep_for(500ms);
    line.set_value(0);
    std::cout << "OFF" << std::endl;
    std::this_thread::sleep_for(500ms);
  }

  return 0 ;
}
```

4. Create a `CMakeLists.txt` file containing the build rules for our program:

```
cmake_minimum_required(VERSION 3.5.1)
project(gpiod)
add_executable(gpiod gpiod.cpp)
target_link_libraries(gpiod gpiodcxx)
```

5. Connect an LED to your Raspberry Pi board using the instructions from the *WiringPI example* section at http://wiringpi.com/examples/blink/.

6. Set up an SSH connection to your Raspberry Pi board. Follow the instructions from the *Raspberry PI documentation* section at https://www.raspberrypi.org/documentation/remote-access/.

7. Copy the contents of the `gpio` folder to the Raspberry Pi board over SSH.

8. Install the `libgpiod-dev` package:

```
$ sudo apt-get install gpiod-dev
```

9. Log in to the board over SSH, then build and run the application:

```
$ cd gpiod && cmake . && make && sudo ./gpiod
```

Your application should run and you can observe the LED blinking.

How it works...

Our application uses a new, recommended way of accessing GPIO devices in Linux. Since it was added only recently, it requires the latest version of the Raspbian distributive, `buster`, to be installed.

The `gpiod` library itself provides high-level wrappers to communicate with GPIO kernel modules using the `ioctl` API. This interface is designed for C languages and on top of it, there is an additional layer for C++ bindings. This layer lives in the `libgpiocxx` library, which is part of the `libgpiod2` package along with the `libgpiod` library for C.

The library uses exceptions to report errors, so the code is simple and not cluttered with checks of return codes. Also, we do not need to bother with releasing the capture's resources; it is done automatically via C++ RAII mechanisms.

When the application starts, it creates an instance of the class chip, which works as an entry point for GPIO communication. Its constructor accepts the name of the device to work with:

```
gpiod::chip chip("gpiochip0");
```

Next, we create an instance of the line, which represents a particular GPIO pin:

```
auto line = chip.get_line(kLedPin);
```

Note that unlike the `wiringPi` implementation, we pass a 17 pin number because `libgpiod` uses native Broadcom SOC Channel (**BCM**) pin numbering:

```
const int kLedPin = 17;
```

After the line instance is created, we need to configure the desired access mode. We construct an instance of the `line_request` structure, passing the name of a consumer (`"test"`) and a constant indicating that the pin is configured for output:

```
line.request({"test",
              gpiod::line_request::DIRECTION_OUTPUT,
              0}, 0);
```

After that, we can change the pin state using the `set_value` method. As in the `wiringPi` example, we set the pin to `1` or `HIGH` for `500ms`, then back to `0` or `LOW` for another `500ms` in a loop:

```
line.set_value(1);
std::cout << "ON" << std::endl;
std::this_thread::sleep_for(500ms);
line.set_value(0);
std::cout << "OFF" << std::endl;
std::this_thread::sleep_for(500ms);
```

The output of this program is identical to the output of the program from the *Controlling devices connected via GPIO* recipe. The code may look more complex, but the new API is more generic and can work on any Linux board, not just Raspberry Pi.

There's more...

More information about `libgpiod` and the GPIO interface, in general, can be found at `https://github.com/brgl/libgpiod`.

Controlling I2C peripheral devices

Connecting devices over GPIO has one downside. A processor has a limited and relatively small number of pins available for GPIO. When you need to work with numerous devices or devices that provide complex functionality, you can run out of pins easily.

A solution is using one of the standard serial buses to connect peripheral devices. One of them is **Inter-Integrated Circuit (I2C)**. This is widely used to connect various low-speed devices because of its simplicity and because a device can be connected with only two wires on the host controller.

The bus is well supported both on hardware and software levels. By using I2C peripherals, developers can control them from user-space applications without writing complex device drivers.

In this recipe, we will learn how to work with an I2C device on a Raspberry Pi board. We will use a popular and inexpensive LCD display. It has 16 pins, which makes it difficult to connect to the Raspberry board directly. However, with an I2C backpack, it only needs four wires to connect.

How to do it...

We will create an application that displays text on a 1602 LCD display attached to our Raspberry Pi board:

1. In your ~/test working directory, create a subdirectory called i2c.
2. Use your favorite text editor to create an i2c.cpp file in the i2c subdirectory.
3. Put the following include directives and constants' definitions into the i2c.cpp file:

```cpp
#include <thread>
#include <system_error>

#include <unistd.h>
#include <fcntl.h>
#include <errno.h>
#include <sys/ioctl.h>
#include <linux/i2c-dev.h>

using namespace std::literals::chrono_literals;

enum class Function : uint8_t {
  clear = 0x01,
  home = 0x02,
  entry_mode_set = 0x04,
  display_control = 0x08,
  cursor_shift = 0x10,
  fn_set = 0x20,
  set_ddram_addr = 0x80
};

constexpr int En = 0b00000100;
constexpr int Rs = 0b00000001;

constexpr int kDisplayOn = 0x04;
constexpr int kEntryLeft = 0x02;
constexpr int kTwoLine = 0x08;
constexpr int kBacklightOn = 0x08;
```

4. Now, we define a new class, `Lcd`, which encapsulates the display control logic. We start with the data fields and the `public` methods:

```
class Lcd {
  int fd;

  public:
    Lcd(const char* device, int address) {
      fd = open(device, O_RDWR);
      if (fd < 0) {
        throw std::system_error(errno,
            std::system_category(),
            "Failed to open RTC device");
      }
      if (ioctl(fd, I2C_SLAVE, address) < 0) {
        close(fd);
        throw std::system_error(errno,
            std::system_category(),
            "Failed to aquire bus address");
      }
      Init();
    }

    ~Lcd() {
      close(fd);
    }

    void Clear() {
      Call(Function::clear);
      std::this_thread::sleep_for(2000us);
    }

    void Display(const std::string& text,
                 bool second=false) {
      Call(Function::set_ddram_addr, second ? 0x40 : 0);
      for(char c : text) {
        Write(c, Rs);
      }
    }
}
```

5. They are followed by the `private` methods. Low-level helper methods go first:

```
private:

    void SendToI2C(uint8_t byte) {
if (write(fd, &byte, 1) != 1) {
throw std::system_error(errno,
std::system_category(),
```

```
        "Write to i2c device failed");
    }
  }

  void SendToLcd(uint8_t value) {
    value |= kBacklightOn;
    SendToI2C(value);
    SendToI2C(value | En);
    std::this_thread::sleep_for(1us);
    SendToI2C(value & ~En);
    std::this_thread::sleep_for(50us);
  }

  void Write(uint8_t value, uint8_t mode=0) {
    SendToLcd((value & 0xF0) | mode);
    SendToLcd((value << 4) | mode);
  }
```

6. Once the helper functions are defined, we add higher-level methods:

```
  void Init() {
    // Switch to 4-bit mode
    for (int i = 0; i < 3; i++) {
      SendToLcd(0x30);
      std::this_thread::sleep_for(4500us);
    }
    SendToLcd(0x20);

    // Set display to two-line, 4 bit, 5x8 character mode
    Call(Function::fn_set, kTwoLine);
    Call(Function::display_control, kDisplayOn);
    Clear();
    Call(Function::entry_mode_set, kEntryLeft);
    Home();
  }

  void Call(Function function, uint8_t value=0) {
    Write((uint8_t)function | value);
  }

  void Home() {
    Call(Function::home);
    std::this_thread::sleep_for(2000us);
  }
};
```

7. Add the `main` function that uses the `Lcd` class:

```cpp
int main (int argc, char* argv[])
{
  Lcd lcd("/dev/i2c-1", 0x27);
  if (argc > 1) {
    lcd.Display(argv[1]);
    if (argc > 2) {
      lcd.Display(argv[2], true);
    }
  }
  return 0 ;
}
```

8. Create a `CMakeLists.txt` file containing the build rules for our program:

```
cmake_minimum_required(VERSION 3.5.1)
project(i2c)
add_executable(i2c i2c.cpp)
```

9. Connect the pins on the `i2c` backpack of your 1602LCD display to the pins on your Raspberry Pi board according to this table:

Raspberry Pi pin name	Physical pin number	1602 I2C pin
GND	6	GND
+5v	2	VSS
SDA.1	3	SDA
SCL.1	5	SCL

10. Set up an SSH connection to your Raspberry Pi board. Follow the instructions from the *Raspberry PI documentation* section at `https://www.raspberrypi.org/documentation/remote-access/ssh/`.

11. Log in to the Raspberry board and run the `raspi-config` tool to enable `i2c`:

```
sudo raspi-config
```

12. In the menu, select **Interfacing Options** | **I2C** | **Yes**.
13. Reboot the board to activate the new settings.
14. Copy the contents of the `i2c` folder to the Raspberry Pi board over SSH.
15. Log in to the board over SSH, then build and run the application:

```
$ cd i2c && cmake . && make && ./i2c Hello, world!
```

Your application should run and you can observe the LED blinking.

How it works...

In this recipe, our peripheral device—an LCD screen—is connected to the board over the I2C bus. It is a form of a serial interface, so the connection only requires four physical wires. An LCD screen, however, can do much more than a simple LED. This means that the communication protocol used to control it is also more complex.

We will use only a fraction of the functionality provided by the 1602 LCD screen. The communication logic is loosely based on the `LiquidCrystal_I2C` library for Arduino, adapted for Raspberry Pi.

We define an `Lcd` class that hides all the complexities of I2C communication and the specifics of the 1602 control protocol in its private methods. Besides a constructor and a destructor, it exposes only two public methods: `Clear` and `Display`.

In Linux, we communicate to I2C devices via device files. To start working with a device, we need to open a device file corresponding to an I2C controller using the regular open call:

```
fd = open(device, O_RDWR);
```

There may be multiple devices attached to the same bus. We need to select the device we what to communicate to. We do this with an `ioctl` call:

```
if (ioctl(fd, I2C_SLAVE, address) < 0) {
```

At this point, the I2C communication is configured and we can issue I2C commands by writing data to the open file descriptor. The commands, however, are specific for each peripheral device. So, after generic I2C initialization, we need to proceed with the LCD initialization.

We put all the LCD-specific initialization into the `Init` private function. It configures the operation modes, the number of rows, and the size of the displayed characters. To do this, we define the helper methods, data types, and constants.

The basic helper function is `SendToI2C`. It is a simple method that writes a byte of data into the file descriptor configured for I2C communication and throws an exception in the case of an error:

```
if (write(fd, &byte, 1) != 1) {
  throw std::system_error(errno,
      std::system_category(),
      "Write to i2c device failed");
}
```

On top of `SendToI2C`, we define another helper method, `SendToLcd`. It sends a sequence of bytes to I2C, forming a command that the LCD controller can interpret. This involves setting different flags and taking care of delays required between chunks of data:

```
SendToI2C(value);
SendToI2C(value | En);
std::this_thread::sleep_for(1us);
SendToI2C(value & ~En);
std::this_thread::sleep_for(50us);
```

The LCD is working in 4-bit mode, which means that each byte sent to the display requires two commands. We define the `Write` method to do it for us:

```
SendToLcd((value & 0xF0) | mode);
SendToLcd((value << 4) | mode);
```

Finally, we define all possible commands supported by the device and put them into the `Function` enum class. A `Call` helper function can be used to invoke the functions in a type-safe way:

```
void Call(Function function, uint8_t value=0) {
  Write((uint8_t)function | value);
}
```

Finally, we use these helper functions to define public methods to clear the screen and display a string.

Since all the complexity of the communication protocol is encapsulated in the `Lcd` class, our `main` function is relatively simple.

It creates an instance of the class, passing in a device filename and a device address that we are going to use. By default, a 1620 LCD with an I2C backpack has a `0x27` address:

```
Lcd lcd("/dev/i2c-1", 0x27);
```

The constructor of the `Lcd` class performs all initialization and as soon as the instance is created, we can invoke the `Display` function. Instead of hardcoding the string to display, we use data passed by a user through the command-line parameters. The first parameter is displayed in the first row. If the second parameter is provided, it is also displayed in the second row of the display:

```
lcd.Display(argv[1]);
if (argc > 2) {
  lcd.Display(argv[2], true);
}
```

Our program is ready and we can copy it over to the Raspberry Pi board and build it there. But before running it, we need to wire the display to the board and enable I2C support.

We use the `raspi-config` tool to enable I2C. We need to do it only once, but a reboot is required unless I2C has not been previously enabled:

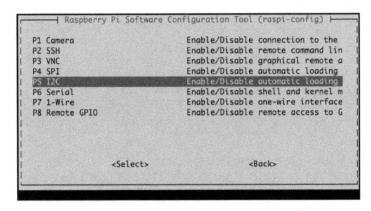

Finally, we can run our application. It will display the following output on the LCD display:

Now, we know how to control devices connected via an I2C bus from Linux user-space programs.

There's more...

More information about working with I2C devices can be found at the *Interfacing with I2C devices* page, available at https://elinux.org/Interfacing_with_I2C_Devices.

Reducing Power Consumption

10

There are many applications for embedded systems that require them to be battery powered. From small **IoT** (short for **internet of things**) devices collecting data from sensors, pushing it into the cloud for processing, to autonomous vehicles and robots—these systems should be as power efficient as possible so that they can operate for a long time without a steady external power supply.

Power efficiency means the smart control of the power consumption of all parts of a system, from the peripheral devices to the memory and the processor. The efficiency of power control depends significantly on the choice of hardware components and the system design. If a processor does not support dynamic voltage control or a peripheral device cannot enter power-saving mode when idle, then not much can be done on the software side. If, however, hardware components implement standard specifications, such as an **advanced configuration and power interface** (**ACPI**), then a lot of the burden of power management can be offloaded to the operating system kernel.

In this chapter, we will explore different power-saving modes of modern hardware platforms and how they can be utilized. We will learn how to manage the power state of external devices and reduce the power consumption of processors by writing more efficient software.

We will cover the following topics:

- Exploring power-saving modes in Linux
- Waking up using **RTC** (short for **real-time clock**)
- Controlling the autosuspend of USB devices
- Configuring CPU frequency
- Using events for waiting
- Profiling power consumption with PowerTOP

The recipes from this chapter will help you efficiently utilize the power-saving capabilities of modern operating systems and write code that is optimized for battery-powered devices.

Technical requirements

For running code examples in this chapter, you need to have a Raspberry PI box revision 3 or above.

Exploring power-saving modes in Linux

When a system is in the idle state and does not have work to do, it can be put in a sleep state to save power. Similar to human sleep, it cannot do anything until it is woken up by external event, for example an alarm clock.

Linux supports multiple sleep modes. The choice of sleep mode and the amount of power it can save depends on the hardware support and the time it takes to enter the mode and wake up from it.

The supported modes are as follows:

- **Suspend-to-idle** (**S2I**): This is a light sleep mode that can be implemented purely in software and does not require any support from the hardware. The devices are put into low-power mode and time keeping is suspended to let the processor spend more time in a power-efficient idle state. A system is woken up by an interrupt from any of the peripheral devices.
- **Standby**: This is similar to S2I, but provides more power saving by taking all non boot CPUs offline. Interruption from some devices can wake the system up.
- **Suspend-to-RAM** (**STR** or **S3**): All components of the system (except memory), including CPUs, go into low-power mode. The system state is maintained in memory until it is woken up by an interrupt from a limited set of devices. This mode requires hardware support.
- **Hibernation** or **suspend-to-disk**: This provides the greatest power saving, since all the system components can be powered off. When entering this state, a snapshot of the memory is taken and written to persistent storage (disk or flash). After that, the system can be turned off. As part of the boot process, on wake up, the saved snapshot is restored and the system resumes its work.

In this recipe, we will learn how to query the sleep modes supported on a particular system and how to switch to one of them.

How to do it...

In this recipe, we will use simple bash commands to access sleep modes supported by a Linux system running in **QEMU** (short for **quick emulator**).

1. Run the Raspberry Pi QEMU as described in `Chapter 3`, *Working with Different Architectures*.
2. Log in as user `pi`, using the password `raspberry`.
3. Run `sudo` to gain root access:

   ```
   $ sudo bash
   #
   ```

4. To get the list of supported sleep modes, run the following command:

   ```
   # cat /sys/power/state
   ```

5. Now switch to one of the supported modes:

   ```
   # echo freeze > /sys/power/state
   ```

6. The system goes to sleep, but we have not instructed it as to how to wake up. Close the QEMU window now.

How it works...

Power management is part of the Linux kernel; that is why we cannot use a Docker container to work with it. Docker virtualization is lightweight and uses the kernel of the host operating system.

We cannot use the real Raspberry Pi board either, because it does not provide any sleep modes at all because of hardware limitations. QEMU, however, provides full virtualization, including power management in the kernel we use to emulate Raspberry Pi.

Linux provides access to its power management functions through the sysfs interface. Applications can read and write text files in the `/sys/power` directory. Access to power-management functions is limited for the root user; that is why we need to get the root shell once we log into the system:

```
$ sudo bash
```

Now we can get the list of supported sleep modes. To do this, we read the
`/sys/power/state` file:

```
$ cat /sys/power/state
```

The file consists of a single line of text. Each word represents a sleep mode that is
supported, with the modes separated by spaces. We can see that the QEMU kernel supports
two modes: `freeze` and `mem`:

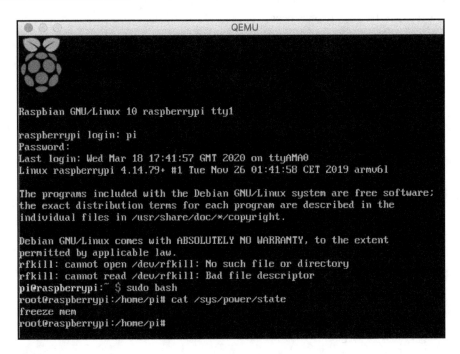

Freeze represents the S2I state we discussed in the preceding section. The meaning of `mem` is
defined by the content of the `/sys/power/mem_sleep` file. In our system, it contains only
`[s2idle]`, representing the same S2I state as `freeze`.

Let's switch our emulator to `freeze` mode. We write the word `freeze` to
`/sys/power/state`, and immediately the QEMU window turns black and frozen:

We were able to put the emulated Linux system to sleep, but cannot wake it up—there are no sources of interrupts that it can understand. We learned about different sleep modes and the kernel API to work with them. Based on the requirements of your embedded system, you can use these modes to reduce power consumption.

There's more...

More information about sleep modes can be found in the corresponding section of the *Linux Kernel Guide* at `https://www.kernel.org/doc/html/v4.19/admin-guide/pm/sleep-states.html`.

Waking up using RTC

In the preceding recipe, we were able to put our QEMU system to sleep but were not able to wake it up. We need a device that can send an interrupt to the system when most of its internal components are powered off.

The **RTC (Real-time clock)** is one such device. One of its functions is to keep the internal clock running when the system is off, and to do this, it has its own battery. RTC power consumption is similar to an electronic watch; it uses the same 3 V battery and can function on its power for years.

RTC can work as an alarm clock, sending an interrupt to the CPU at a given time. This makes it an ideal device for waking up a system on schedule.

In this recipe, we will learn how to wake up a Linux system at a specific time using the built-in RTC.

How to do it...

In this recipe, we will set a wake-up time to 1 minute in advance and put the system to sleep:

1. Log in to any Linux system that has an RTC clock—any Linux laptop can work. Unfortunately, Raspberry Pi does not have an onboard RTC, and cannot be woken up without additional hardware.

2. Get root permissions using `sudo`:

```
$ sudo bash
#
```

3. Instruct RTC to wake up the system in `1` minute:

```
# date '+%s' -d '+1 minute' > /sys/class/rtc/rtc0/wakealarm
```

4. Put the system to sleep:

```
# echo freeze > /sys/power/state
```

5. Wait for a minute. Your system will wake up.

How it works...

Like many other functions exposed by the Linux kernel, RTC can be accessed via sysfs interfaces. To set an alarm that will send a wake-up interrupt to the system, we need to write a **POSIX** (short for **Portable Operating System Interface**) timestamp to the `/sys/class/rtc/rtc0/wakealarm` file.

The POSIX timestamp, which we discuss in more detail in `Chapter 11`, *Time Points and Intervals*, is defined as the number of seconds elapsed since the Epoch, or 00:00 January 1, 1970.

Though we can write a program to read the current timestamp using the `time` function, add 60, and write the result to the `wakealarm` file, we can do this in one line using the Unix shell and the `date` command, which is available on any modern Unix system.

The date utility can not only format the current time using different formats, but it can also interpret dates and times in different formats.

We instruct `date` to interpret the time string `+1 minute` and use the formatting pattern `%s` to output it as a POSIX timestamp. We redirect its standard output to the `wakealarm` file, effectively passing it to the RTC driver:

```
date '+%s' -d '+1 minute' > /sys/class/rtc/rtc0/wakealarm
```

Now, knowing that in 60 seconds the alarm will go off, we can put the system to sleep. As in the previous recipe, we write the desired sleep mode to the `/sys/power/state` file:

```
# echo freeze > /sys/power/state
```

The system goes to sleep. You will notice that the screen turns off. If you connected to the Linux box using **Secure Shell** (**SSH**), the command line freezes. However, in one minute it wakes up, the screen turns on, and the Terminal is responsive again.

This technique is very efficient for tasks such as gathering data from sensors on a regular, infrequent basis, such as hourly or daily. The system spends most of the time powered off, waking up only to collect data and store it or send it to the cloud, and then it goes to sleep again.

There's more...

An alternative way to set RTC alarms is by using the `rtcwake` utility.

Controlling the autosuspend of USB devices

Turning an external device off is one of the most efficient ways to save power. It is, however, not always easy to understand when a device can be turned off safely. Peripheral devices such as network cards or memory cards can perform internal data processing; otherwise, the caching and powering off of the device at an arbitrary point can cause data loss.

To mitigate this problem, many external devices that are connected over the USB can switch themselves into low-power consumption mode when requested by the host. This way, they can perform all necessary steps to handle internal data safely before entering the suspended state.

Since Linux provides access to peripheral devices only through its API, it knows when a device is in use by applications and kernel services. If a device is not in use for a certain amount of time, the power-management system within the Linux kernel can instruct the device to enter power-saving mode automatically—explicit requests from userspace applications are not needed. This feature is called **autosuspend**. The kernel, however, allows applications to control the device's idle time, after which autosuspend kicks in.

In this recipe, we will learn how to enable autosuspend and modify the autosuspend interval for a particular USB device.

How to do it...

We are going to enable autosuspend and modify its autosuspend time for a USB device connected to your Linux box:

1. Log in to your Linux box (Raspberry Pi, Ubuntu, and Docker containers won't work).
2. Switch to the root account:

   ```
   $ sudo bash
   #
   ```

3. Get the current autosuspend status for all USB devices that are connected:

   ```
   # for f in /sys/bus/usb/devices/*/power/control; do echo "$f"; cat $f; done
   ```

4. Enable autosuspend for one of the devices:

   ```
   # echo auto > /sys/bus/usb/devices/1-1.2/power/control
   ```

5. Read the autosuspend interval for the device:

   ```
   # cat /sys/bus/usb/devices/1-1.2/power/autosuspend_delay_ms
   ```

6. Modify the autosuspend interval:

   ```
   # echo 5000 > /sys/bus/usb/devices/1-1.2/power/autosuspend_delay_ms
   ```

7. Check the current power mode of the device:

   ```
   # cat /sys/bus/usb/devices/1-1.2/power/runtime_status
   ```

   The same operations can be programmed in C++ using the standard file API.

How it works...

Linux exposes its power management API via the sysfs filesystem, which makes it possible to read the current status and modify the settings of any device using standard file read and write operations. As a result, we can use any programming language that supports basic file operations to control peripheral devices in Linux.

To simplify our examples, we are going to use the Unix shell, but exactly the same logic can be programmed in C++ when necessary.

First, we check the `autosuspend` settings for all attached USB devices. In Linux, the parameters of each USB device are exposed as a directory under the `/sysfs/bus/usb/devices/` folder. Each device directory, in turn, has a set of files that represent the device parameters. All parameters related to power management are grouped in the `power` subdirectory.

To read the status of `autosuspend`, we need to read the `control` file in the `power` directory of a device. Using Unix shell wildcard substitution, we can read this file for all USB devices:

```
# for f in /sys/bus/usb/devices/*/power/control; do echo "$f"; cat $f; done
```

For each directory matching the wildcard, we display the full path of the control file and its content. The result depends on the devices that are connected and may look like the following:

```
~ — igor@raspberrypi: ~ — ssh pi
root@raspberrypi:/home/igor# for f in /sys/bus/usb/devices/*/power/control; do e
cho "$f"; cat $f; done
/sys/bus/usb/devices/1-1.1/power/control
on
/sys/bus/usb/devices/1-1.2/power/control
on
/sys/bus/usb/devices/1-1/power/control
auto
/sys/bus/usb/devices/usb1/power/control
on
root@raspberrypi:/home/igor#
```

The reported status may either be autosuspend or `on`. If the status is reported as autosuspend, then the automatic power management is enabled; otherwise, the device is always kept on.

In our case, devices `usb1`, `1-1.1`, and `1-1.2` are on. Let's modify the configuration of `1-1.2` to use autosuspend. To do it, we just write a string `_auto_` to the corresponding `_control_` file.

```
# echo auto > /sys/bus/usb/devices/1-1.2/power/control
```

Running the read loop over all devices again shows that the 1-1.2 device is now in autosuspend mode:

```
 ~ — igor@raspberrypi: ~ — ssh pi
[root@raspberrypi:/home/igor# for f in /sys/bus/usb/devices/*/power/control; do e
cho "$f"; cat $f; done
/sys/bus/usb/devices/1-1.1/power/control
on
/sys/bus/usb/devices/1-1.2/power/control
on
/sys/bus/usb/devices/1-1/power/control
auto
/sys/bus/usb/devices/usb1/power/control
on
root@raspberrypi:/home/igor# echo auto > /sys/bus/usb/devices/1-1.2/power/contro
l
[root@raspberrypi:/home/igor# for f in /sys/bus/usb/devices/*/power/control; do e
cho "$f"; cat $f; done
/sys/bus/usb/devices/1-1.1/power/control
on
/sys/bus/usb/devices/1-1.2/power/control
auto
/sys/bus/usb/devices/1-1/power/control
auto
/sys/bus/usb/devices/usb1/power/control
on
root@raspberrypi:/home/igor# 
```

When is it going to be suspended? We can read this from the autosuspend_delay_ms file in the power subdirectory:

```
# cat /sys/bus/usb/devices/1-1.2/power/autosuspend_delay_ms
```

It shows that the device will be suspended after 2000 milliseconds of idleness:

```
 ~ — igor@raspberrypi: ~ — ssh pi
[root@raspberrypi:/home/igor# cat  /sys/bus/usb/devices/1-1.2/power/autosuspend_d
elay_ms
2000
root@raspberrypi:/home/igor# 
```

Let's change it to 5 seconds. We write 5000 in the autosuspend_delay_ms file:

```
# echo 5000 > /sys/bus/usb/devices/1-1.2/power/autosuspend_delay_ms
```

Reading it again shows that the new value is accepted:

```
●  ●  ●                    ⌂ ~ — igor@raspberrypi: ~ — ssh pi
root@raspberrypi:/home/igor# cat  /sys/bus/usb/devices/1-1.2/power/autosuspend_d
elay_ms
2000
root@raspberrypi:/home/igor# echo 5000 > /sys/bus/usb/devices/1-1.2/power/autosu
spend_delay_ms
root@raspberrypi:/home/igor# cat  /sys/bus/usb/devices/1-1.2/power/autosuspend_d
elay_ms
5000
root@raspberrypi:/home/igor#
```

Now let's check the current power state of the device. We can read it from the `runtime_status` file:

```
# cat /sys/bus/usb/devices/1-1.2/power/runtime_status
```

The status is reported as `active`:

```
●  ●  ●                    ⌂ ~ — igor@raspberrypi: ~ — ssh pi
root@raspberrypi:/home/igor# cat  /sys/bus/usb/devices/1-1.2/power/runtime_statu
s
active
root@raspberrypi:/home/igor#
```

> Please note that the kernel does not control the power state of devices directly; it only requests them to change the state. Even if a device is requested to switch into suspend mode, it may refuse to do it for various reasons—for example, it may not support the power-saving mode at all.

Accessing the power-management setting of any device through the sysfs interface is a powerful way to tweak the power consumption of the embedded system running Linux OS.

There's more...

There is no direct way to turn a USB device off immediately; however, in many cases, it can be done by writing 0 into the `autosuspend_delay_ms` file. A zero autosuspend interval is interpreted by the kernel as an immediate suspend request to the device.

More details on the USB power management in Linux can be found in the corresponding section of the Linux kernel documentation, available at `https://www.kernel.org/doc/html/v4.13/driver-api/usb/power-management.html`

Configuring CPU frequency

The CPU frequency is an important parameter of the system that determines its performance and its power consumption. The higher the frequency, the more instructions the CPU can perform per second. But it comes with a cost. Higher frequency implies a higher power consumption that, in turn, means more heat that needs to be dissipated to avoid the processor overheating.

Modern processors are able to use different operating frequencies depending on their load. For computationally intense tasks, they use their maximum frequency to achieve the maximum performance, but when the system is mostly idle, they switch to lower frequencies to reduce both the power consumption and thermal impact.

Proper frequency selection is managed by the operating system. In this recipe, we will learn how to set the CPU frequency range and select a frequency governor in Linux to fine-tune the CPU frequency to your needs.

How to do it...

We are going to use simple shell commands to adjust the parameters of CPU frequency on a Raspberry PI box:

1. Log in to a Raspberry Pi or another nonvirtualized Linux system.
2. Switch to the root account:

   ```
   $ sudo bash
   #
   ```

3. Get the current frequency of all CPU cores available in the system:

   ```
   # cat /sys/devices/system/cpu/*/cpufreq/scaling_cur_freq
   ```

4. Get all of the frequencies supported by the CPU:

   ```
   # cat
   /sys/devices/system/cpu/cpu0/cpufreq/scaling_available_frequencies
   ```

5. Get the available CPU-frequency governors:

   ```
   # cat
   /sys/devices/system/cpu/cpu0/cpufreq/scaling_available_governors
   ```

6. Now let's check which frequency governor is currently in use:

```
# cat /sys/devices/system/cpu/cpu0/cpufreq/scaling_governor
```

7. Adjust the minimum frequency of the CPU to the highest supported:

```
# echo 1200000 >
/sys/devices/system/cpu/cpu0/cpufreq/scaling_min_freq
```

8. Display the current frequencies again to understand the effect:

```
# cat /sys/devices/system/cpu/*/cpufreq/scaling_cur_freq
```

9. Adjust the minimum frequency to the lowest supported:

```
# echo 600000 >
/sys/devices/system/cpu/cpu0/cpufreq/scaling_min_fre
```

10. Now let's check how the CPU frequency depends on the governor in use. Select a `performance` governor and get the current frequency:

```
# echo performance >
/sys/devices/system/cpu/cpu0/cpufreq/scaling_governor
# cat /sys/devices/system/cpu/*/cpufreq/scaling_cur_freq
```

11. Select the `powersave` governor and observe the result:

```
# echo powersave >
/sys/devices/system/cpu/cpu0/cpufreq/scaling_governor
# cat /sys/devices/system/cpu/*/cpufreq/scaling_cur_freq
```

You can use a regular file API to implement the same logic in C++.

How it works...

Similar to USB power management, the CPU-frequency management system API is exposed via sysfs. We can read and modify its parameters as regular text files.

We can find all settings related to CPU cores under the `/sys/devices/system/cpu/` directory. Configuration parameters are grouped by CPU cores in subdirectories named after each code index, such as `cpu1`, `cpu2`, and so on.

We are interested in several parameters related to CPU frequencies management that live in the `cpufreq` subdirectory of each core. Let's read the current frequency of all available cores:

```
# cat /sys/devices/system/cpu/*/cpufreq/scaling_cur_freq
```

We can see that all cores have the same frequency, 600 MHz (the `cpufreq` subsystem uses KHz as a measurement unit for frequency):

```
● ● ●                        ⬆ ~ — igor@raspberrypi: ~ — ssh pi
[root@raspberrypi:/home/igor# cat /sys/devices/system/cpu/*/cpufreq/scaling_cur_f]
req
600000
600000
600000
600000
root@raspberrypi:/home/igor# ▮
```

Next, we figure out all the frequencies supported by our CPU:

```
# cat /sys/devices/system/cpu/cpu0/cpufreq/scaling_available_frequencies
```

The ARM processor of Raspberry Pi 3 supports only two frequencies, 600 MHz and 1.2 GHz:

```
● ● ●                        ⬆ ~ — igor@raspberrypi: ~ — ssh pi
[root@raspberrypi:/home/igor# cat /sys/devices/system/cpu/*/cpufreq/scaling_cur_f]
req
600000
600000
600000
600000
[root@raspberrypi:/home/igor# cat /sys/devices/system/cpu/cpu0/cpufreq/scaling_av]
ailable_frequencies
600000 1200000
root@raspberrypi:/home/igor# ▮
```

We cannot set the desired frequency directly. Linux manages the CPU frequencies internally through a so-called **governor**, and only allows us to adjust two parameters:

- A range of frequencies available for the governor
- The type of governor

Though this looks like a limitation, these two parameters give enough flexibility to implement fairly complex policies. Let's check how the modification of both of these parameters affects the CPU frequency.

First, let's figure out which governors are supported and which is currently in use:

```
root@raspberrypi:/home/igor# cat /sys/devices/system/cpu/*/cpufreq/scaling_cur_f
req
600000
600000
600000
600000
root@raspberrypi:/home/igor# cat /sys/devices/system/cpu/cpu0/cpufreq/scaling_av
ailable_frequencies
600000 1200000
root@raspberrypi:/home/igor# cat /sys/devices/system/cpu/cpu0/cpufreq/scaling_av
ailable_governors
conservative ondemand userspace powersave performance schedutil
root@raspberrypi:/home/igor# cat /sys/devices/system/cpu/cpu0/cpufreq/scaling_go
vernor
ondemand
root@raspberrypi:/home/igor#
```

The current governor is `ondemand`. It adjusts the frequency based on the system load. At the moment, the Raspberry Pi board is pretty idle, and so it uses the lowest frequency, 600 MHz. But what if we make the lowest frequency equal to the highest frequency?

```
# echo 1200000 > /sys/devices/system/cpu/cpu0/cpufreq/scaling_min_freq
```

After we updated the `scaling_min_freq` parameter of one core, the frequency of all cores was changed to the maximum:

```
● ● ●                    ⬆ ~ — igor@raspberrypi: ~ — ssh pi
[root@raspberrypi:/home/igor# cat /sys/devices/system/cpu/*/cpufreq/scaling_cur_f]
req
600000
600000
600000
600000
[root@raspberrypi:/home/igor# cat /sys/devices/system/cpu/cpu0/cpufreq/scaling_av]
ailable_frequencies
600000 1200000
[root@raspberrypi:/home/igor# cat /sys/devices/system/cpu/cpu0/cpufreq/scaling_av]
ailable_governors
conservative ondemand userspace powersave performance schedutil
[root@raspberrypi:/home/igor# cat /sys/devices/system/cpu/cpu0/cpufreq/scaling_go]
vernor
ondemand
[root@raspberrypi:/home/igor# echo 1200000 > /sys/devices/system/cpu/cpu0/cpufreq]
/scaling_min_freq
[root@raspberrypi:/home/igor# cat /sys/devices/system/cpu/*/cpufreq/scaling_cur_f]
req
1200000
1200000
1200000
1200000
root@raspberrypi:/home/igor# ▮
```

Since all four cores belong to the same CPU, we cannot change their frequencies independently; changing the frequency of one core affects all cores. We can, however, control the frequencies of separate CPUs independently.

Now we revert the minimum frequency back to 600 MHz and change the governor. Instead of the `ondemand` governor that adjusts the frequency, we selected the `performance` governor, aiming to deliver maximal performance unconditionally:

```
echo performance > /sys/devices/system/cpu/cpu0/cpufreq/scaling_g;overnor
```

It's no surprise that it raised the frequency up to the maximum supported frequency:

On the other hand, the `powersave` governor aims to save as much power as possible as it always sticks to the lowest-supported frequency regardless of the load:

As you can see, adjusting both the frequency ranges and the frequency governor allows you to flexibly fine-tune the frequency depending on the nature of the system and reduce the power consumed by the CPU.

There's more...

Besides `ondemand`, `performance`, and `powersave`, there are other governors that provide even more flexible tuning of CPU frequency from userspace applications. You can find more details about the available governors and their properties in the corresponding section of Linux CPUFreq at `https://www.kernel.org/doc/Documentation/cpu-freq/governors.txt`

Using events for waiting

Waiting is an extremely common pattern in software development. Applications have to wait for user input or for data to be ready for processing. Embedded programs communicate with peripheral devices and need to know when data can be read from the device and when the device is ready to accept data.

Often, developers use variations of the polling technique for waiting. They check a device-specific availability flag in a loop, and when it is set to true by the device, they proceed with reading or writing data.

Though this approach is easy to implement, it is inefficient from the perspective of power consumption. When a processor is constantly busy looping around a flag check, it cannot be put into a more power-efficient mode by the operating system power manager. Based on the load, the Linux `ondemand` frequency governor that we discussed earlier can even decide to increase the CPU frequency despite the fact that it is a wait in disguise. Additionally, polling requests may prevent the target device or the device bus from staying in power-saving mode until data is ready.

That is why instead of polling programs that care about energy efficiency, it should rely on interrupts and events generated by the operating system.

In this recipe, we will learn how to use the operating system events to wait for a specific USB device to be connected.

How to do it...

We are going to create an application that can monitor USB devices and wait until a specific device appears:

1. In your working ~/test directory create a subdirectory called udev.
2. Use your favorite text editor to create a udev.cpp file in the udev subdirectory.
3. Put the essential includes and the namespace definition into the udev.cpp file:

```cpp
#include <iostream>
#include <functional>

#include <libudev.h>
#include <poll.h>

namespace usb {
```

4. Now, let's define the Device class:

```cpp
class Device {
  struct udev_device *dev{0};

  public:
    Device(struct udev_device* dev) : dev(dev) {
    }

    Device(const Device& other) : dev(other.dev) {
      udev_device_ref(dev);
    }

    ~Device() {
        udev_device_unref(dev);
    }

    std::string action() const {
        return udev_device_get_action(dev);
     }

    std::string attr(const char* name) const {
      const char* val = udev_device_get_sysattr_value(dev,
            name);
      return val ? val : "";
    }
};
```

5. After that, add the definition of the `Monitor` class:

```cpp
class Monitor {
  struct udev_monitor *mon;

public:
  Monitor() {
    struct udev* udev = udev_new();
    mon = udev_monitor_new_from_netlink(udev, "udev");
    udev_monitor_filter_add_match_subsystem_devtype(
        mon, "usb", NULL);
    udev_monitor_enable_receiving(mon);
  }

  Monitor(const Monitor& other) = delete;

  ~Monitor() {
    udev_monitor_unref(mon);
  }

  Device wait(std::function<bool(const Device&)> process) {
    struct pollfd fds[1];
    fds[0].events = POLLIN;
    fds[0].fd = udev_monitor_get_fd(mon);

    while (true) {
        int ret = poll(fds, 1, -1);
        if (ret < 0) {
          throw std::system_error(errno,
              std::system_category(),
              "Poll failed");
        }
        if (ret) {
          Device d(udev_monitor_receive_device(mon));
          if (process(d)) {
            return d;
          };
        }
    }
  }
};
};
```

6. After `Device` and `Monitor` are defined in the `usb` namespace, add a simple `main` function that shows how to use them:

```
int main() {
  usb::Monitor mon;
  usb::Device d = mon.wait([](auto& d) {
    auto id = d.attr("idVendor") + ":" +
              d.attr("idProduct");
    auto produce = d.attr("product");
    std::cout << "Check [" << id << "] action: "
              << d.action() << std::endl;
    return d.action() == "bind" &&
           id == "8086:0808";
  });
  std::cout << d.attr("product")
            << " connected, uses up to "
            << d.attr("bMaxPower") << std::endl;
  return 0;
}
```

7. Create a `CMakeLists.txt` file containing the build rules for our program:

```
cmake_minimum_required(VERSION 3.5.1)
project(udev)
add_executable(usb udev.cpp)
target_link_libraries(usb udev)
```

8. Copy the `udev` directory into your home directory on your Linux box using `ssh`.

9. Log in to your Linux box, change the directory to `udev`, and build the program using `cmake`:

$cd ~/udev; cmake. && make

You can now build and run the application.

How it works...

To get system notifications about events on USB devices, we are using a library called `libudev`. It provides only a plain C interface, and so we created simple C++ wrappers to make coding easier.

For our wrapper classes, we declared a `namespace` named `usb`:

```
namespace usb {
```

It contains two classes. The first class is `Device`, which gives us a C++ interface to a low-level `libudev` object called `udev_device`.

We defined a constructor that created an instance of `Device` from a `udev_device` pointer and a destructor to release the `udev_device`. Internally, `libudev` uses reference counting for its object, and so our destructor calls a function to decrease the reference count of the `udev_device`:

```
~Device() {
    udev_device_unref(dev);
}

Device(const Device& other) : dev(other.dev) {
  udev_device_ref(dev);
}
```

This way, we can copy the `Device` instances without memory or file descriptor leaks.

Besides the constructors and the destructor, the `Device` class has only two methods: `action` and `attr`. The `action` method returns the most recent USB device action:

```
std::string action() const {
    return udev_device_get_action(dev);
  }
```

The `attr` method returns any sysfs attribute associated with the device:

```
std::string attr(const char* name) const {
  const char* val = udev_device_get_sysattr_value(dev,
        name);
  return val ? val : "";
}
```

The `Monitor` class also has a constructor and a destructor, but we made it noncopyable by disabling the copy constructor:

```
Monitor(const Monitor& other) = delete;
```

The constructor initializes the `libudev` instance using a static variable to ensure it is initialized only once:

```
struct udev* udev = udev_new();
```

It also sets up the monitoring filter and enables monitoring:

```
udev_monitor_filter_add_match_subsystem_devtype(
    mon, "usb", NULL);
udev_monitor_enable_receiving(mon);
```

The `wait` method contains the most important monitoring logic. It accepts a function-like `process` object that is called each time an event is detected:

```
Device wait(std::function<bool(const Device&)> process) {
```

The function should return `true` if the event and the device it originates from are what we need; otherwise, it returns `false` to indicate that `wait` should keep working.

Internally, the `wait` function creates a file descriptor that is used to deliver device events to the program:

```
fds[0].fd = udev_monitor_get_fd(mon);
```

Then it sets up the monitoring loop. Despite its name, the `poll` function does not check the status of devices constantly; it waits for events on the specified file descriptors. We pass −1 as a timeout, indicating that we intend to wait for events forever:

```
int ret = poll(fds, 1, -1);
```

The `poll` function returns only in the case of an error or a new USB event. We handle an error condition by throwing an exception:

```
if (ret < 0) {
  throw std::system_error(errno,
      std::system_category(),
      "Poll failed");
}
```

For each event, we create a new instance of `Device` and pass it to the `process`. If `process` returns `true`, we exit the wait loop, returning the instance of `Device` to the caller:

```
Device d(udev_monitor_receive_device(mon));
if (process(d)) {
  return d;
};
```

Let's see how we can use these classes in our application. In the `main` function, we create an instance of `Monitor` and invoke its `wait` function. We use a lambda function to process each action:

```
usb::Device d = mon.wait([](auto& d) {
```

In the lambda function, we print information about all of the events:

```
std::cout << "Check [" << id << "] action: "
          << d.action() << std::endl;
```

We also check for the specific action and device `id`:

```
return d.action() == "bind" &&
       id == "8086:0808";
```

Once found, we display information about its function and power requirements:

```
std::cout << d.attr("product")
          << " connected, uses up to "
          << d.attr("bMaxPower") << std::endl;
```

Running this application initially does not produce any output:

```
⬤ ◯ ◯              ⌂ ~ — igor@raspberrypi: ~/udev — ssh pi
igor@raspberrypi:~/udev $ ./usb
```

However, once we insert a USB device (a USB microphone in my case), we can see the following output:

```
⬤ ◯ ◯              ⌂ ~ — igor@raspberrypi: ~/udev — ssh pi
igor@raspberrypi:~/udev $ ./usb
Check [8086:0808] action: add
Check [:] action: add
Check [:] action: add
Check [:] action: add
Check [:] action: bind
Check [:] action: bind
Check [:] action: bind
Check [8086:0808] action: bind
Should not
USB PnP Sound Device connected, uses up to 100mA
igor@raspberrypi:~/udev $
```

The application can wait for a specific USB device and handle it after it is connected. It does this without busy looping, relying on the information provided by the operating system. As a result, the application spends most of the time sleeping while the `poll` call is blocked by the operating system.

There's more...

There are a number of C++ wrappers for `libudev`. You can use one of these or create your own using the code from the recipe as a starting point.

Profiling power consumption with PowerTOP

In complex operating systems such as Linux that run multiple userspace and kernel space services and control many peripheral devices at once, it is not always easy to find components that can cause excessive power drain. Even when inefficiency is identified, fixing it may be difficult.

One of the solutions is to use a power profiler tool, such as PowerTOP. It can diagnose issues with power consumption in a Linux system and allows the user to tweak system parameters that can save power.

In this recipe, we will learn how to install and use PowerTOP on a Raspberry Pi system.

How to do it...

In this recipe, we will run PowerTOP in interactive mode and analyze its output:

1. Log in to your Raspberry Pi system as user `pi`, using the password `raspberry`.
2. Run `sudo` to gain root access:

   ```
   $ sudo bash
   #
   ```

3. Install PowerTOP from the repository:

   ```
   # apt-get install powertop
   ```

4. Staying in a root shell, run PowerTOP:

```
# powertop
```

The PowerTOP UI will show up in your Terminal. Use the *Tab* key to navigate between its screens.

How it works...

PowerTOP is a tool created by Intel to diagnose power issues in a Linux system. It is part of the Raspbian distribution and can be installed using the `apt-get` command:

```
# apt-get install powertop
```

When we run it without parameters, it starts in an interactive mode and lists all of the processes and kernel tasks, ordered by their power usage and the frequency of the events they generate. As we discussed in the *Using events for waiting* recipe, the more often a program has to wake up the processor, the less energy efficient it is:

```
● ◉ ◉                    ~ — igor@raspberrypi: ~ — ssh pi
PowerTOP 2.8       Overview    Idle stats   Frequency stats    Device stats    Tunab

Summary: 0.0 wakeups/second,  0.0 GPU ops/seconds, 0.0 VFS ops/sec and 9.2% CPU

              Usage        Events/s    Category     Description
          53.5 ms/s       0.00        Process      powertop
          11.7 ms/s       0.00        Interrupt    [56] dwc_otg_hcd:usb1
           6.0 ms/s       0.00        Interrupt    [56] dwc_otg
           2.9 ms/s       0.00        Process      lxpanel --profile LXDE-pi
           3.8 ms/s       0.00        Interrupt    [56] dwc_otg_pcd
           2.0 ms/s       0.00        Process      [migration/0]
           1.8 ms/s       0.00        Process      [migration/3]
           1.7 ms/s       0.00        Process      [migration/2]
           1.5 ms/s       0.00        Interrupt    [7] sched(softirq)
           0.8 ms/s       0.00        Interrupt    [162] arch_timer
         685.0 µs/s       0.00        Interrupt    [9] RCU(softirq)
         591.7 µs/s       0.00        Process      /usr/lib/xorg/Xorg :0 -se
         583.7 µs/s       0.00        Process      [migration/1]
         394.6 µs/s       0.00        Process      [kworker/u8:1]
         340.6 µs/s       0.00        Timer        txdone_hrtimer
         309.2 µs/s       0.00        Interrupt    [6] tasklet(softirq)
         308.8 µs/s       0.00        Timer        tick_sched_timer

<ESC> Exit | <TAB> / <Shift + TAB> Navigate |
```

Using the *Tab* key, we can switch to other reporting modes. For example, **Device stats** shows how much energy or CPU time the devices consume:

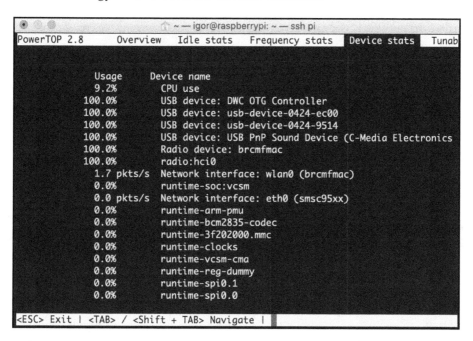

Another interesting tab is **Tunab**. PowerTOP can check a number of settings that affect power consumption and flags those that are suboptimal:

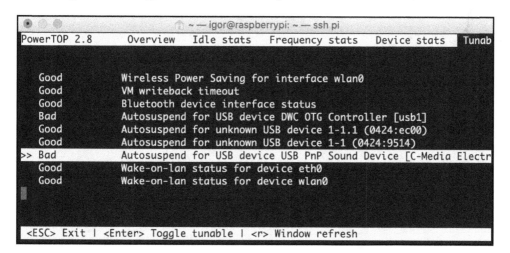

As you can see, two of the USB devices are marked as Bad because they do not use autosuspend. By pressing the *Enter* key, PowerTOP enables autosuspend, displaying a command line that can be used from a script to make it permanent. After autosuspend is enabled, the tunable status changes to Good:

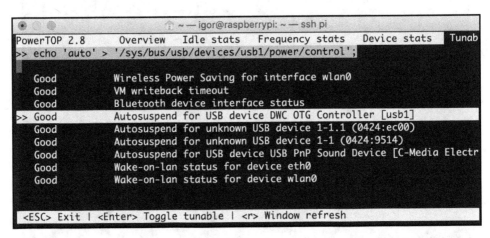

A number of system parameters can be tuned to save power. Sometimes they are obvious, like using autosuspend on USB devices. Sometimes they are not, such as using timeout on the kernel that is used to flush the file cache to disk. Using power diagnostic and optimization tools such as PowerTOP helps you to tune your system for maximum power efficiency.

There's more...

Besides its interactive mode, PowerTOP has other modes to help you optimize power use, such as calibration, workload, and auto-tune. More information about PowerTOP features, usage scenarios, and the interpretation of results can be found in the *PowerTOP User Guide* at https://01.org/sites/default/files/page/powertop_users_guide_201412.pdf.

11
Time Points and Intervals

Embedded applications handle events and control processes happening in the physical world—that is why the correct handling of time and delays is crucial for them. Switching traffic lights; generation of sound tones; synchronization of data from multiple sensors—all these tasks rely on proper time measurements.

Plain C does not provide any standard functions to work with time. It is expected that application developers will use a time API specific for the target operating system—Windows, Linux, or macOS. For bare-metal embedded systems, developers have to create custom functions to work with time, based on a low-level timer API specific for the target platform. As a result, the code is hard to port to other platforms.

To overcome the portability issue, C++ (starting with C++11) defines data types and functions to work with time and time intervals. This API, referenced as an `std::chrono` library, helps developers work with time in a uniform way in any environment and on any target platform.

In this chapter, we will learn how to work with timestamps, time intervals, and delays in our applications. We will discuss some of the common pitfalls related to time management, along with the proper workarounds for them.

We will cover the following topics:

- Exploring the C++ Chrono library
- Measuring time intervals
- Working with delays
- Using the monotonic clock
- Using **Portable Operating System Interface (POSIX)** timestamps

Using these recipes, you will be able to write portable code for time handling that works on any embedded platform.

Exploring the C++ Chrono library

Starting from C++11, the C++ Chrono library provides standardized data types and functions to work with clocks, time points, and time intervals. In this recipe, we will explore the basic capabilities of the Chrono library, and learn how to work with time points and intervals.

We will also learn how to use C++ literals for a more readable representation of time intervals.

How to do it...

We are going to create a simple application that creates three time points and compares them to each other.

1. In your `~/test` working directory, create a subdirectory called `chrono`.
2. Use your favorite text editor to create a `chrono.cpp` file in the `chrono` subdirectory.
3. Put the following code snippet into the file:

```
#include <iostream>
#include <chrono>

using namespace std::chrono_literals;

int main() {
   auto a = std::chrono::system_clock::now();
   auto b = a + 1s;
   auto c = a + 200ms;

   std::cout << "a < b ? " << (a < b ? "yes" : "no") << std::endl;
   std::cout << "a < c ? " << (a < c ? "yes" : "no") << std::endl;
   std::cout << "b < c ? " << (b < c ? "yes" : "no") << std::endl;

   return 0;
}
```

4. Create a `CMakeLists.txt` file containing build rules for our program:

```
cmake_minimum_required(VERSION 3.5.1)
project(chrono)
add_executable(chrono chrono.cpp)

set(CMAKE_SYSTEM_NAME Linux)
```

```
set(CMAKE_SYSTEM_PROCESSOR arm)

SET(CMAKE_CXX_FLAGS "--std=c++14")
set(CMAKE_CXX_COMPILER /usr/bin/arm-linux-gnueabi-g++)
```

You can now build and run the application.

How it works...

Our application creates three different time points. The first one is created using the now function of the system clock:

```
auto a = std::chrono::system_clock::now();
```

Two others are derived from the first one by adding fixed time intervals of 1 second and 200 milliseconds:

```
auto b = a + 1s;
auto c = a + 200ms;
```

Please note how we specified the time units next to the numeric values. We used a feature called C++ literals. The Chrono library defines such literals for basic time units. To use these definitions, we added the following:

```
using namespace std::chrono_literals;
```

This was added before our main function.

Next, we compared these time points to each other:

```
std::cout << "a < b ? " << (a < b ? "yes" : "no") << std::endl;
std::cout << "a < c ? " << (a < c ? "yes" : "no") << std::endl;
std::cout << "b < c ? " << (b < c ? "yes" : "no") << std::endl;
```

When we run the application, we see the following output:

```
user@3324138cc2c7: /mnt/chrono — bash
user@3324138cc2c7:/mnt/chrono$ ./chrono
a < b ? yes
a < c ? yes
b < c ? no
user@3324138cc2c7:/mnt/chrono$
```

As expected, time point a is earlier than both b and c, where time point c—which is a + 200 milliseconds—is earlier than b (a + 1 second). String literals help write more readable code, and C++ Chrono provides a rich set of functions to work with time. We will learn how to work with them in the next recipes.

There's more...

Information about all data types, templates, and functions defined in the Chrono library can be found in the Chrono reference at `https://en.cppreference.com/w/cpp/chrono`

Measuring time intervals

Every embedded application interacting with peripheral hardware or responding to external events has to deal with timeouts and reaction times. To do this properly, developers need the ability to measure time intervals with sufficient precision.

The C++ Chrono library provides an `std::chrono::duration` templated class for handling durations of arbitrary span and precision. In this recipe, we will learn how to use this class to measure the time interval between two timestamps and check it against a reference duration.

How to do it...

Our application will measure the duration of simple console output and compare it to the previous values in the loop.

1. In your `~/test` working directory, create a subdirectory called `intervals`.
2. Use your favorite text editor to create an `intervals.cpp` file in the `intervals` subdirectory.
3. Copy the following code snippet into the `intervals.cpp` file:

```
#include <iostream>
#include <chrono>

int main() {
  std::chrono::duration<double, std::micro> prev;
  for (int i = 0; i < 10; i++) {
    auto start = std::chrono::steady_clock::now();
    std::cout << i << ": ";
```

```
auto end = std::chrono::steady_clock::now();
std::chrono::duration<double, std::micro> delta = end - start;
std::cout << "output duration is " << delta.count() <<" us";
if (i) {
  auto diff = (delta - prev).count();
  if (diff >= 0) {
    std::cout << ", " << diff << " us slower";
  } else {
    std::cout << ", " << -diff << " us faster";
  }
}
std::cout << std::endl;
prev = delta;
}
return 0;
}
```

4. Finally, create a CMakeLists.txt file containing build rules for our program:

```
cmake_minimum_required(VERSION 3.5.1)
project(interval)
add_executable(interval interval.cpp)

set(CMAKE_SYSTEM_NAME Linux)
set(CMAKE_SYSTEM_PROCESSOR arm)

SET(CMAKE_CXX_FLAGS "--std=c++11")
set(CMAKE_CXX_COMPILER /usr/bin/arm-linux-gnueabi-g++)
```

You can now build and run the application.

How it works...

On each iteration of the application loop, we measure the performance of one output operation. To do so, we capture a timestamp before the operation and another timestamp after the operation is complete:

```
auto start = std::chrono::steady_clock::now();
std::cout << i << ": ";
auto end = std::chrono::steady_clock::now();
```

We use C++11 `auto` to let the compiler infer data types for the timestamps. Now, we need to calculate a time interval between these timestamps. Subtracting one timestamp from another does the job. We explicitly define the result variable as an `std::chrono::duration` class that tracks a microsecond in a `double` value:

```
std::chrono::duration<double, std::micro> delta = end - start;
```

We use another `duration` variable of the same type to hold the previous value. On each iteration except the first one, we calculate the difference between these two durations:

```
auto diff = (delta - prev).count();
```

The duration and the difference are printed to the Terminal on each iteration. When we run the application, we get this output:

```
user@3324138cc2c7: /mnt/interval — bash
user@3324138cc2c7:/mnt/interval$ ./interval
0: output duration is 32.3 us
1: output duration is 6.3 us, 26 us faster
2: output duration is 4.2 us, 2.1 us faster
3: output duration is 4.3 us, 0.1 us slower
4: output duration is 4.4 us, 0.1 us slower
5: output duration is 4.2 us, 0.2 us faster
6: output duration is 4.1 us, 0.1 us faster
7: output duration is 4.2 us, 0.1 us slower
8: output duration is 4.2 us, 0 us slower
9: output duration is 3.8 us, 0.4 us faster
user@3324138cc2c7:/mnt/interval$
```

As we can see, modern C++ provides convenient ways of handling time intervals in applications. Thanks to overloaded operators, it is easy to get a duration between two time points and add, subtract, or compare durations.

There's more...

Starting from C++20, the Chrono library supports direct writing of durations into output streams and parsing durations from input streams. There is no need to serialize durations into integer or float values explicitly. This makes handling durations even more convenient for C++ developers.

Working with delays

Periodic data processing is a common pattern in many embedded applications. The code does not need to work all the time. If we know in advance when processing is needed, an application or a worker thread can be inactive most of the time, waking up and processing data only when needed. It saves power consumption or lets other applications running on the device use the CPU resources when the application is idle.

There are several techniques to organize periodic processing. A worker thread that runs a loop with a delay in it is one of the simplest and most common of them.

C++ provides standard functions to add a delay to the current execution thread. In this recipe, we will learn two ways of adding a delay into an application and discuss their pros and cons.

How to do it...

We are going to create an application with two processing loops. These loops use different functions to pause the execution of the current thread.

1. In your ~/test working directory, create a subdirectory called delays.
2. Use your favorite text editor to create a delays.cpp file in the delays subdirectory.
3. Let's start by adding a first function, sleep_for, along with the necessary inclusions:

```
#include <iostream>
#include <chrono>
#include <thread>

using namespace std::chrono_literals;

void sleep_for(int count, auto delay) {
  for (int i = 0; i < count; i++) {
    auto start = std::chrono::system_clock::now();
    std::this_thread::sleep_for(delay);
    auto end = std::chrono::system_clock::now();
    std::chrono::duration<double, std::milli> delta = end - start;
    std::cout << "Sleep for: " << delta.count() << std::endl;
  }
}
```

4. It is followed by a second function, `sleep_until`:

```
void sleep_until(int count,
                 std::chrono::milliseconds delay) {
  auto wake_up = std::chrono::system_clock::now();
  for (int i = 0; i < 10; i++) {
    wake_up += delay;
    auto start = std::chrono::system_clock::now();
    std::this_thread::sleep_until(wake_up);
    auto end = std::chrono::system_clock::now();
    std::chrono::duration<double, std::milli> delta = end - start;
    std::cout << "Sleep until: " << delta.count() << std::endl;
  }
}
```

5. Next, add a simple `main` function that invokes them:

```
int main() {
  sleep_for(10, 100ms);
  sleep_until(10, 100ms);
  return 0;
}
```

6. Finally, create a `CMakeLists.txt` file containing the build rules for our program:

```
cmake_minimum_required(VERSION 3.5.1)
project(delays)
add_executable(delays delays.cpp)

set(CMAKE_SYSTEM_NAME Linux)
set(CMAKE_SYSTEM_PROCESSOR arm)

SET(CMAKE_CXX_FLAGS "--std=c++14")
set(CMAKE_CXX_COMPILER /usr/bin/arm-linux-gnueabi-g++)
```

You can now build and run the application.

How it works...

In our application, we created two functions, `sleep_for` and `sleep_until`. They are almost identical, except `sleep_for` uses `std::this_thread::sleep_for` to add a delay, while `sleep_until` uses `std::this_thread::sleep_until`.

Let's take a closer look at the `sleep_for` function. It takes two parameters—`count` and `delay`. The first parameter defines a number of iterations in its loop, and the second parameter specifies a delay. We use `auto` as a data type of the `delay` parameter, letting C++ infer the actual data type for us.

The function body consists of a single loop:

```
for (int i = 0; i < count; i++) {
```

On each iteration, we run the `delay` and measure its actual duration by taking timestamps before and after the `delay`. The `std::this_thread::sleep_for` function accepts a time interval as a parameter:

```
auto start = std::chrono::system_clock::now();
std::this_thread::sleep_for(delay);
auto end = std::chrono::system_clock::now();
```

The actual delay is measured in milliseconds, and we use a `double` value as a milliseconds counter:

```
std::chrono::duration<double, std::milli> delta = end - start;
```

The `wait_until` function is only slightly different. It uses the `std::current_thred::wait_until` function, which accepts a time point to wake up instead of a time interval. We introduce an additional `wake_up` variable to track the wake-up time point:

```
auto wake_up = std::chrono::system_clock::now();
```

Initially, it is set to the current time, and on each iteration, it adds the delay passed as a function parameter to its value:

```
wake_up += delay;
```

The rest of the function is identical to the `sleep_for` implementation, except the `delay` function:

```
std::this_thread::sleep_until(wake_up);
```

We run both functions, using the same number of iterations and the same delay. Please note how we use C++ string literals to pass milliseconds into the functions to make the code more readable. To use string literals, we added the following:

```
sleep_for(10, 100ms);
sleep_until(10, 100ms);
```

This was done above the function definitions, like so:

```
using namespace std::chrono_literals;
```

Do different delay functions make any difference? We use the same delay in both implementations, after all. Let's run the code and compare the results:

```
user@3324138cc2c7: /mnt/delays — bash
user@3324138cc2c7:/mnt/delays$ ./delays
Sleep for: 102.319
Sleep for: 100.342
Sleep for: 101.227
Sleep for: 101.148
Sleep for: 100.99
Sleep for: 100.499
Sleep for: 101.072
Sleep for: 100.521
Sleep for: 100.908
Sleep for: 102.753
Sleep until: 100.573
Sleep until: 99.8844
Sleep until: 100.116
Sleep until: 99.597
Sleep until: 100.062
Sleep until: 100.196
Sleep until: 99.8845
Sleep until: 99.672
Sleep until: 104.222
Sleep until: 97.3192
user@3324138cc2c7:/mnt/delays$
```

Interestingly, we can see that all actual delays for `sleep_for` are greater than 100 milliseconds, while some results for `sleep_until` fall below this value. Our first function, `delay_for`, does not account for the time needed to print data to the console. `sleep_for` is a good choice when you know exactly how long you need to wait. However, if your goal is to wake up with specific periodicity, `sleep_until` might be a better choice.

There's more...

There are other subtle differences between `sleep_for` and `sleep_until`. The system timer is often not too precise and might be adjusted by time synchronization services such as **Network Time Protocol daemon (ntpd)**. These clock adjustments do not affect `sleep_for`, but `sleep_until` takes them into account. Use it if your application relies on a specific time rather than a time interval; for example, if you need to redraw the digits on a clock display every second.

Using the monotonic clock

The C++ Chrono library provides three types of clocks:

- System clock
- Steady clock
- High-resolution clock

The high-resolution clock is often implemented as an alias of the system clock or the steady clock. The system clock and the steady clock, however, are quite different.

The system clock reflects the system time and hence is not monotonic. It can be adjusted at any time by time synchronization services such as **Network Time Protocol (NTP)**, and, as a result, can even go backward.

This makes the system clock a poor choice for dealing with precise durations. The steady clock is monotonic; it is never adjusted and never goes backward. This property has its cost—it is not related to wall clock time and is usually represented as the time since the last reboot.

The steady clock should not be used for persistent timestamps that need to remain valid after reboots—for example, serialized into a file or saved into a database. Also, the steady clock should not be used for any time calculations involving time from different sources, such as remote systems or peripheral devices.

In this recipe, we will learn how to use the steady clock to implement a simple software watchdog. When running a background worker thread, it is important to know if it works correctly or hangs because of a coding error or an unresponsive peripheral device. The thread periodically updates a timestamp, while a monitoring routine compares the timestamp with the current time, and, if the threshold is exceeded, performs a certain recovery action.

How to do it...

In our application, we are going to create a simple iterative function that runs in the
background, along with the monitoring loop running in the main thread.

1. In your ~/test working directory, create a subdirectory called monotonic.
2. Use your favorite text editor to create a monotonic.cpp file in
   the monotonic subdirectory.
3. Let's add headers and define global variables used by our routines:

```cpp
#include <iostream>
#include <chrono>
#include <atomic>
#include <mutex>
#include <thread>

auto touched = std::chrono::steady_clock::now();
std::mutex m;
std::atomic_bool ready{ false };
```

4. They are followed by the code of the background worker thread routine:

```cpp
void Worker() {
  for (int i = 0; i < 10; i++) {
    std::this_thread::sleep_for(
        std::chrono::milliseconds(100 + (i % 4) * 10));
    std::cout << "Step " << i << std::endl;
    {
      std::lock_guard<std::mutex> l(m);
      touched = std::chrono::steady_clock::now();
    }
  }
  ready = true;
}
```

5. Add the main function that contains the monitoring routine:

```cpp
int main() {
  std::thread t(Worker);
  std::chrono::milliseconds threshold(120);
  while(!ready) {
    auto now = std::chrono::steady_clock::now();
    std::chrono::milliseconds delta;
    {
      std::lock_guard<std::mutex> l(m);
      auto delta = now - touched;
      if (delta > threshold) {
```

```
            std::cout << "Execution threshold exceeded" << std::endl;
        }
    }
    std::this_thread::sleep_for(std::chrono::milliseconds(10));

    }
    t.join();
    return 0;
}
```

6. Finally, create a CMakeLists.txt file containing build rules for our program:

```
cmake_minimum_required(VERSION 3.5.1)
project(monotonic)
add_executable(monotonic monotonic.cpp)
target_link_libraries(monotonic pthread)

set(CMAKE_SYSTEM_NAME Linux)
set(CMAKE_SYSTEM_PROCESSOR arm)

SET(CMAKE_CXX_FLAGS "--std=c++11")
set(CMAKE_CXX_COMPILER /usr/bin/arm-linux-gnueabi-g++)
```

You can now build and run the application.

How it works...

Our application is multithreaded—it consists of the main thread that runs the monitoring and the background worker thread. We use three global variables for their synchronization.

The touched variable is holding the timestamp that is to be periodically updated by the Worker thread. Since the timestamp is accessed by both threads, access needs to be protected. We use an m mutex for this purpose. Finally, to indicate that the worker thread has finished its job, an atomic variable, ready, is used.

The worker thread is a loop that contains artificial delays inside. The delay is calculated based on the step number, resulting in delays from 100 milliseconds to 130 milliseconds:

```
std::this_thread::sleep_for(
        std::chrono::milliseconds(100 + (i % 4) * 10));
```

On each iteration, the `Worker` thread updates the timestamp. A lock guard is used to synchronize access to the timestamp:

```
{
    std::lock_guard<std::mutex> l(m);
    touched = std::chrono::steady_clock::now();
}
```

The monitoring routine runs in a loop while the `Worker` thread is running. On each iteration, it calculates the time interval between the current time and the last update:

```
std::lock_guard<std::mutex> l(m);
auto delta = now - touched;
```

If it is larger than the threshold, the function prints a warning message, as shown:

```
if (delta > threshold) {
    std::cout << "Execution threshold exceeded" << std::endl;
}
```

In many cases, applications may invoke a recovery function to reset a peripheral device or restart the thread. We add a delay of 10 milliseconds in the monitoring loop:

```
std::this_thread::sleep_for(std::chrono::milliseconds(10));
```

This helps us to reduce resource consumption yet achieve an acceptable reaction time. Running the application produces the following output:

We can see several warnings in the output, indicating that some iterations in the worker thread took more time than the threshold of 120 milliseconds. It is predictable since the worker function is written this way. It is important that we use a monotonic std::chrono::steady_clock function for monitoring purposes. Using the system clock could lead to the spurious invocations of the recovery function during the clock adjustments.

There's more...

C++20 defines several other types of clocks, such as gps_clock, representing **Global Positioning System** (**GPS**) time, or file_clock, to work with file timestamps. These clocks may, or may not, be steady, or monotonic. Use an is_steady member function to check if a clock is monotonic or not.

Using POSIX timestamps

POSIX timestamps are a traditional internal representation of time in Unix-based operating systems. A POSIX timestamp is defined as the number of seconds since the epoch, or 00:00:00 **Coordinated Universal Time** (**UTC**), January 1, 1970.

Because of its simplicity, this representation is widely used in network protocols, file metadata, or serialization.

In this recipe, we will learn how to convert C++ time points to POSIX timestamps, and create C++ time points from POSIX timestamps.

How to do it...

We are going to create an application that converts a time point into a POSIX timestamp and then recovers a time point from this timestamp.

1. In your ~/test working directory, create a subdirectory called timestamps.
2. Use your favorite text editor to create a timestamps.cpp file in the timestamps subdirectory.
3. Put the following code snippet into the file:

```
#include <iostream>
#include <chrono>
```

```
int main() {
  auto now = std::chrono::system_clock::now();

  std::time_t ts = std::chrono::system_clock::to_time_t(now);
  std::cout << "POSIX timestamp: " << ts << std::endl;

  auto restored = std::chrono::system_clock::from_time_t(ts);

  std::chrono::duration<double, std::milli> delta = now - restored;
  std::cout << "Recovered time delta " << delta.count() <<
std::endl;
  return 0;
}
```

4. Create a CMakeLists.txt file containing build rules for our program:

```
cmake_minimum_required(VERSION 3.5.1)
project(timestamps)
add_executable(timestamps timestamps.cpp)

set(CMAKE_SYSTEM_NAME Linux)
set(CMAKE_SYSTEM_PROCESSOR arm)

SET(CMAKE_CXX_FLAGS "--std=c++11")
set(CMAKE_CXX_COMPILER /usr/bin/arm-linux-gnueabi-g++)
```

You can now build and run the application.

How it works...

Firstly, we create a time point object for the current time, using the system clock:

```
auto now = std::chrono::system_clock::now();
```

Since POSIX timestamps represent the time since the epoch, we cannot use the steady clock. The system clock, however, knows how to convert its internal representation into POSIX format. It provides a to_time_t static function for this purpose:

```
std::time_t ts = std::chrono::system_clock::to_time_t(now);
```

The result is defined as having type std::time_t, but this is an integral integer type, not an object. Unlike a time point instance, we can write it directly into an output stream:

```
std::cout << "POSIX timestamp: " << ts << std::endl;
```

Let's try to recover a time point from this integer timestamp. We use a `from_time_t` static function:

```
auto restored = std::chrono::system_clock::from_time_t(ts);
```

Now, we have two timestamps. Are they the same? Let's calculate and display the difference:

```
std::chrono::duration<double, std::milli> delta = now - restored;
std::cout << "Recovered time delta " << delta.count() << std::endl;
```

When we run the application, we get the following output:

```
user@3324138cc2c7: /mnt/timestamps — bash
user@3324138cc2c7:/mnt/timestamps$ ./timestamps
POSIX timestamp: 1578081946
Recovered time delta 903.05
user@3324138cc2c7:/mnt/timestamps$ ▯
```

The timestamps are different, but the difference is always less than 1,000. Since POSIX timestamps are defined as the number of seconds since the epoch, we lost the fine granularity time, such as milliseconds and microseconds.

Despite such limitations, POSIX timestamps remain an important and widely used transport representation of time, and we learned how to convert them into an internal C++ representation when needed.

There's more...

In many cases, it is sufficient to work with POSIX timestamps directly. Since they are represented as numbers, a simple numeric comparison can be used to decide which timestamp is newer or older. Similarly, subtracting one timestamp from another gives a time interval in seconds between them. If performance is a bottleneck, this approach can be preferable to comparing to native C++ time points.

12
Error Handling and Fault Tolerance

It is hard to overestimate the importance of error handling in regards to embedded software. Embedded systems should work without supervision in varying physical conditions, such as controlling external peripheral devices that may fail over or not always provide reliable communication lines. And in many cases, a failure of the system is either expensive or plain unsafe.

In this chapter, we will learn about common strategies and best practices that will help you write reliable and fault-tolerant embedded applications.

We will cover the following recipes in this chapter:

- Working with error codes
- Using exceptions for error handling
- Using constant references when catching exceptions
- Tackling static objects
- Working with watchdogs
- Exploring heartbeats for highly available systems
- Implementing software debouncing logic

These recipes will help you understand the importance of error handling design, learn best practices, and avoid pitfalls in this domain.

Working with error codes

When designing a new function, developers often need a mechanism to indicate that the function can't accomplish its work because of some kind of error. It might be invalid, an unexpected result being received from a peripheral device, or a resource allocation issue.

One of the most traditional and widespread ways to report an error condition is through error codes. This is an efficient and ubiquitous mechanism that does not depend on the programming language or the operating system. Due to its efficiency, versatility, and ability to cross various platform boundaries, it is highly used in embedded software development.

Designing a function interface that returns either a value or an error code may be tricky, especially if the value and the error code have different types. In this recipe, we will explore several approaches to designing such types of function interfaces.

How to do it...

We are going to create a simple program with three implementations of a function called `Receive`. All three implementations have identical behavior but a different interface. Follow these steps:

1. In your working directory, that is, `~/test`, create a subdirectory called `errcode`.
2. Use your favorite text editor to create a file called `errcode.cpp` in the `errcode` subdirectory.
3. Add the implementation of the first function to the `errcode.cpp` file:

```
#include <iostream>
int Receive(int input, std::string& output) {
  if (input < 0) {
    return -1;
  }

  output = "Hello";
  return 0;
}
```

4. Next, we add the second implementation:

```
std::string Receive(int input, int& error) {
  if (input < 0) {
    error = -1;
    return "";
  }
  error = 0;
  return "Hello";
}
```

5. The third implementation of the `Receive` function is as follows:

```
std::pair<int, std::string> Receive(int input) {
  std::pair<int, std::string> result;
  if (input < 0) {
    result.first = -1;
  } else {
    result.second = "Hello";
  }
  return result;
}
```

6. Now, we define a helper function called `Display` to display a result:

```
void Display(const char* prefix, int err, const std::string&
result) {
  if (err < 0) {
    std::cout << prefix << " error: " << err << std::endl;
  } else {
    std::cout << prefix << " result: " << result << std::endl;
  }
}
```

7. Then, we add a function called `Test` that invokes all three implementations:

```
void Test(int input) {
  std::string outputResult;
  int err = Receive(input, outputResult);
  Display(" Receive 1", err, outputResult);

  int outputErr = -1;
  std::string result = Receive(input, outputErr);
  Display(" Receive 2", outputErr, result);

  std::pair<int, std::string> ret = Receive(input);
  Display(" Receive 3", ret.first, ret.second);
}
```

8. The `main` function ties everything together:

```
int main() {
  std::cout << "Input: -1" << std::endl;
  Test(-1);
  std::cout << "Input: 1" << std::endl;
  Test(1);

  return 0;
}
```

9. Finally, we create a `CMakeLists.txt` file containing the build rules for our program:

```
cmake_minimum_required(VERSION 3.5.1)
project(errcode)
add_executable(errcode errcode.cpp)
set(CMAKE_SYSTEM_NAME Linux)
set(CMAKE_SYSTEM_PROCESSOR arm)

SET(CMAKE_CXX_FLAGS "--std=c++11")
set(CMAKE_CXX_COMPILER /usr/bin/arm-linux-gnueabi-g++)
```

10. You can now build and run the application.

How it works...

In our application, we defined three different implementations of a function that receives data from some device. It should return the received data as a string, but in the case of an error, it should return an integer error code representing the reason for the error.

Since the result and the error code have different types, we can't reuse the same value for both. To return multiple values in C++, we either need to use output parameters or create a compound data type.

Our implementations explore both these strategies. We use C++ function overloading to define the `Receive` function with the same name, but different types of arguments and return values.

The first implementation returns an error code and stores the result in an output parameter result:

```
int Receive(int input, std::string& output)
```

The output parameter is a string passed by reference to let the function modify its content. The second implementation flips the parameters around. It returns a received string as a result and accepts an error code as an output parameter:

```
std::string Receive(int input, int& error)
```

Since we want the error code to be set from within the function, we also pass it by reference. Finally, the third implementation combines and returns both the result and the error code in a C++ `pair`:

```
std::pair<int, std::string> Receive(int input)
```

The function always creates an `std::pair<int, std::string>` instance. Since we do not pass any values to its constructor, the object is default-initialized. The integer element is set to `0`, and the string element is set to an empty string.

This approach does not require an `output` parameter and is more readable, but has a slightly higher overhead to construct and then destroy a `pair` object.

When all three implementations are defined, we test all of them in the `Test` function. We pass the same parameter to each of the implementations and display the result. We expect each of them to generate the same result.

There are two invocations of `Test`. First, we pass -1 as a parameter, which should trigger an error path, and then we pass 1, which activates a normal operation path:

```
std::cout << "Input: -1" << std::endl;
Test(-1);
std::cout << "Input: 1" << std::endl;
Test(1);
```

When we run our program, we see the following output:

All three implementations correctly return either the result or error code based on the input parameters. You can use any of the approaches in your applications based on the overall design guidelines or your personal preferences.

There's more...

As part of the C++17 standard, a template called `std::optional` was added to the standard library. It can represent an optional value that may be missing. It can be used as a return value from a function that may fail. However, it can't represent a reason for failure, only a Boolean value indicating whether the value is valid or not. For more information, please check the `std::optional` reference at `https://en.cppreference.com/w/cpp/utility/optional`.

Using exceptions for error handling

While the error codes remain the most widespread technique of error handling in embedded programming, C++ offers another mechanism for this purpose, called exceptions.

Exceptions aim to simplify error handling and make it more reliable. When using error codes, developers have to check the result of each function for errors and propagate the result to the calling functions. This clutters the code with lots of if-else constructs, making the function logic more obscure.

When using exceptions, developers do not need to check for errors after every function invocation. Exceptions propagate through the call stack automatically, until they reach the code that can handle it properly by logging, retrying, or terminating the application.

While exceptions are the default error handling mechanism of the C++ standard library, communicating with peripheral devices or the underlying operating system layer still involves error codes. In this recipe, we will learn how to bridge the low-level error handling to the C++ exceptions using the `std::system_error` exception class.

How to do it...

We are going to create a simple application that communicates to a device over a serial link. Follow these steps:

1. In your working directory, that is, `~/test`, create a subdirectory called `except`.
2. Use your favorite text editor to create a file called `except.cpp` in the `except` subdirectory.

3. Put the required includes in the `except.cpp` file:

```
#include <iostream>
#include <system_error>
#include <fcntl.h>
#include <unistd.h>
```

4. Next, we define a `Device` class that abstracts the communication to the device. We start with the constructor and the destructor:

```
class Device {
  int fd;

public:
  Device(const std::string& deviceName) {
    fd = open(deviceName.c_str(), O_RDWR);
    if (fd < 0) {
      throw std::system_error(errno, std::system_category(),
                              "Failed to open device file");
    }
  }

  ~Device() {
    close(fd);
  }
```

5. Then, we add a method that sends data to the device, as follows:

```
  void Send(const std::string& data) {
    size_t offset = 0;
    size_t len = data.size();
    while (offset < data.size() - 1) {
      int sent = write(fd, data.data() + offset,
                       data.size() - offset);
      if (sent < 0) {
        throw std::system_error(errno,
                                std::system_category(),
                                "Failed to send data");
      }
      offset += sent;
    }
  }
};
```

6. After our class has been defined, we add the `main` function, which uses it:

```cpp
int main() {
  try {
    Device serial("/dev/ttyUSB0");
    serial.Send("Hello");
  } catch (std::system_error& e) {
    std::cout << "Error: " << e.what() << std::endl;
    std::cout << "Code: " << e.code() << " means \""
              << e.code().message()
              << "\"" << std::endl;
  }

  return 0;
}
```

7. Finally, we create a `CMakeLists.txt` file containing the build rules for our program:

```cmake
cmake_minimum_required(VERSION 3.5.1)
project(except)
add_executable(except except.cpp)

set(CMAKE_SYSTEM_NAME Linux)
set(CMAKE_SYSTEM_PROCESSOR arm)

SET(CMAKE_CXX_FLAGS "--std=c++11")
set(CMAKE_CXX_COMPILER /usr/bin/arm-linux-gnueabi-g++)
```

8. You can now build and run the application.

How it works...

Our application communicates with an external device connected over a serial link. In POSIX operating systems, communication to devices is similar to operations with regular files and uses the same API; that is, the `open`, `close`, `read`, and `write` functions.

All these functions return error codes to indicate various error conditions. Instead of using them directly, we wrap the communication in a class called `Device`.

Its constructor tries to open a file referred to by the `deviceName` constructor parameter. The constructor checks for the error code and, if it indicates an error, creates and throws an `std::system_error` exception:

```
throw std::system_error(errno, std::system_category(),
                        "Failed to open device file");
```

We construct the `std::system_error` instance using three parameters. The first one is an error code we want to wrap in an exception. We use the value of the `errno` variable that's set by the `open` function when it returns an error. The second parameter is an error category. Since we use an error code specific to the operating system, we use an instance of `std::system_category`. The first parameter is a message we want to associate with the exception. It can be anything that helps us identify the error if it occurs.

In a similar way, we define the `Send` function, which sends data to the device. It is a wrapper around the `write` system function, and if `write` returns an error, we create and throw an `std::system_error` instance. The only difference is the message string since we want to differentiate between these two cases in our logs:

```
throw std::system_error(errno, std::system_category(),
                        "Failed to send data");
}
```

After the `Device` class has been defined, we can use it. Instead of opening a device and checking for errors, and then writing to the device and checking for errors again, we just create an instance of the `Device` class and send data to it:

```
Device serial("/dev/ttyUSB0");
serial.Send("Hello");
```

All error handling lies in the `catch` block after the main logic. If a system error is thrown, we log it to the standard output. Additionally, we print information about the error code, embedded in the exception:

```
} catch (std::system_error& e) {
  std::cout << "Error: " << e.what() << std::endl;
  std::cout << "Code: " << e.code() << " means \"" << e.code().message()
      << "\"" << std::endl;
}
```

When we build and run the application, it shows the following output, if no device is connected as `/dev/ttyUSB0`:

```
user@3324138cc2c7: /mnt/except — bash
user@3324138cc2c7:/mnt/except$ ./except
Error: Failed to open device file: No such file or directory
Code: system:2 means "No such file or directory"
user@3324138cc2c7:/mnt/except$
```

As expected, the error condition was detected and we can see all the required details, including the underlying operating system error code and its description. Note that the code that communicates with the device using the wrapper class is uncluttered and readable.

There's more...

The C++ standard library comes with a number of predefined exceptions and error categories. For more details, check the C++ error handling reference at `https://en.cppreference.com/w/cpp/error`.

Using constant references when catching exceptions

C++ exceptions provide a powerful foundation for exception handling design. They are flexible and may be used in multiple different ways. You can throw exceptions of any type, including pointers and integers. You can catch exceptions by value or by reference. A wrong choice when it comes to selecting a data type may lead to performance hits or resource leaks.

In this recipe, we will analyze potential pitfalls and learn how to use constant references in catch blocks for efficient and safe error handling.

How to do it...

We are going to create a sample application that throws and catches a custom exception and analyze how the data type choice affects efficiency. Follow these steps:

1. In your working directory, that is, `~/test`, create a subdirectory called `catch`.
2. Use your favorite text editor to create a file called `catch.cpp` in the `catch` subdirectory.
3. Put the definition of the `Error` class in the `catch.cpp` file:

```cpp
#include <iostream>

class Error {
  int code;

  public:
    Error(int code): code(code) {
      std::cout << " Error instance " << code << " was created"
                << std::endl;
    }
    Error(const Error& other): code(other.code) {
      std::cout << " Error instance " << code << " was cloned"
                << std::endl;
    }
    ~Error() {
      std::cout << " Error instance " << code << " was destroyed"
                << std::endl;
    }
};
```

4. Next, we add helper functions to test three different ways of throwing and handling errors. We start with the function that catches exceptions by value:

```cpp
void CatchByValue() {
  std::cout << "Catch by value" << std::endl;
  try {
    throw Error(1);
  }
  catch (Error e) {
    std::cout << " Error caught" << std::endl;
  }
}
```

5. Then, we add a function that throws a pointer and catches the exception by pointer, as follows:

```cpp
void CatchByPointer() {
  std::cout << "Catch by pointer" << std::endl;
  try {
    throw new Error(2);
  }
  catch (Error* e) {
    std::cout << " Error caught" << std::endl;
  }
}
```

6. Next, we add a function that uses a const reference to catch exceptions:

```cpp
void CatchByReference() {
  std::cout << "Catch by reference" << std::endl;
  try {
    throw Error(3);
  }
  catch (const Error& e) {
    std::cout << " Error caught" << std::endl;
  }
}
```

7. After all the helper functions have been defined, we add the main function to tie everything together:

```cpp
int main() {
  CatchByValue();
  CatchByPointer();
  CatchByReference();
  return 0;
}
```

8. We put the build rules for our application into a CMakeLists.txt file:

```cmake
cmake_minimum_required(VERSION 3.5.1)
project(catch)
add_executable(catch catch.cpp)
set(CMAKE_SYSTEM_NAME Linux)
set(CMAKE_SYSTEM_PROCESSOR arm)

SET(CMAKE_CXX_FLAGS "--std=c++11")

set(CMAKE_CXX_COMPILER /usr/bin/arm-linux-gnueabi-g++)
```

9. We can now build and run the application.

How it works...

In our application, we defined a custom class called `Error` that we are going to use when throwing and catching exceptions. This class provides a constructor, a copy constructor, and a destructor that only logs information to the console. We need it to evaluate the efficiency of different exception catching approaches.

The `Error` class only contains the `code` data field, which is used to differentiate between instances of the class:

```
class Error {
    int code;
```

We evaluate three approaches for exception handling. The first one, `CatchByValue`, is the most straightforward. We create and throw an instance of the `Error` class:

```
throw Error(1);
```

Then, we catch it by value:

```
catch (Error e) {
```

The second implementation, `CatchByPointer`, creates an instance of `Error` dynamically using the `new` operator:

```
throw new Error(2);
```

We use a pointer to catch the exception:

```
catch (Error* e) {
```

Finally, `CatchByReference` throws an exception similar to `CatchByValue`, but it uses a `const` reference to `Error` when catching it:

```
catch (const Error& e) {
```

Does it make any difference? When we run our program, we get the following output:

```
user@3324138cc2c7: /mnt/catch — bash
user@3324138cc2c7:/mnt/catch$ ./catch
Catch by value
 Error instance 1 was created
 Error instance 1 was cloned
 Error caught
 Error instance 1 was destroyed
 Error instance 1 was destroyed
Catch by pointer
 Error instance 2 was created
 Error caught
Catch by reference
 Error instance 3 was created
 Error caught
 Error instance 3 was destroyed
user@3324138cc2c7:/mnt/catch$ []
```

As you can see, when catching an object by value, a copy of the exception object was created. Though not critical in a sample application, this inefficiency can cause performance issues in a high-load application.

There is no inefficiency when catching exceptions by pointer, but we can see that the object destructor was not invoked, causing a memory leak. This can be avoided by calling `delete` from the `catch` block, but this is error-prone since it is not always clear who is responsible for destroying an object referenced by a pointer.

The reference approach is the safest and most efficient one. There is no memory leak and unnecessary copying. Also, making the reference constant gives the compiler a hint that it is not going to be changed and thus can be better optimized under the hood.

There's more...

Error handling is a complex area with a number of best practices, hints, and recommendations. Consider reading the C++ exceptions and error handling FAQ at `https://isocpp.org/wiki/faq/exceptions` to master your exception handling skills.

Tackling static objects

In C++, object constructors throw exceptions if an object can't be instantiated properly. Normally, this does not cause any issues. An exception originating from an object constructed on the stack, or an object created dynamically using the `new` keyword, can be handled by the try-catch block around the code where the object was created.

It gets more complicated for static objects, though. Such objects are instantiated before the execution enters the `main` function, so they cannot be wrapped in a try-catch block of the program. The C++ compiler handles this situation by calling the `std::terminate` function, which prints an error message and terminates the program. Even if the exception is non-fatal, there is no way to recover.

There are several ways to not get into this pitfall. As a general rule, only simple, integral data types should be allocated statically. If you still need to have a complex static object, make sure its constructor does not throw exceptions.

In this recipe, we will learn how to implement a constructor for static objects.

How to do it...

We will create a custom class that allocates a specified amount of memory and statically allocates two instances of the class. Follow these steps:

1. In your working directory, that is, `~/test`, create a subdirectory called `static`.
2. Use your favorite text editor to create a file called `static.cpp` in the `static` subdirectory.
3. Let's define a class named `Complex`. Put its private field and the constructor in the `static.cpp` file:

```cpp
#include <iostream>
#include <stdint.h>
class Complex {
  char* ptr;

  public:
    Complex(size_t size) noexcept {
      try {
        ptr = new(std::nothrow) char[size];
        if (ptr) {
          std::cout << "Successfully allocated "
                    << size << " bytes" << std::endl;
        } else {
          std::cout << "Failed to allocate "
                    << size << " bytes" << std::endl;
        }
      } catch (...) {
        // Do nothing
      }
    }
```

4. Then, define a destructor and the `IsValid` method:

```cpp
~Complex() {
  try {
    if (ptr) {
      delete[] ptr;
      std::cout << "Deallocated memory" << std::endl;
    } else {
      std::cout << "Memory was not allocated"
                << std::endl;
    }
  } catch (...) {
    // Do nothing
  }
}

bool IsValid() const { return nullptr != ptr; }
};
```

5. After the class has been defined, we define two global objects, `small` and `large`, and the `main` function, which uses them:

```cpp
Complex small(100);
Complex large(SIZE_MAX);
int main() {
  std::cout << "Small object is "
            << (small.IsValid()? "valid" : "invalid")
            << std::endl;
  std::cout << "Large object is "
            << (large.IsValid()? "valid" : "invalid")
            << std::endl;

  return 0;
}
```

6. Finally, we create a `CMakeLists.txt` file containing the build rules for our program:

```
cmake_minimum_required(VERSION 3.5.1)
project(static)
add_executable(static static.cpp)
set(CMAKE_SYSTEM_NAME Linux)
set(CMAKE_SYSTEM_PROCESSOR arm)

SET(CMAKE_CXX_FLAGS "--std=c++11")
set(CMAKE_CXX_COMPILER /usr/bin/arm-linux-gnueabi-g++)
```

7. You can now build and run the application.

How it works...

Here, we defined the `Complex` class, and we intend to allocate instances of this class statically. To be safe, we need to make sure that neither the constructor nor the destructor of this class can throw exceptions.

However, both the constructor and the destructor invoke operations that may potentially throw exceptions. The constructor performs memory allocation, while the destructor writes logs to standard output.

The constructor allocates memory using the `new` operator, which throws an `std::bad_alloc` exception if memory can't be allocated. We use an `std::nothrow` constant to select a non-throwing implementation of `new`. Instead of throwing an exception, `new` will return `nullptr` if it can't allocate any memory:

```
ptr = new(std::nothrow) char[size];
```

We wrap the body of the constructor in the `try` block to catch all exceptions. The `catch` block is empty – if the constructor fails, we can't do much:

```
} catch (...) {
        // Do nothing
}
```

Since we do not allow any exceptions to propagate to the upper level, we mark our constructor as non-throwing using a C++ keyword, that is, `noexcept`:

```
Complex(size_t size) noexcept {
```

However, we need to know whether an object was created properly. For this purpose, we define a method called `IsValid`. It returns `true` if the memory was allocated, or `false` otherwise:

```
bool IsValid() const { return nullptr != ptr; }
```

The destructor does the reverse. It deallocates the memory and logs the status of deallocation to the console. As for the constructor, we do not want any exceptions to be propagated to the upper level, so we wrap the destructor body in a try-catch block:

```
try {
    if (ptr) {
      delete[] ptr;
      std::cout << "Deallocated memory" << std::endl;
    } else {
      std::cout << "Memory was not allocated" << std::endl;
    }
```

```
} catch (...) {
  // Do nothing
}
```

Now, we declare two global objects, `small` and `large`. Global objects are allocated statically. The size of the objects is artificially selected in a way that the `small` object will be allocated properly, but the allocation of the `large` object should fail:

```
Complex small(100);
Complex large(SIZE_MAX);
```

In our `main` function, we check and print whether the objects are valid or not:

```
std::cout << "Small object is " << (small.IsValid()? "valid" : "invalid")
          << std::endl;
std::cout << "Large object is " << (large.IsValid()? "valid" : "invalid")
          << std::endl;
```

When we run our program, we see the following output:

```
igor@raspberrypi:~ $ ./static
Successfully allocated 100 bytes
Failed to allocate 4294967295 bytes
Small object is valid
Large object is invalid
Memory was not allocated
Deallocated memory
igor@raspberrypi:~ $
```

As we can see, the small object was allocated and deallocated properly. Initialization of the large object failed, but since it was designed to not throw any exceptions, it did not cause the abnormal termination of our application. You can use a similar technique for statically allocated objects to write robust and safe applications.

Working with watchdogs

Embedded applications are built to work without supervision. This includes the ability to recover from errors. If an application crashes, it can be restarted automatically. But what should we do if an application hangs by entering an endless loop or due to a deadlock?

Hardware or software watchdogs are used to prevent such situations. Applications should periodically notify or *feed* them to indicate that they keep operating normally. If a watchdog is not fed within a specific time interval, it terminates an application or restarts the system.

Many different implementations of watchdogs exist, but their interfaces are essentially the same. They provide a function that applications can use to reset the watchdog timer.

In this recipe, we will learn how to create a simple software watchdog on top of POSIX signals subsystems. The same technique can be used to work with hardware watchdog timers or more sophisticated software watchdog services.

How to do it...

We will create an application that will define the Watchdog class and provide an example of its usage. Follow these steps:

1. In your working directory, that is, ~/test, create a subdirectory called watchdog.

2. Use your favorite text editor to create a file called watchdog.cpp in the watchdog subdirectory.

3. Put the required includes in the watchdog.cpp file:

```cpp
#include <chrono>
#include <iostream>
#include <thread>

#include <unistd.h>

using namespace std::chrono_literals;
```

4. Next, we define the Watchdog class itself:

```cpp
class Watchdog {
  std::chrono::seconds seconds;

  public:
    Watchdog(std::chrono::seconds seconds):
      seconds(seconds) {
        feed();
    }

    ~Watchdog() {
      alarm(0);
    }
```

```
        void feed() {
          alarm(seconds.count());
        }
};
```

5. Add the `main` function, which serves as a usage example for our watchdog:

```
int main() {
  Watchdog watchdog(2s);
  std::chrono::milliseconds delay = 700ms;
  for (int i = 0; i < 10; i++) {
    watchdog.feed();
    std::cout << delay.count() << "ms delay" << std::endl;
    std::this_thread::sleep_for(delay);
    delay += 300ms;
  }
}
```

6. Add a `CMakeLists.txt` file containing the build rules for our program:

```
cmake_minimum_required(VERSION 3.5.1)
project(watchdog)
add_executable(watchdog watchdog.cpp)

set(CMAKE_SYSTEM_NAME Linux)
set(CMAKE_SYSTEM_PROCESSOR arm)

SET(CMAKE_CXX_FLAGS "--std=c++14")

set(CMAKE_CXX_COMPILER /usr/bin/arm-linux-gnueabi-g++)
```

7. You can now build and run the application.

How it works...

We need a mechanism to terminate our application when it hangs. Though we could spawn a special monitoring thread or process, there is another, simpler way to do this—POSIX signals.

Any process running in a POSIX operating system can receive a number of signals. To deliver a signal to the process, the operating system stops the normal execution of the process and invokes a corresponding signal handler.

One of the signals that can be delivered to the process is called `alarm` and, by default, its handler just terminates the application. This is exactly what we need to implement a watchdog.

The constructor of our `Watchdog` class accepts one parameter, `seconds`:

```
Watchdog(std::chrono::seconds seconds):
```

It is a time interval for our watchdog and it is immediately passed into the `feed` method to activate the watchdog timer:

```
feed();
```

The `feed` method invokes a POSIX function `alarm` that sets the timer. If the timer is already set, it updates it with a new value:

```
void feed() {
    alarm(seconds.count());
}
```

Finally, we invoke the same `alarm` function in the destructor to disable the timer by passing a value of `0`:

```
alarm(0);
```

Now, each time we invoke the `feed` function, we shift the time when the process will receive the `alarm` signal. If, however, we do not invoke this function before the timer expires, it triggers the `alarm` handler, which terminates our process.

To check it out, we've created a simple example. It is a loop that has 10 iterations. On each iteration, we display a message and sleep for a specific interval. The interval is initially 700 ms and on each iteration, it increases by 300 ms; for example, 700 ms, 1,000 ms, 1,300 ms, and so on:

```
delay += 300ms;
```

Our watchdog is set to a 2-second interval:

```
Watchdog watchdog(2s);
```

Let's run the application and check how it works. It produces the following output:

```
●  ●  ●                    ⌂ ~ — igor@raspberrypi: ~ — ssh pi
igor@raspberrypi:~ $ ./watchdog || echo "Failure, restart required"
700ms delay
1000ms delay
1300ms delay
1600ms delay
1900ms delay
2200ms delay
Alarm clock
Failure, restart required
igor@raspberrypi:~ $ ▮
```

As we can see, the application was terminated after the sixth iteration, after the delay exceeded the watchdog interval. Moreover, since it was terminated abnormally, its return code is non-zero. If the application is spawned by another application or script, this is an indicator that the application needs to be restarted.

The watchdog technique is a simple and efficient way to build robust embedded applications.

Exploring heartbeats for highly available systems

In the preceding recipe, we learned how to prevent software from hanging using watchdog timers. A similar technique can be used to implement a highly available system, which consists of one or more software or hardware components that can perform the same function. If one of the components fails, another one can take over.

The component that is currently active should periodically advertise its health status to other, passive components using messages that are called **heartbeats**. When it reports an unhealthy status or doesn't report it within a specific amount of time, a passive component detects it and activates itself. When the failed component recovers, it can either transition into passive mode, monitoring the now active component for failures, or initiate a failback procedure to claim the active status back.

In this recipe, we will learn how to implement a simple heartbeat monitor in our application.

How to do it...

We will create an application that defines a `Watchdog` class and provide an example of its usage. Follow these steps:

1. In your working directory, that is, `~/test`, create a subdirectory called `heartbeat`.

2. Use your favorite text editor to create a file called `heartbeat.cpp` in the `heartbeat` subdirectory.

3. Put the required includes in the `heatbeat.cpp` file:

```cpp
#include <chrono>
#include <iostream>
#include <system_error>
#include <thread>

#include <unistd.h>
#include <poll.h>
#include <signal.h>

using namespace std::chrono_literals;
```

4. Next, we define an `enum` to report the health status of the active worker:

```cpp
enum class Health : uint8_t {
  Ok,
  Unhealthy,
  ShutDown
};
```

5. Now, let's create a class that encapsulates the heartbeat reporting and monitoring. We start with the class definition, its private fields, and its constructor:

```cpp
class Heartbeat {
  int channel[2];
  std::chrono::milliseconds delay;

  public:
    Heartbeat(std::chrono::milliseconds delay):
        delay(delay) {
      int rv = pipe(channel);
      if (rv < 0) {
        throw std::system_error(errno,
                         std::system_category(),
                         "Failed to open pipe");
```

```
      }
    }
```

6. Next, we add a method to report the health status:

```
void Report(Health status) {
    int rv = write(channel[1], &status, sizeof(status));
    if (rv < 0) {
      throw std::system_error(errno,
                    std::system_category(),
                    "Failed to report health status");
    }
}
```

7. This is followed by a health monitoring method:

```
bool Monitor() {
    struct pollfd fds[1];
    fds[0].fd = channel[0];
    fds[0].events = POLLIN;
    bool takeover = true;
    bool polling = true;
    while(polling) {
      fds[0].revents = 0;
      int rv = poll(fds, 1, delay.count());
      if (rv) {
        if (fds[0].revents & (POLLERR | POLLHUP)) {
          std::cout << "Polling error occured"
                    << std::endl;
          takeover = false;
          polling = false;
          break;
        }

        Health status;
        int count = read(fds[0].fd, &status,
                      sizeof(status));
        if (count < sizeof(status)) {
          std::cout << "Failed to read heartbeat data"
                    << std::endl;
          break;
        }
        switch(status) {
          case Health::Ok:
            std::cout << "Active process is healthy"
                    << std::endl;
            break;
          case Health::ShutDown:
```

```
                    std::cout << "Shut down signalled"
                                  << std::endl;
                    takeover = false;
                    polling = false;
                    break;
                default:
                    std::cout << "Unhealthy status reported"
                                  << std::endl;
                    polling = false;
                    break;
                }
            } else if (!rv) {
                std::cout << "Timeout" << std::endl;
                polling = false;
            } else {
                if (errno != EINTR) {
                    std::cout << "Error reading heartbeat data, retrying"
    << std::endl;
                }
            }
        }
        return takeover;
    }
};
```

8. Once the heartbeat logic has been defined, we create some functions so that we can use it in our test application:

```
void Worker(Heartbeat& hb) {
  for (int i = 0; i < 5; i++) {
    hb.Report(Health::Ok);
    std::cout << "Processing" << std::endl;
    std::this_thread::sleep_for(100ms);
  }
  hb.Report(Health::Unhealthy);
}

int main() {
  Heartbeat hb(200ms);
  if (fork()) {
    if (hb.Monitor()) {
      std::cout << "Taking over" << std::endl;
      Worker(hb);
    }
  } else {
    Worker(hb);
  }
}
```

9. Next, we add a `CMakeLists.txt` file containing the build rules for our program:

```
cmake_minimum_required(VERSION 3.5.1)
project(heartbeat)
add_executable(heartbeat heartbeat.cpp)

set(CMAKE_SYSTEM_NAME Linux)
set(CMAKE_SYSTEM_PROCESSOR arm)

SET(CMAKE_CXX_FLAGS "--std=c++14")

set(CMAKE_CXX_COMPILER /usr/bin/arm-linux-gnueabi-g++)
```

10. You can now build and run the application.

How it works...

The heartbeats mechanism needs some kind of communication channel to let one component report its status to other components. In a system that is built around multiple processing units, the best choice would be network-based communication over sockets. Our application is running on a single node, and we can use one of the local IPC mechanisms instead.

We are going to use POSIX pipes mechanisms for our heartbeat transport. When a pipe is created, it provides two file descriptors for communication—one is used to read data, while the other is used to write data.

Besides the communication transport, we need to choose the time interval for taking over. If a monitoring process does not receive a heartbeat message within this interval, it should consider another component as unhealthy or failed, and perform some takeover action.

We start by defining the possible health statuses of our applications. We use the C++ `enum class` to make the stats strictly typed, as follows:

```
enum class Health : uint8_t {
  Ok,
  Unhealthy,
  ShutDown
};
```

Our application is simple and has only three statuses: `Ok`, `Unhealthy`, and `ShutDown`. The `ShutDown` status is an indicator that the active process is going to shut down normally and that no takeover action is needed.

Then, we define the `Heartbeat` class, which encapsulates all message exchange, health reporting, and monitoring functions.

It has two data fields that represent the monitoring time interval and the POSIX pipe that's being used for message exchange:

```
int channel[2];
std::chrono::milliseconds delay;
```

The constructor creates the pipe and throws an exception in the event of a failure:

```
int rv = pipe(channel);
if (rv < 0) {
   throw std::system_error(errno,
                           std::system_category(),
                           "Failed to open pipe");
```

The health reporting method is a simple wrapper around the `write` function. It writes the status, represented as an unsigned 8-bit integer value, to the `write` file descriptor of the pipe:

```
int rv = write(channel[1], &status, sizeof(status));
```

The monitoring method is more complex. It uses the POSIX `poll` function to wait for data in one or more file descriptors. In our case, we are interested in data from only one file descriptor—the read side of the pipe. We fill the `fds` structure used by `pol` with file descriptors and the types of events we are interested in:

```
struct pollfd fds[1];
fds[0].fd = channel[0];
fds[0].events = POLLIN | POLLERR | POLLHUP;
```

Two Boolean flags control the polling loop. The `takeover` flag indicates whether the takeover action should be performed when we exit the loop, while the `polling` flag indicates whether the loop should exist or not:

```
bool takeover = true;
bool polling = true;
```

On each iteration of the loop, we poll for new data in the socket using the `poll` function. We use a monitoring interval passed into the constructor as a polling timeout:

```
int rv = poll(fds, 1, delay.count());
```

The result of the `poll` function indicates one of three possible outcomes:

- If it is greater than zero, we have new data available to read from the communication pipe. We read the status from the communication channel and analyze it.
- If the status is `Ok`, we log it and go to the next iteration of polling.
- If the status is `ShutDown`, we need to exit the polling loop, but also prevent the `takeover` action. To do this, we set our Boolean flags accordingly:

```
case Health::ShutDown:
  std::cout << "Shut down signalled"
            << std::endl;
  takeover = false;
  polling = false;
```

For any other health status, we break from the loop with the `takeover` flag set to `true`:

```
  std::cout << "Unhealthy status reported"
            << std::endl;
  polling = false;
```

`poll` returns zero in the case of a timeout. Similar to the `Unhealthy` status, we need to break from the loop and perform the `takeover` action:

```
} else if (!rv) {
  std::cout << "Timeout" << std::endl;
  polling = false;
```

Finally, if the value returned by `poll` is less than zero, it indicates an error. There are several reasons why a system call can fail, with a very common one being when it is interrupted by a signal. This is not a real error; we only need to call `poll` again. For all other cases, we write a log message and keep polling.

The monitoring method blocks while the monitoring loop is running, and it returns a Boolean value to let the caller know whether the takeover action should be performed or not:

```
bool Monitor() {
```

Now, let's try to use this class in a toy example. We'll define a `Worker` function that accepts a reference to the `Heartbeat` instance and represents the job to be done:

```
void Worker(Heartbeat& hb) {
```

On each iteration of the inner loop, the `Worker` reports its health status:

```
hb.Report(Health::Ok);
```

At some point, it reports its status as `Unhealthy`:

```
hb.Report(Health::Unhealthy);
```

In the `main` function, we create an instance of the `Heartbeat` class with a 200 ms polling interval:

```
Heartbeat hb(200ms);
```

Then, we spawn two independent processes. A parent process starts monitoring and, if a takeover is needed, runs the `Worker` method:

```
if (hb.Monitor()) {
    std::cout << "Taking over" << std::endl;
    Worker(hb);
}
```

The child simply runs the `Worker` method. Let's run the application and check how it works. It produces the following output:

```
user@f00a13ab012c:/mnt/heartbeat$ ./heartbeat
Active process is healthy
Processing
Processing
Active process is healthy
Processing
Active process is healthy
Active process is healthy
Processing
Processing
Active process is healthy
Unhealthy status reported
Taking over
Processing
Processing
Processing
Processing
Processing
user@f00a13ab012c:/mnt/heartbeat$
```

As we can see, the `Worker` method reports that it processes data, and the monitor detects its status as healthy. However, after the `Worker` method reports its status as `Unhealthy`, the monitor detects it immediately and reruns the worker again to keep processing. This strategy can be used to build a more elaborate health monitoring and failure recovery logic to implement high availability in a system you have designed and developed.

There's more...

In our example, we used two identical components that run simultaneously and monitor each other. However, if one of the components contains a software bug that, under certain conditions, causes the component to malfunction, there's a high chance that another identical component could suffer from this issue too. In safety-critical systems, you may need to develop two completely different implementations. This approach increases the cost and development time but results in the higher reliability of the system.

Implementing software debouncing logic

One of the common tasks of embedded applications is interacting with external physical controls such as buttons or switches. Though such objects have only two states – on and off – detecting the moment a button or switch changes state is not as simple as it may look.

When a physical button is pressed, it takes some time before the contact is established firmly. During this time, spurious interrupts can be triggered as if the button is bouncing between on and off states. Instead of reacting to every interrupt, an application should be able to filter out the spurious transitions. This is called **debouncing**.

Though it can be implemented at the hardware level, the most common approach is to do this through software. In this recipe, we will learn how to implement a simple and generic debouncing function that can be used with any type of input.

How to do it...

We will create an application that defines a generic debouncing function along with a test input. This function can be used for any practical purpose by replacing the test input with real input. Follow these steps:

1. In your working directory, that is, ~/test, create a subdirectory called debounce.
2. Use your favorite text editor to create a file called debounce.cpp in the debounce subdirectory.
3. Let's add includes and a function called debounce to the debounce.cpp file:

```
#include <iostream>
#include <chrono>
#include <thread>
```

```
using namespace std::chrono_literals;

bool debounce(std::chrono::milliseconds timeout, bool
(*handler)(void)) {
  bool prev = handler();
  auto ts = std::chrono::steady_clock::now();
  while (true) {
    std::this_thread::sleep_for(1ms);
    bool value = handler();
    auto now = std::chrono::steady_clock::now();
    if (value == prev) {
      if (now - ts > timeout) {
        break;
      }
    } else {
      prev = value;
      ts = now;
    }
  }
  return prev;
}
```

4. Then, we add the `main` function, which shows how to use it:

```
int main() {
  bool result = debounce(10ms, []() {
    return true;
  });
  std::cout << "Result: " << result << std::endl;
}
```

5. Add a `CMakeLists.txt` file containing the build rules for our program:

```
cmake_minimum_required(VERSION 3.5.1)
project(debounce)
add_executable(debounce debounce.cpp)

set(CMAKE_SYSTEM_NAME Linux)
set(CMAKE_SYSTEM_PROCESSOR arm)

SET(CMAKE_CXX_FLAGS "--std=c++14")

set(CMAKE_CXX_COMPILER /usr/bin/arm-linux-gnueabi-g++)
```

6. You can now build and run the application.

How it works...

Our goal is to detect when a button has stopped bouncing between on and off states. We assume that if all consecutive attempts to read the button state return the same value (either on or off) within a specific interval of time, we can tell whether the button is really on or off.

We use this logic to implement the `debounce` function. Since we want to make the debouncing logic as generic as possible, the function should not know how to read the state of a button. That is why the function accepts two arguments:

```
bool debounce(std::chrono::milliseconds timeout, bool (*handler)(void)) {
```

The first argument, `timeout`, defines that specific interval of time we need to wait to report a state change. The second argument, `handler`, is a function or a function-like object that knows how to read the state of the button. It is defined as a pointer to a Boolean function without arguments.

The `debounce` function runs a loop. On each iteration, it calls the handler to read the state of the button and compares it with the previous value. If the values are equal, we check the time since the most recent state change. If it exceeds the timeout, we exit the loop and return:

```
auto now = std::chrono::steady_clock::now();
    if (value == prev) {
      if (now - ts > timeout) {
        break;
      }
    }
```

If the values are not equal, we reset the time for the most recent state change and keep waiting:

```
} else {
      prev = value;
      ts = now;
    }
```

To minimize the CPU load and let other processes do some work, we add a 1-millisecond delay between reads. If the function is intended to be used on a microcontroller that does not run a multitasking operating system, this delay is not needed:

```
std::this_thread::sleep_for(1ms);
```

Our `main` function contains a usage example for the `debounce` function. We use the C++ lambda to define a simple rule to read the button. It always returns `true`:

```
bool result = debounce(10ms, []() {
    return true;
});
```

We pass `10ms` as a `debounce` timeout. If we run our program, we will see the following output:

```
user@3324138cc2c7: /mnt/debounce — bash
user@3324138cc2c7:/mnt/debounce$ ./debounce
Result: 1
user@3324138cc2c7:/mnt/debounce$
```

The `debounce` function works for 10 ms and returns `true` since there were no spurious state changes in the test input. In the case of real input, it may take more time until the button state stabilizes. This simple yet efficient debouncing function can be applied to a variety of real inputs.

13
Guidelines for Real-Time Systems

Real-time systems are a class of embedded systems where the time of reaction is critical. The consequences of not reacting in time vary between different applications. Based on severity, real-time systems are classified as follows:

- **Hard real time**: Missing a deadline is not acceptable and considered a system failure. These are usually mission-critical systems in airplanes, cars, and power plants.
- **Firm real time**: Missing a deadline is acceptable in rare cases. The usefulness of the result is zero after the deadline. Think about a live streaming service. A video frame delivered too late can only be discarded. This is tolerable provided it happens infrequently.
- **Soft real time**: Missing a deadline is acceptable. The usefulness of results degrades after the deadline, causing degradation of the overall quality, and should be avoided. Such an example is capturing and synchronizing data from multiple sensors.

Real-time systems are not necessarily required to be super fast. What they need is predictable reaction time. If a system can normally respond to an event within 10 milliseconds, but it often takes much longer, it is not a real-time system. If a system responds within 1 second guaranteed, this constitutes hard real time.

Determinism and predictability are the main traits of real-time systems. In this chapter, we will explore potential sources of unpredictable behavior and ways to mitigate them.

This chapter covers the following topics:

- Using real-time schedulers in Linux
- Using statically allocated memory
- Avoiding exceptions for error handling
- Exploring real-time operating systems

The recipes in this chapter will help you better understand the specifics of real-time systems and learn some best practices of software development for this kind of embedded system.

Using real-time schedulers in Linux

Linux is a general-purpose operating system that is commonly used in various embedded devices because of its versatility. It can be tailored to the particular hardware and is free.

Linux is not a real-time operating system and is not the best choice for implementing a hard real-time system. However, it can be used efficiently to build a soft real-time system, since it provides a real-time scheduler for time-critical applications.

In this recipe, we will learn how to use the real-time scheduler in Linux in our application.

How to do it...

We are going to create an application that uses the real-time scheduler:

1. In your working directory, ~/test, create a subdirectory called realtime.
2. Use your favorite text editor to create a realtime.cpp file in the realtime subdirectory.
3. Add all the necessary includes and namespaces:

```cpp
#include <iostream>
#include <system_error>
#include <thread>
#include <chrono>

#include <pthread.h>

using namespace std::chrono_literals;
```

4. Next, add a function that configures a thread to use the real-time scheduler:

```cpp
void ConfigureRealtime(pthread_t thread_id, int priority) {
    sched_param sch;
    sch.sched_priority = 20;
    if (pthread_setschedparam(thread_id,
                        SCHED_FIFO, &sch)) {
        throw std::system_error(errno,
                std::system_category(),
                "Failed to set real-time priority");
    }
}
```

5. Next, we define a thread function that we want to run with normal priority:

```cpp
void Measure(const char* text) {
    struct timespec prev;
    timespec_get(&prev, TIME_UTC);
    struct timespec delay{0, 10};
    for (int i = 0; i < 100000; i++) {
        nanosleep(&delay, nullptr);
    }
    struct timespec ts;
    timespec_get(&ts, TIME_UTC);
    double delta = (ts.tv_sec - prev.tv_sec) +
        (double)(ts.tv_nsec - prev.tv_nsec) / 1000000000;
    std::clog << text << " completed in "
                << delta << " sec" << std::endl;
}
```

6. This is followed by a real-time thread function and a `main` function that starts both threads:

```cpp
void RealTimeThread(const char* txt) {
    ConfigureRealtime(pthread_self(), 1);
    Measure(txt);
}

int main() {
    std::thread t1(RealTimeThread, "Real-time");
    std::thread t2(Measure, "Normal");
    t1.join();
    t2.join();
}
```

7. Finally, we create a `CMakeLists.txt` file containing build rules for our program:

```
cmake_minimum_required(VERSION 3.5.1)
project(realtime)
add_executable(realtime realtime.cpp)
target_link_libraries(realtime pthread)

SET(CMAKE_CXX_FLAGS "--std=c++14")
set(CMAKE_CXX_COMPILER /usr/bin/arm-linux-gnueabihf-g++)
```

8. You can now build and run the application.

How it works...

Linux has several scheduling policies that it applies to application processes and threads. `SCHED_OTHER` is the default Linux time-sharing policy. It is intended for all threads and does not provide real-time mechanisms.

In our application, we use another policy, `SCHED_FIFO`. This is a simple scheduling algorithm. All threads that use this scheduler can only be preempted by a thread with a higher priority. If the thread goes to sleep, it is placed at the back of the queue of those threads with the same priority.

The priority of a thread with a `SCHED_FIFO` policy is always higher than the priority of any thread with a `SCHED_OTHER` policy, and as soon as a `SCHED_FIFO` thread becomes runnable, it immediately preempts a running `SCHED_OTHER` thread. From a practical standpoint, if there is only one `SCHED_FIFO` thread running in the system, it can use as much CPU time as it requires. The deterministic behavior and high priority of the `SCHED_FIFO` scheduler make it a good fit for real-time applications.

To assign a real-time priority to a thread, we define a `ConfigureRealtime` function. This accepts two parameters—a thread ID and the desired priority:

```
void ConfigureRealtime(pthread_t thread_id, int priority) {
```

The function populates data for the `pthread_setschedparam` function that uses the low-level API of the operating system to change the scheduler and the priority of a thread:

```
if (pthread_setschedparam(thread_id,
                          SCHED_FIFO, &sch)) {
```

We define a `Measure` function that runs a busy loop, invoking a `nanosleep` function with parameters requiring it to sleep for 10 nanoseconds – way too short to yield execution to another thread:

```
struct timespec delay{0, 10};
for (int i = 0; i < 100000; i++) {
   nanosleep(&delay, nullptr);
}
```

This function captures timestamps before and after the loop and calculates the elapsed time in seconds:

```
struct timespec ts;
timespec_get(&ts, TIME_UTC);
double delta = (ts.tv_sec - prev.tv_sec) +
     (double)(ts.tv_nsec - prev.tv_nsec) / 1000000000;
```

Next, we define the `RealTimeThread` function as a wrapper around the `Measure` function. This sets the priority of the current thread to real time and immediately invokes `Measure`:

```
ConfigureRealtime(pthread_self(), 1);
Measure(txt);
```

In the `main` function, we start two threads, passing text literals as parameters to differentiate their output. If we run the program on a Raspberry Pi device, we can see the following output:

Real-time threads took four times lesser time because this was not preempted by normal threads. This technique can be efficiently used to meet the soft real-time requirements in the Linux environment.

Using statically allocated memory

As has already been discussed in Chapter 6, *Memory Management*, dynamic memory allocation should be avoided in real-time systems because generic memory allocators are not time-bound. While, in most cases, memory allocation does not take much time, it is not guaranteed. It is not acceptable for real-time systems.

The most straightforward way to avoid dynamic memory allocation is to replace it with static allocation. C++ developers often use std::vector to store sequences of elements. On account of its similarity with C arrays, it is efficient and easy to use and its interface is consistent with other containers in the standard library. Since vectors have a variable number of elements, they use dynamic memory allocation extensively. In many situations, however, the std::array class can be used instead of std::vector. It has the same interface, except that the number of its elements is fixed and so its instances can be allocated statically. This makes it a good alternative to std::vector when memory allocation time is critical.

In this recipe, we will learn how std::array can be efficiently used to represent a sequence of elements of fixed size.

How to do it...

We are going to create an application that uses the power of the C++ standard library algorithms to generate and process fixed data frames without using dynamic memory allocation:

1. In your working directory, ~/test, create a subdirectory called array.
2. Use your favorite text editor to create a array.cpp file in the array subdirectory.
3. Add includes and a new type definition to the array.cpp file:

```
#include <algorithm>
#include <array>
#include <iostream>
#include <random>

using DataFrame = std::array<uint32_t, 8>;
```

4. Next, we add a function that generates data frames:

```
void GenerateData(DataFrame& frame) {
  std::random_device rd;
  std::generate(frame.begin(), frame.end(),
  [&rd]() { return rd() % 100; });
}
```

5. This is followed by the function to process data frames:

```
void ProcessData(const DataFrame& frame) {
  std::cout << "Processing array of "
            << frame.size() << " elements: [";
  for (auto x : frame) {
    std::cout << x << " ";
  }
  auto mm = std::minmax_element(frame.begin(),frame.end());
  std::cout << "] min: " << *mm.first
            << ", max: " << *mm.second << std::endl;
}
```

6. Add a `main` function that ties data generation and processing together:

```
int main() {
  DataFrame data;

  for (int i = 0; i < 4; i++) {
    GenerateData(data);
    ProcessData(data);
  }
  return 0;
}
```

7. Finally, we create a `CMakeLists.txt` file containing build rules for our program:

```
cmake_minimum_required(VERSION 3.5.1)
project(array)
add_executable(array array.cpp)

set(CMAKE_SYSTEM_NAME Linux)
set(CMAKE_SYSTEM_PROCESSOR arm)

SET(CMAKE_CXX_FLAGS_RELEASE "--std=c++17")
SET(CMAKE_CXX_FLAGS_DEBUG "${CMAKE_CXX_FLAGS_RELEASE} -g -DDEBUG")

set(CMAKE_C_COMPILER /usr/bin/arm-linux-gnueabihf-gcc)
set(CMAKE_CXX_COMPILER /usr/bin/arm-linux-gnueabihf-g++)
```

```
set(CMAKE_FIND_ROOT_PATH_MODE_PROGRAM NEVER)
set(CMAKE_FIND_ROOT_PATH_MODE_LIBRARY ONLY)
set(CMAKE_FIND_ROOT_PATH_MODE_INCLUDE ONLY)
set(CMAKE_FIND_ROOT_PATH_MODE_PACKAGE ONLY)
```

8. You can now build and run the application.

How it works...

We use the `std::array` template to declare a custom `DataFrame` data type. For our sample application, a `DataFrame` is a sequence of eight 32-bit integers:

```
using DataFrame = std::array<uint32_t, 8>;
```

Now, we can use the new data type in functions to generate and process data frames. Since the data frame is an array, we pass it by reference to the `GenerateData` function to avoid extra copying:

```
void GenerateData(DataFrame& frame) {
```

`GenerateData` fills the data frame with random numbers. Since `std::array` has the same interface as other containers in the standard library, we can use standard algorithms to make the code shorter and more readable:

```
std::generate(frame.begin(), frame.end(),
[&rd]() { return rd() % 100; });
```

We define the `ProcessData` function in a similar manner. It also accepts a `DataFrame`, but it is not supposed to modify it. We use a constant reference to explicitly state that data will not be modified:

```
void ProcessData(const DataFrame& frame) {
```

`ProcessData` prints all values in the data frame, and then finds the minimum and the maximum values in the frame. Unlike built-in arrays, `std::arrays` do not decay to raw pointers when passed to functions, so we can use range-based loop syntax. You may notice that we do not pass the size of the array into the function, and do not use any global constant to query it. It is part of the `std::array` interface. It not only reduces the number of parameters to the function, but also ensures that we cannot pass an incorrect size when calling it:

```
for (auto x : frame) {
  std::cout << x << " ";
}
```

To find the minimum and maximum values, we use the `std::minmax_` element function of the standard library instead of writing a custom loop:

```
auto mm = std::minmax_element(frame.begin(),frame.end());
```

In the `main` function, we create an instance of `DataFrame`:

```
DataFrame data;
```

Then, we run a loop. On each iteration, a new data frame is generated and processed:

```
GenerateData(data);
ProcessData(data);
```

If we run the application, we get the following output:

```
~ — user@f00a13ab012c: /mnt/array — docker exec -ti f0 bash
user@f00a13ab012c:/mnt/array$ ./array
Processing array of 8 elements: [82 42 88 90 59 2 31 20 ] min: 2, max: 90
Processing array of 8 elements: [5 62 67 13 58 46 43 44 ] min: 5, max: 67
Processing array of 8 elements: [3 35 73 37 6 33 86 92 ] min: 3, max: 92
Processing array of 8 elements: [23 66 47 26 76 67 7 11 ] min: 7, max: 76
user@f00a13ab012c:/mnt/array$
```

Our application generated four data frames and processed its data with only a few lines of code and using only statically allocated data. This makes `std::array` a good choice for developers of real-time systems. Moreover, unlike built-in arrays, our functions are type-safe and we can detect and fix a number of coding errors at build time.

There's more...

The C++20 standard introduced a new function, `to_array`, that allows developers to create instances of `std::array` from one-dimensional built-in arrays. See more details and examples on the `to_array` reference page (https://en.cppreference.com/w/cpp/container/array/to_array).

Avoiding exceptions for error handling

A mechanism of exceptions is an integral part of the C++ standard. It is a recommended way to design error handling in C++ programs. It does, however, have limitations that do not always make it acceptable for real-time systems, especially safety-critical ones.

C++ exception handling depends heavily on stack unwinding. Once an exception is thrown, it propagates by the call stack up to the catch block that can handle it. This means that destructors of all local objects in all stack frames in its path are invoked, and it is hard to determine and formally prove the worst-case time of this process.

That is why coding guidelines for safety-critical systems, such as MISRA or JSF, explicitly forbid the use of exceptions for error handling.

This does not mean that C++ developers have to revert to the traditional plain C error codes. In this recipe, we will learn how to use C++ templates to define data types that can hold either the result or the error code of a function call.

How to do it...

We are going to create an application that uses the power of the C++ standard library algorithms to generate and process fixed data frames without using dynamic memory allocation:

1. In your working directory, `~/test`, create a subdirectory called `expected`.
2. Use your favorite text editor to create an `expected.cpp` file in the `expected` subdirectory.
3. Add includes and a new type definition to the `expected.cpp` file:

```cpp
#include <iostream>
#include <system_error>
#include <variant>

#include <unistd.h>
#include <sys/fcntl.h>

template <typename T>
class Expected {
  std::variant<T, std::error_code> v;

public:
  Expected(T val) : v(val) {}
  Expected(std::error_code e) : v(e) {}
```

```
  bool valid() const {
    return std::holds_alternative<T>(v);
  }

  const T& value() const {
    return std::get<T>(v);
  }

  const std::error_code& error() const {
    return std::get<std::error_code>(v);
  }
};
```

4. Next, we add a wrapper for the open POSIX function:

```
Expected<int> OpenForRead(const std::string& name) {
  int fd = ::open(name.c_str(), O_RDONLY);
  if (fd < 0) {
    return Expected<int>(std::error_code(errno,
                            std::system_category()));
  }
  return Expected<int>(fd);
}
```

5. Add the `main` function that shows how to use the `OpenForRead` wrapper:

```
int main() {
  auto result = OpenForRead("nonexistent.txt");
  if (result.valid()) {
    std::cout << "File descriptor"
              << result.value() << std::endl;
  } else {
    std::cout << "Open failed: "
              << result.error().message() << std::endl;
  }
  return 0;
}
```

6. Finally, we create a `CMakeLists.txt` file containing build rules for our program:

```
cmake_minimum_required(VERSION 3.5.1)
project(expected)
add_executable(expected expected.cpp)

set(CMAKE_SYSTEM_NAME Linux)
#set(CMAKE_SYSTEM_PROCESSOR arm)
```

```
SET(CMAKE_CXX_FLAGS "--std=c++17")

#set(CMAKE_C_COMPILER /usr/bin/arm-linux-gnueabihf-gcc)
#set(CMAKE_CXX_COMPILER /usr/bin/arm-linux-gnueabihf-g++)

set(CMAKE_FIND_ROOT_PATH_MODE_PROGRAM NEVER)
set(CMAKE_FIND_ROOT_PATH_MODE_LIBRARY ONLY)
set(CMAKE_FIND_ROOT_PATH_MODE_INCLUDE ONLY)
set(CMAKE_FIND_ROOT_PATH_MODE_PACKAGE ONLY)
```

7. You can now build and run the application.

How it works...

In our application, we create a data type that can hold either an expected value or an error code in a type-safe way. C++17 provides a type-safe union class, `std::variant`, which we are going to use as an underlying data type for our templated class, `Expected`.

The `Expected` class encapsulates an `std::variant` field that can hold one of two data types, either templated type `T` or `std::error_code`, which is a standard C++ generalization of error codes:

```
std::variant<T, std::error_code> v;
```

Although it is possible to work with `std::variant` directly, we expose public methods that make it more convenient. The `valid` method returns `true` if the result holds the templated type, otherwise `false`:

```
bool valid() const {
    return std::holds_alternative<T>(v);
}
```

The `value` and `error` methods are used to access returned values or error code, respectively:

```
const T& value() const {
    return std::get<T>(v);
}

const std::error_code& error() const {
    return std::get<std::error_code>(v);
}
```

Once the `Expected` class is defined, we create an `OpenForReading` function that uses it. This invokes the open system function and, based on the return value, creates an instance of `Expected` that holds either a file descriptor or error code:

```
if (fd < 0) {
    return Expected<int>(std::error_code(errno,
                          std::system_category()));
}
return Expected<int>(fd);
```

In the `main` function, when we call `OpenForReading` for non-existing files, it is expected to fail. When we run the application, we can see the following output:

Our `Expected` class allows us to write functions that may return error codes, and do it in a type-safe way. Compile time-type validation helps developers to avoid many issues common to traditional error codes, making our applications more robust and safe.

There's more...

Our implementation of the `Expected` data type is a variation of the `std::expected` class (`http://www.open-std.org/jtc1/sc22/wg21/docs/papers/2018/p0323r7.html`) proposed for standardization, but not approved. One of the implementations of `std::expected` can be found on GitHub at `https://github.com/TartanLlama/expected`.

Exploring real-time operating systems

As has already been discussed in this chapter, Linux is not a real-time system. It is a good choice for soft real-time tasks, but despite the fact that it provides a real-time scheduler, its kernel is too complex to guarantee the level of determinism needed for hard real-time applications.

Time-critical applications require either a real-time operating system to run, or are designed and implemented to run on bare metal, with no operating system at all.

Real-time operating systems are usually much simpler than general-purpose operating systems such as Linux. Also, they require tailoring to the particular hardware platform, usually a microcontroller.

There are a number of real-time operating systems, with most of them being proprietary and not free. FreeRTOS is a good starting point to explore the capabilities of real-time operating systems. Unlike most of the alternatives, it is open source and free to use since it is distributed under the MIT license. It is ported to a number of microcontrollers and small microprocessors, but even if you do not have the specific hardware, Windows and POSIX simulators are available.

In this recipe, we will learn how to download and run the FreeRTOS POSIX simulator.

How to do it...

We are going to download and build a FreeRTOS simulator in our build environment:

1. Switch to your Ubuntu Terminal and change the current directory to /mnt:

   ```
   $ cd /mnt
   ```

2. Download the source code of the FreeRTOS simulator:

   ```
   $ wget -O simulator.zip
   http://interactive.freertos.org/attachments/token/r6d5gt3998niuc4/?
   name=Posix_GCC_Simulator_6.0.4.zip
   ```

3. Extract the downloaded archive:

   ```
   $ unzip simulator.zip
   ```

4. Change the current directory to
   Posix_GCC_Simulator/FreeRTOS_Posix/Debug:

   ```
   $ cd Posix_GCC_Simulator/FreeRTOS_Posix/Debug
   ```

5. Fix the minor mistake in makefile by running the following command:

   ```
   $ sed -i -e 's/\(.*gcc.*\)-lrt\(.*\)/\1\2 -lrt/' makefile
   ```

6. Build the simulator from the source code:

```
$ make
```

7. Start it:

```
$ ./FreeRTOS_Posix
```

At this point, the simulator is running.

How it works...

As we already know, the kernels of real-time operating systems are usually much simpler than the kernels of general-purpose operating systems. The same is also true for FreeRTOS.

As a consequence of this simplicity, the kernel can be built and run as a process in a general-purpose operating system, such as Linux or Windows. When used from within another operating system, it stops being truly real time, but can be used as a starting point to explore the FreeRTOS API and start working on applications that can later be run in the real-time environment of the target hardware platform.

In this recipe, we downloaded and built the FreeRTOS kernel for the POSIX operating system.

The build stage is straightforward. Once the code has been downloaded and extracted from the archive, we run make, and this builds a single executable, FreeRTOS-POSIX. Before running the make command, we fix a mistake in makefile by placing the -lrt option at the end of the GCC command line. We do this by running sed:

```
$ sed -i -e 's/\(.*gcc.*\)-lrt\(.*\)/\1\2 -lrt/' makefile
```

Running the application starts the kernel and pre-packaged applications:

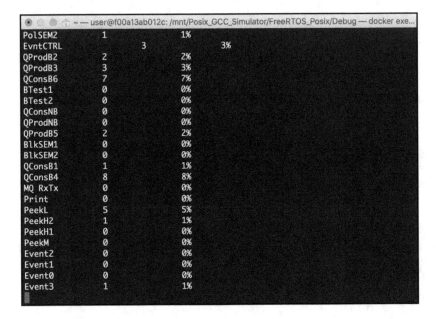

We were able to run FreeRTOS in our build environment. You can dive deeper into its code base and documentation to get a better understanding of the internals and APIs of real-time operating systems.

There's more...

If you work in the Windows environment, there is a better supported Windows version of the FreeRTOS simulator. It can be downloaded from `https://www.freertos.org/FreeRTOS-Windows-Simulator-Emulator-for-Visual-Studio-and-Eclipse-MingW.html`, along with documentation and tutorials.

Guidelines for Safety-Critical Systems

14

The requirements for the code quality of embedded systems are usually higher than in other software domains. Since lots of embedded systems work without supervision or control expensive industrial equipment, the cost of error is high. It becomes even higher in safety-critical systems where software or hardware failure may lead to injuries or even death. Software for such systems must follow specific guidelines that aim to minimize the chances of bugs not being found during the debugging and testing stages.

In this chapter, we'll explore some of the requirements and best practices for safety-critical systems through the following recipes:

- Using the return values of all functions
- Using static code analyzers
- Using preconditions and postconditions
- Exploring formal validation of code correctness

These recipes will help you understand the requirements and guidelines for safety-critical systems, as well as the tools and methods used for certification and conformance testing.

Using the return values of all functions

Neither the C nor C++ languages require developers to use the value returned by any function. It is totally acceptable to define a function that returns an integer and then invoke it in the code, ignoring its return value.

Such flexibility often causes software errors that may be difficult to diagnose and fix. Most commonly, it happens for functions returning error code. Developers may forget to add error condition checks for functions that are used often and rarely fail, such as `close`.

One of the most widely used coding standards for safety-critical systems is MISRA. It defines requirements for C and C++ languages—MISRA C and MISRA C++, respectively. A recently introduced Adaptive AUTOSAR defines coding guidelines for the automotive industry. It is expected that the Adaptive AUTOSAR guidelines will be used as a base for the updated MISRA C++ guidelines in the near future.

Both MISRA and AUTOSAR coding guidelines (`https://www.autosar.org/fileadmin/ user_upload/standards/adaptive/17-03/AUTOSAR_RS_CPP14Guidelines.pdf`) for C++ require developers to use values returned by all non-void functions and methods. The corresponding rule is defined as follows:

"Rule A0-1-2 (required, implementation, automated): The value returned by a function having a non-void return type that is not an overloaded operator shall be used."

In this recipe, we will learn how to use this rule in our code.

How to do it...

We are going to create two classes that save two timestamps in a file. One timestamp indicates when an instance was created, while the other indicates when the instance was destroyed. This is useful for code profiling, to measure how much time we have spent in a function or any other code block of interest. Follow these steps:

1. In your working directory, that is, `~/test`, create a subdirectory called `returns`.
2. Use your favorite text editor to create a file called `returns.cpp` in the `returns` subdirectory.
3. Add the first class to the `returns.cpp` file:

```cpp
#include <system_error>

#include <unistd.h>
#include <sys/fcntl.h>
#include <time.h>

[[nodiscard]] ssize_t Write(int fd, const void* buffer,
                            ssize_t size) {
  return ::write(fd, buffer, size);
}

class TimeSaver1 {
  int fd;

public:
```

```
    TimeSaver1(const char* name) {
      int fd = open(name, O_RDWR|O_CREAT|O_TRUNC, 0600);
      if (fd < 0) {
        throw std::system_error(errno,
                                std::system_category(),
                                "Failed to open file");
      }
      Update();
    }

    ~TimeSaver1() {
      Update();
      close(fd);
    }

private:
  void Update() {
    time_t tm;
    time(&tm);
    Write(fd, &tm, sizeof(tm));
  }
};
```

4. Next, we add the second class:

```
class TimeSaver2 {
  int fd;

public:
  TimeSaver2(const char* name) {
    fd = open(name, O_RDWR|O_CREAT|O_TRUNC, 0600);
    if (fd < 0) {
      throw std::system_error(errno,
                              std::system_category(),
                              "Failed to open file");
    }
    Update();
  }

  ~TimeSaver2() {
    Update();
    if (close(fd) < 0) {
      throw std::system_error(errno,
                              std::system_category(),
                              "Failed to close file");
    }
  }
```

```
    private:
      void Update() {
        time_t tm = time(&tm);
        int rv = Write(fd, &tm, sizeof(tm));
        if (rv < 0) {
          throw std::system_error(errno,
                                  std::system_category(),
                                  "Failed to write to file");
        }
      }
};
```

5. The `main` function creates instances of both classes:

```
int main() {
  TimeSaver1 ts1("timestamp1.bin");
  TimeSaver2 ts2("timestamp2.bin");
  return 0;
}
```

6. Finally, we create a `CMakeLists.txt` file containing the build rules for our program:

```
cmake_minimum_required(VERSION 3.5.1)
project(returns)
add_executable(returns returns.cpp)

set(CMAKE_SYSTEM_NAME Linux)
set(CMAKE_SYSTEM_PROCESSOR arm)

SET(CMAKE_CXX_FLAGS "--std=c++17")
set(CMAKE_CXX_COMPILER /usr/bin/arm-linux-gnueabi-g++)
```

7. You can now build and run the application.

How it works...

We have now created two classes, `TimeSaver1` and `TimeSaver2`, which look almost identical and do identical jobs. Both classes open a file in their constructors and call the `Update` function, which writes a timestamp into an open file.

Similarly, their destructors invoke the same `Update` function to add a second timestamp and close the file descriptor.

`TimeSaver1`, however, breaks the *A0-1-2* rule and is unsafe. Let's take a closer look at this. Its `Update` function invokes two functions, `time` and `write`. Both functions may fail, returning proper error code, but our implementation ignores it:

```
time(&tm);
Write(fd, &tm, sizeof(tm));
```

Also, the destructor of `TimeSaver1` closes the open file by calling the `close` function. This may also fail, returning an error code, which we ignore:

```
close(fd);
```

The second class, `TimeSaver2`, complies with the requirement. We assign the result of the `time` call to the `tm` variable:

```
time_t tm = time(&tm);
```

If `Write` returns an error, we throw an exception:

```
int rv = Write(fd, &tm, sizeof(tm));
if (rv < 0) {
  throw std::system_error(errno,
                          std::system_category(),
                          "Failed to write to file");
}
```

Similarly, we throw an exception if `close` returns an error:

```
if (close(fd) < 0) {
  throw std::system_error(errno,
                          std::system_category(),
                          "Failed to close file");
}
```

To mitigate this kind of issue, the C++17 standard introduced a special attribute called `[[nodiscard]]`. If a function is declared with this attribute, or it returns a class or enumeration marked as `nodiscard`, the compiler should display a warning if its return value is discarded. To use this feature, we created a custom wrapper around the `write` function and declared it `nodiscard`:

```
[[nodiscard]] ssize_t Write(int fd, const void* buffer,
                            ssize_t size) {
  return ::write(fd, buffer, size);
}
```

We can see this in the compiler output when we build our application, which also means we have the opportunity to fix it:

```
● ● ●                ⌂ ~ — user@f00a13ab012c: /mnt/returns — docker exec -ti f0 bash
[user@f00a13ab012c:/mnt/returns$ make
Scanning dependencies of target returns
[ 50%] Building CXX object CMakeFiles/returns.dir/returns.cpp.o
/mnt/returns/returns.cpp: In member function 'void TimeSaver1::Update()':
/mnt/returns/returns.cpp:34:10: warning: ignoring return value of 'ssize_t Write
(int, const void*, ssize_t)', declared with attribute nodiscard [-Wunused-resul
]
     Write(fd, &tm, sizeof(tm));
           ^~~~~~~~~~~~~~~~~~~
/mnt/returns/returns.cpp:7:23: note: declared here
  [[nodiscard]] ssize_t Write(int fd, const void* buffer, ssize_t size) {
                        ^~~~~
/mnt/returns/returns.cpp: In destructor 'TimeSaver2::~TimeSaver2()':
/mnt/returns/returns.cpp:55:53: warning: throw will always call terminate() [-Wt
erminate]
                             "Failed to close file");
                                                   ^
/mnt/returns/returns.cpp:55:53: note: in C++11 destructors default to noexcept
[100%] Linking CXX executable returns
[100%] Built target returns
user@f00a13ab012c:/mnt/returns$ ▏
```

In fact, the compiler was able to recognize and report another issue in our code that we will discuss in the next recipe.

If we build and run the application, we won't see any output since all writes go to files. We can run the `ls` command to check that the program produces a result, as follows:

```
$ ls timestamp*
```

From this, we get the following output:

```
● ● ●              ⌂ ~ — user@f00a13ab012c: /mnt/returns — docker exec -ti f0 bash
[user@f00a13ab012c:/mnt/returns$ ./returns
[user@f00a13ab012c:/mnt/returns$ ls -l timestamp*
-rw------- 1 user user  0 Mar  6 21:11 timestamp1.bin
-rw------- 1 user user 16 Mar  6 21:11 timestamp2.bin
user@f00a13ab012c:/mnt/returns$ ▏
```

As expected, two files are created by our program. They should be identical, but they are not. The file created by `TimeSaver1` is empty, meaning its implementation has an issue.

The file generated by `TimeSaver2` is valid, but does that mean that its implementation is 100 percent correct? Not necessarily, as we'll see in the next recipe.

There's more...

More information about the `[[nodiscard]]` attribute can be found on its reference page (`https://en.cppreference.com/w/cpp/language/attributes/nodiscard`). Starting from C++20, the `nodiscard` attribute can include a string literal, explaining why the value should not be discarded; for example, `[[nodiscard("Check for write errors")]]`.

It is important to understand that compliance with safety guidelines does make your code safer, but does not guarantee it. In our implementation of `TimeSaver2`, we use the value returned by `time`, but we do not check whether it is valid. Instead, we write to the output file unconditionally. Similarly, if `write` returns a non-zero number, it can still write less data to the file than requested. Even if your code formally matches the guidelines, it may contain related issues.

Using static code analyzers

All safety guidelines are defined as extensive sets of specific requirements to the source code or design of the application. Many of these requirements can be checked automatically by using static code analyzers.

Static code analyzers are tools that can analyze the source code and warn developers if they detect code patterns that violate code quality requirements. They are extremely efficient when it comes to error detection and prevention. Since they can be run before the code is built, a lot of errors are fixed at the earliest stage of development, without involving the time-consuming testing and debugging process.

Besides error detection and prevention, static code analyzers are used to prove that the code complies with target requirements and guidelines during the certification process.

In this recipe, we will learn how to use a static code analyzer in our applications.

How to do it...

We are going to create a simple program and run one of the many open source code analyzers that are available to check for potential issues. Follow these steps:

1. Go to the ~/test/returns directory, which we created as part of the previous recipe.

2. Install the cppcheck tool from the repository. Make sure you are under the root account, not user:

   ```
   # apt-get install cppcheck
   ```

3. Change to the user account again:

   ```
   # su - user
   $
   ```

4. Run cppcheck against the returns.cpp file:

   ```
   $ cppcheck --std=posix --enable=warning returns.cpp
   ```

5. Analyze its output.

How it works...

The code analyzer can parse the source code of our applications and test it against a number of patterns representing bad coding practices.

A lot of code analyzers exist, from open source and free to use to expensive commercial products for enterprise use.

The **MISRA** coding standard that was mentioned in *Using the Return Values of All Functions* recipe is a commercial standard. This means that you need to buy a license to use it and, similarly, buy a certified code analyzer that can test code for MISRA compliance.

For learning purposes, we will use an open source code analyzer called cppcheck. It is widely used and already included in the Ubuntu repository. We can install it in the same way as any other Ubuntu package:

```
# apt-get install cppcheck
$ cppcheck --std=posix --enable=warning returns.cpp
```

Now, we pass the source filename as a parameter. The check is fast and generates the following report:

```
● ● ●                    ~ — user@f00a13ab012c: /mnt/returns — docker exec -ti f0 bash
user@f00a13ab012c:/mnt/returns$ cppcheck --std=posix --enable=warning returns.cp
p
Checking returns.cpp ...
[returns.cpp:49]: (warning) Class TimeSaver2 is not safe, destructor throws exce
ption
[returns.cpp:18]: (error) Resource leak: fd
user@f00a13ab012c:/mnt/returns$ ▌
```

As we can see, it has detected two issues in our code, even before we have tried to build it. The first issue is in our safer, enhanced `TimeSaver2` class! To make it comply with A0-1-2 requirements, we need to check for the status code returned by `close` and throw an exception if an error occurs. However, we do this in a destructor, breaking C++ error handling mechanisms.

The second issue that was detected by the code analyzer is a resource leak. This explains why `TimeSaver1` generates empty files. When opening a file, we accidentally assign the file descriptor to the local variable instead of the instance variable, that is, `fd`:

```
int fd = open(name, O_RDWR|O_CREAT|O_TRUNC, 0600);
```

Now, we can fix them and rerun `cppcheck` to make sure the issues have gone and that no new issues are introduced. Using code analyzers as part of the development workflow makes your code safer and your performance faster since you can detect and prevent issues in the early stages of the development cycle.

There's more...

Though `cppcheck` is an open source tool, it supports a number of MISRA checks. This does not make it a certified tool for the validation of conformance to MISRA guidelines but allows you to understand how close your code is to the MISRA requirements and how much effort might be needed to make it compliant.

The MISRA check is implemented as an add-on; you can run it according to the instructions that can be found in the add-ons section of the GitHub repository for `cppcheck` (`https://github.com/danmar/cppcheck/tree/master/addons`).

Using preconditions and postconditions

In the previous recipe, we learned how to use static code analyzers to prevent coding errors at the early stages of development. Another powerful tool for error prevention is **programming by contract**.

Programming by contract is a practice in which developers explicitly define contracts or expectations for input values of a function or module, its results, and intermediate states. While intermediate states depend on implementation, the contracts for the input and output values can be defined as part of the public interface. These expectations are called **preconditions** and **preconditions**, respectively, and help avoid programming errors caused by vaguely defined interfaces.

In this recipe, we will learn how to define preconditions and postconditions in our C++ code.

How to do it...

To test how preconditions and postconditions work, we will partially reuse the code of the TimeSaver1 class we used in the previous recipe. Follow these steps:

1. In your working directory, that is, ~/test, create a subdirectory called assert.
2. Use your favorite text editor to create a file called assert.cpp in the assert subdirectory.
3. Add the modified version of the TimeSaver1 class to the assert.cpp file:

```cpp
#include <cassert>
#include <system_error>

#include <unistd.h>
#include <sys/fcntl.h>
#include <time.h>

class TimeSaver1 {
  int fd = -1;

public:
  TimeSaver1(const char* name) {
    assert(name != nullptr);
    assert(name[0] != '\0');

    int fd = open(name, O_RDWR|O_CREAT|O_TRUNC, 0600);
    if (fd < 0) {
```

```
        throw std::system_error(errno,
                                std::system_category(),
                                "Failed to open file");
    }
    assert(this->fd >= 0);
  }

  ~TimeSaver1() {
    assert(this->fd >= 0);
    close(fd);
  }
};
```

4. This is followed by a simple `main` function:

```
int main() {
  TimeSaver1 ts1("");
  return 0;
}
```

5. Put the build rules into the `CMakeLists.txt` file:

```
cmake_minimum_required(VERSION 3.5.1)
project(assert)
add_executable(assert assert.cpp)

set(CMAKE_SYSTEM_NAME Linux)
set(CMAKE_SYSTEM_PROCESSOR arm)

SET(CMAKE_CXX_FLAGS "--std=c++11")
set(CMAKE_CXX_COMPILER /usr/bin/arm-linux-gnueabi-g++)
```

6. You can now build and run the application.

How it works...

Here, we reused some of the code from the `TimeSaver1` class from the previous recipe. For simplicity, we removed the `Update` method, leaving only its constructor and destructor.

We intentionally kept the same error that was discovered by the static code analyzer in the previous recipe to check whether precondition and postcondition checks can be used to prevent such issues.

Our constructor accepts a filename as a parameter. We do not have any particular restrictions on the filename, except that it should be valid. Two obviously invalid filenames are as follows:

- A null pointer as a name
- An empty name

We put these rules as preconditions using the `assert` macro:

```
assert(name != nullptr);
assert(name[0] != '\0');
```

To use this macro, we need to include a header file, that is, `cassert`:

```
#include <cassert>
```

Next, we use the filename to open the file and store it in the `fd` variable. We assign it to the local variable, that is, `fd`, instead of the instance variable, `fd`. This is a coding error we want to detect:

```
int fd = open(name, O_RDWR|O_CREAT|O_TRUNC, 0600);
```

Finally, we put postconditions in the constructor. The only postcondition, in our case, is that the instance variable, `fd`, should be valid:

```
assert(this->fd >= 0);
```

Note how we prefix it with this to disambiguate it from local variables. In the same way, we add a precondition to the destructor:

```
assert(this->fd >= 0);
```

We don't add any postconditions here because after the destructor returns, the instance is not valid anymore.

Now, let's test our code. In the `main` function, we create an instance of `TimeSaver1`, passing an empty filename as a parameter:

```
TimeSaver1 ts1("");
```

After we've built and run our program, we will see the following output:

```
user@f00a13ab012c: /mnt/assert — docker exec -ti f0 bash
[user@f00a13ab012c:/mnt/assert$ ./assert
assert: /mnt/assert/assert.cpp:14: TimeSaver1::TimeSaver1(const char*): Assertio
n `name[0] != '\0'' failed.
Aborted
user@f00a13ab012c:/mnt/assert$
```

The precondition check in the constructor has detected the violation of contracts and terminated the application. Let's change the filename to a valid one:

```
TimeSaver1 ts1("timestamp.bin");
```

We build and run the application once again and get a different output:

```
user@f00a13ab012c: /mnt/assert — docker exec -ti f0 bash
user@f00a13ab012c:/mnt/assert$ ./assert
assert: /mnt/assert/assert.cpp:21: TimeSaver1::TimeSaver1(const char*): Assertio
n `this->fd >= 0' failed.
Aborted
user@f00a13ab012c:/mnt/assert$
```

Now, all the preconditions have been met, but we violated the postcondition since we failed to update the instance variable, `fd`. Change line 16 by removing the type definition before `fd`, like so:

```
fd = open(name, O_RDWR|O_CREAT|O_TRUNC, 0600);
```

Rebuilding and running the program again yields an empty output:

```
user@f00a13ab012c: /mnt/assert — docker exec -ti f0 bash
[user@f00a13ab012c:/mnt/assert$ ./assert
user@f00a13ab012c:/mnt/assert$
```

This indicates that all the expectations for the input parameters and results have been met. Even in a rudimentary form, programming using the contract helped us prevent two coding issues. That is why this technique is widely used in all areas of software development and in safety-critical systems in particular.

There's more...

More elaborate support for programming by contract was expected to be added to the C++20 standard. However, it has been deferred to a later standard. A description of the proposal can be found in the paper *A Contract Design* (http://www.open-std.org/jtc1/sc22/wg21/docs/papers/2016/p0380r1.pdf) by G. Dos Reis, J. D. Garcia, J. Lakos, A. Meredith, N. Myers, B. Stroustrup.

Exploring the formal validation of code correctness

Static code analyzers and the programming-by-contract methodology help developers significantly reduce the number of coding errors in their code. However, this is not sufficient in safety-critical software development. It is important to formally prove that the design of a software component is correct.

There are a number of fairly complex methods to do this, along with tools to automate this process. In this recipe, we will explore one of the tools for formal software validation, called CPAchecker (https://cpachecker.sosy-lab.org/index.php).

How to do it...

We are going to download and install CPAcheck to our build environment, and then run it against a sample program. Follow these steps:

1. Open a Terminal with your build environment included.
2. Make sure you have root permissions. If not, press *Ctrl + D* to exit from the *user* session back to the *root* session.
3. Install the Java runtime:

   ```
   # apt-get install openjdk-11-jre
   ```

4. Switch to the user session and change directory to /mnt:

   ```
   # su - user
   $ cd /mnt
   ```

5. Download and unpack the CPACheck archive, as follows:

```
$ wget -O -
https://cpachecker.sosy-lab.org/CPAchecker-1.9-unix.tar.bz2 | tar
xjf -
```

6. Change directory to CPAchecker-1.9-unix:

```
$ cd CPAchecker-1.9-unix
```

7. Run CPAcheck against an example file:

```
./scripts/cpa.sh -default doc/examples/example.c
```

8. Download the example file that intentionally contains a bug:

```
$ wget
https://raw.githubusercontent.com/sosy-lab/cpachecker/trunk/doc/exa
mples/example_bug.c
```

9. Run the checker against the new example:

```
./scripts/cpa.sh -default example_bug.c
```

10. Switch to your web browser and open the ~/test/CPAchecker-1.9-unix/output/Report.html report file that was generated by the tool.

How it works...

To run CPAcheck, we need to install the Java runtime. This is available in the Ubuntu repository, and we use apt-get to install it.

The next step is to download CPAcheck itself. We use the wget tool to download the archive file and feed it to tar utility immediately to extract it. When completed, the tool can be found in the CPAchecker-1.9-unix directory.

We use one of the pre-packaged example files to check how the tool works:

```
./scripts/cpa.sh -default doc/examples/example.c
```

It generates the following output:

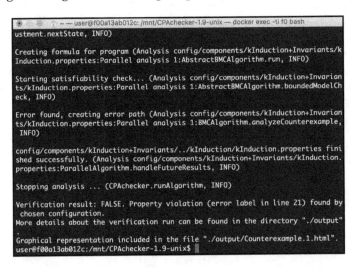

We can see, the tool has not discovered any issues with this file. There is no similar file that contains bugs in the `CPAcheck` archive, but we can download it from its site:

```
$ wget
https://raw.githubusercontent.com/sosy-lab/cpachecker/trunk/doc/examples/ex
ample_bug.c
```

We run the tool again and get the following output:

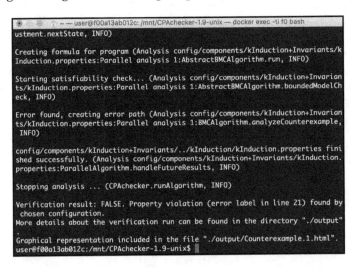

Now, the result is different: an error was detected. We can open an HTML report generated by the tool for further analysis. Besides logs and statistics, it also displays a flow automation graph:

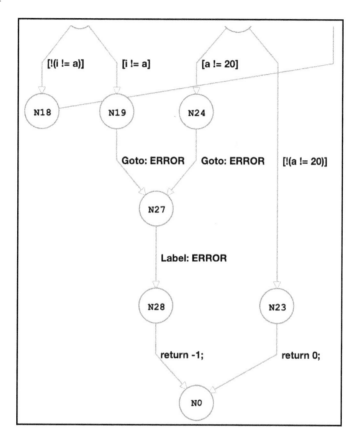

Formal validation methods and tools are complex and can deal with relatively simple applications, but they guarantee the correctness of application logic in all cases.

There's more...

You can find more information about CPAchecker on its website (https://cpachecker.sosy-lab.org/index.php).

15
Microcontroller Programming

In previous chapters, we mostly covered topics applicable to relatively powerful embedded systems that have megabytes of memory and run Linux operating systems. Now, we are going to explore the other side of the embedded system spectrum—microcontrollers.

As we discussed in the introduction, microcontrollers are commonly used to perform simple, often real-time tasks, such as collecting data or providing a high-level API to a specific device. Microcontrollers are inexpensive, consume little energy, and can work in a wide range of environmental conditions, making them a perfect choice for IoT applications.

The other side of their low cost is their capabilities. Normally, they have onboard memory that is measured in kilobytes and do not have hardware memory mapping. They do not run any operating system at all, or run a simple real-time operating system like FreeRTOS.

There are many models of microcontrollers, tailored for specific applications. In this chapter, we will learn how to use the Arduino development environment. The recipes were created for the Arduino UNO board built on top of an ATmega328 microcontroller, which is widely used for education and prototyping purposes, but they will work for other Arduino boards as well.

We will cover the following topics:

- Setting up the development environment
- Compiling and uploading a program
- Debugging microcontroller code

These recipes will help with setting up the environment and starting development for microcontrollers.

Setting up the development environment

The Arduino UNO board comes with an integrated development environment, or IDE, called the Arduino IDE. It can be downloaded for free from `https://www.arduino.cc/` `website`.

In this recipe, we will learn how to set it up and connect your Arduino board.

How to do it...

We are going to install the Arduino IDE, connect the Arduino UNO board to your computer, and then establish the communication between the IDE and the board:

1. In your browser, open the downloads (`https://www.arduino.cc/en/Main/` `Software`) page and choose an installation option that matches your operating system.
2. Once the download is complete, follow the installation instructions from the *Getting started* (`https://www.arduino.cc/en/Guide/HomePage`) page.
3. Connect your Arduino board to your computer using a USB cable. It will power on automatically.
4. Run the Arduino IDE.
5. Now, we need to establish communication between the IDE and the board. Switch to the Arduino IDE window. In the application menu, select **Tools -> Port**. This will open a sub-menu with serial port options available. Choose the one that has Arduino in its name.
6. In the **Tools** menu, click the **Board** item and then select a model of your Arduino board.
7. Select the **Tools -> Board Info** menu item.

How it works...

Arduino boards come with a free IDE that can be downloaded from the manufacturer's site. The IDE installation is straightforward and is not different from the installation of any other software for your platform.

All code is written, compiled, and debugged in the IDE, but the resulting compiled images should be flashed to the target board and executed there. For this, the IDE should be able to communicate with the board.

The board is connected to the computer running the IDE via USB. The USB cable provides not only communication but also power for the board. As soon as the board is connected to the computer, it turns on and starts working.

The IDE uses a serial interface for communication with the board. Since there can be multiple serial ports already configured on your computer, one of the steps to set up the communication is to choose one of the available ports. Usually, it is the one that has Arduino in its name:

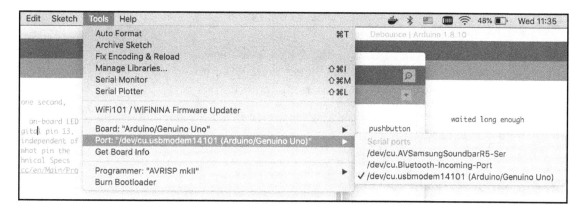

Finally, once the port has been selected, we let the IDE know the type of Arduino board we use. Once done, we can check whether communication between the board and the IDE actually works. When we invoke the **Board Info** menu item, the IDE displays a dialog window with information pertaining to the connected board:

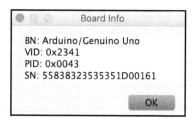

If the dialog does not show up, this indicates a problem. The board may be disconnected or damaged, or the wrong port may have been selected. Otherwise, we are ready to build and run our first program.

There's more...

If something goes wrong, consider reading the troubleshooting section (`https://www.arduino.cc/en/Guide/Troubleshooting`) on the Arduino site.

Compiling and uploading a program

In the previous recipe, we learned how to set up the development environment. Now, let's compile and run our first program.

The Arduino UNO board itself does not have a screen, but we need some way to know that our program is doing something. It does, however, have a built-in LED that we can control from our program without connecting any peripherals to the board.

In this recipe, we will learn how to compile and run a program that blinks a built-in LED on an Arduino UNO board.

How to do it...

We are going to compile and upload to the board an existing example application that comes with the IDE:

1. Connect the Arduino board to your computer and open the Arduino IDE.
2. In the Arduino IDE, open the **File** menu and choose **Examples -> 01. Basics -> Blink**.
3. A new window will open. In this window, click the **Upload** button.
4. Observe how the built-in LED on the board starts flashing.

How it works...

Arduino is a platform widely used for educational purposes. It is designed to be easy to use and comes with a bunch of examples. For our first program, we have chosen an application that does not require the board to be wired with external peripherals. Once we launch the IDE, we select the **Blink** application from the examples available, as follows:

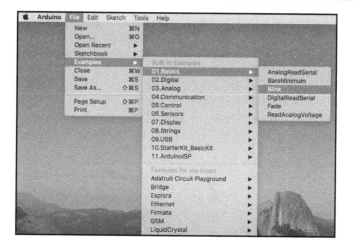

This opens a window with the program code:

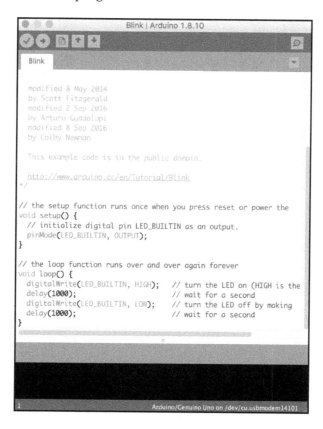

Aside from the source code of the program, we can also see a black console window and a status bar, indicating that the Arduino UNO board is connected via the `/dev/cu.usbmodem14101` serial port. The device name depends on the board model, and the port name may look different in Windows or Linux.

Above the source code, we can see several buttons. The second button, a right-pointing arrow, is the **Upload** button. Once we press it, the IDE starts building the application and then uploads the resulting binary to the board. We can see the build status in the console window:

The application starts immediately after uploading. If we take a look at the board, we can see that the built-in yellow LED has started blinking. We were able to build and run our first Arduino application.

There's more...

After uploading, your program is stored in the flash memory on the board. If you power off your board and then power it on again, the program starts running even if you do not have an IDE running.

Debugging microcontroller code

Compared with more powerful embedded platforms, such as the Raspberry PI, the debugging capabilities of Arduino are limited. The Arduino IDE does not provide an integrated debugger, and the Arduino board itself does not have a built-in screen. It does, however, have UART, and provides a serial interface that can be used for debugging purposes.

In this recipe, we will learn how to use the Arduino serial interface for debugging and reading user input.

How to do it...

We will implement a simple program for the Arduino controller that waits for user input on the serial port and turns the built-in LED on or off depending on the data:

1. Open Arduino IDE and select **New** in its **File** menu. A new **Sketch** window will show up.
2. Paste the following code snippet into the **Sketch** window:

```
void setup() {
 pinMode(LED_BUILTIN, OUTPUT);
 Serial.begin(9600);
 while (!Serial);
}

void loop() {
  if (Serial.available() > 0) {
      int inByte = Serial.read();
      if (inByte == '1') {
        Serial.print("Turn LED on\n");
        digitalWrite(LED_BUILTIN, HIGH);
      } else if (inByte == '0') {
        Serial.print("Turn LED off\n");
        digitalWrite(LED_BUILTIN, LOW);
      } else {
```

```
        Serial.print("Ignore byte ");
        Serial.print(inByte);
        Serial.print("\n");
    }
    delay(500);
  }
}
```

3. Click the **Upload** button to build and run the code.
4. Select **Serial Monitor** in the **Tools** menu of the Arduino IDE. A **Serial Monitor** window will appear.
5. In the **Serial Monitor** window, enter 1010110.

How it works...

We create a new Arduino sketch that consists of two functions. The first function, setup, is invoked on the program startup and is used to provide the initial configuration of the application.

In our case, we need to initialize the serial interface. The most important parameter of serial communication is its speed in bits per second. Both the microcontroller and the IDE should agree to use the same speed, otherwise the communication will not work. By default, the serial monitor uses 9,600 bits per second, and we use this value in our program:

```
Serial.begin(9600);
```

It is possible to use higher communication speeds though. The serial monitor has a dropdown in the bottom-right corner of the screen that allows other speeds to be selected. If you decide to use other speeds, the code should be modified accordingly.

We also configure pin 13, corresponding to the built-in LED, for output:

```
pinMode(LED_BUILTIN, OUTPUT);
```

We use the constant, LED_BUILTIN, instead of 13, to make the code more understandable. The second function, loop, defines an endless loop of the Arduino program. For each iteration, we read a byte from the serial port:

```
if (Serial.available() > 0) {
    int inByte = Serial.read();
```

It the byte is 1, we turn the LED on and write a message back to the serial port:

```
Serial.print("Turn LED on\n");
digitalWrite(LED_BUILTIN, HIGH);
```

Similarly, for 0, we turn the LED off:

```
Serial.print("Turn LED off\n");
digitalWrite(LED_BUILTIN, LOW);
```

All other values are ignored. After each byte read from the port, we add a 500 microsecond delay. This way, we can define different blinking patterns. For example, if we send 1001001, the LED will turn on for 0.5 seconds, then off for 1 second, on for 0.5 seconds, off for 1 second, and finally, on again.

If we run the code and enter 1001001 in the serial monitor, we can see the following output:

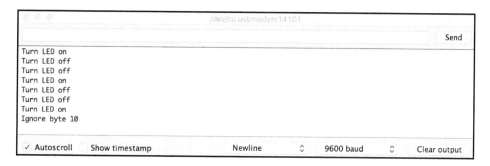

The LED is blinking as expected and, apart from that, we can see debug messages in the serial monitor. In this way, we can debug real, more complex applications.

Other Books You May Enjoy

If you enjoyed this book, you may be interested in these other books by Packt:

Hands-On Embedded Programming with C++17

Maya Posch

ISBN: 978-1-78862-930-0

- Choose the correct type of embedded platform to use for a project
- Develop drivers for OS-based embedded systems
- Use concurrency and memory management with various microcontroller units (MCUs)
- Debug and test cross-platform code with Linux
- Implement an infotainment system using a Linux-based single board computer
- Extend an existing embedded system with a Qt-based GUI
- Communicate with the FPGA side of a hybrid FPGA/SoC system

Hands-On Embedded Programming with Qt

John Werner

ISBN: 978-1-78995-206-3

- Understand how to develop Qt applications using Qt Creator on Linux
- Explore various Qt GUI technologies to build resourceful and interactive applications
- Understand Qt's threading model to maintain a responsive UI
- Get to grips with remote target load and debug using Qt Creator
- Become adept at writing IoT code using Qt
- Learn a variety of software best practices to ensure that your code is efficient

Leave a review - let other readers know what you think

Please share your thoughts on this book with others by leaving a review on the site that you bought it from. If you purchased the book from Amazon, please leave us an honest review on this book's Amazon page. This is vital so that other potential readers can see and use your unbiased opinion to make purchasing decisions, we can understand what our customers think about our products, and our authors can see your feedback on the title that they have worked with Packt to create. It will only take a few minutes of your time, but is valuable to other potential customers, our authors, and Packt. Thank you!

Index

embedded system
  connecting 43
  connecting to 44
  diagnostics 29, 30
  exploring 10
  logging 29, 30
  performance, implications 14
  software, deploying 27, 28
  software, running 28, 29
  types 11
  versus desktop 10
  versus web applications 10
  working 45, 46
emulators
  working with 35, 37, 38
endianness of platform
  detecting 67, 69, 70
endianness, types
  bi-endian 15
  big-endian 15
  little-endian 15
endianness
  about 14, 15, 65
  converting 70, 71, 73, 74, 75
Error class 319
error codes
  working with 308, 309, 310, 311, 312
error handling FAQ
  reference link 320
error handling
  exceptions, avoiding 350, 351, 352, 353
  exceptions, using 312, 313, 314
events
  using 278, 279, 281, 282, 284, 285
exception handling
  constant references, using 316, 317, 318
  working 319, 320
exceptions
  used, for error handling 312, 313, 314
  working 314, 315, 316

F

field programmable gate arrays (FPGAs) 13
firmware 10
fixed-width integer types

about 17
  exploring 62, 63
  working 64
FlatBuffers library
  download link 232
  using 231, 232
  working 234, 235
flatc 231
formal validation, of correctness
  exploring 370, 371, 372, 373
FreeRTOS simulator
  reference link 356
function objects
  reference link 226
functions
  return values, using of 357, 359, 360, 362

G

GDB commands
  using 113
gdbserver
  about 50
  used, for debugging 127, 128
  using, for remote debugging 50, 51, 52, 53
General Purpose Input-Output (GPIO)
  used, for connecting controlling devices 237,
    238, 239, 240, 241
getter methods 231
Global Positioning System (GPS) 303
GNU Compiler Collection (GCC) 81
GNU Project Debugger (GDB)
  about 103
  application, running in 104, 105, 106, 107, 108,
    109, 110, 111, 112, 113
  used, for analyzing core dumps 126
governor 275
governor, properties
  reference link 278
GPIO pins
  controlling, with libgpiod 250, 251, 252, 253

H

hardware architecture
  alignment 16, 17
  endianness 14, 15